D0404152

Corpora in Applied Linguistics

07/25/02

THE CAMBRIDGE APPLIED LINGUISTICS SERIES

Series editors: Michael H. Long and Jack C. Richards

This series presents the findings of recent work in applied linguistics which are of direct relevance to language teaching and learning and of particular interest to applied linguists, researchers, language teachers, and teacher trainers:

Corpora in Applied Linguistics

Susan Hunston

University of Birmingham

PUBLISHED BY THE PRESS SYNDICATE OF THE UNIVERSITY OF CAMBRIDGE
The Pitt Building, Trumpington Street, Cambridge, United Kingdom

CAMBRIDGE UNIVERSITY PRESS
The Edinburgh Building, Cambridge CB2 2RU, United Kingdom
40 West 20th Street, New York, NY 10011–4211, USA
477 Williamstown Road, Port Melbourne, VIC 3207, Australia
Ruiz de Alarcón 13, 28014 Madrid, Spain
Dock House, The Waterfront, Cape Town 8001, South Africa

http://www.cambridge.org

© Cambridge University Press 2002

This book is in copyright. Subject to statutory exception
and to the provisions of relevant collective licensing agreements,
no reproduction of any part may take place without
the written permission of Cambridge University Xress.

First published 2002

Printed in the United Kingdom at the University Xress, Cambridge

Typeset in Sabon 10.5/12pt   System 3b2   [CE]

A catalogue record for this book is available from the British Library

ISBN 0 521 80171 0 hardback
ISBN 0 521 80583 X paperback

For Doreen and Peter Hunston

Contents

Series editors' preface

The use and uses of linguistic corpora in applied linguistics have expanded rapidly over the past 20 years, in part because of the advent of improved, more accessible systems of electronic storage and analysis, and also because of an ever-growing appreciation of the huge potential of corpus work. Among the pioneers in this effort has been the team in the English Department at the University of Birmingham, led for many years by Professor John Sinclair, and known among other things for its prolific publications surrounding the COBUILD Project. Dr Susan Hunston has long been a core member of that team, including several years as a Senior Grammarian with COBUILD, and has steadily become one of corpus analysis' most widely recognised experts. In *Corpora in Applied Linguistics*, she provides an original and authoritative introduction to modern uses of corpus studies, and does so in a clear fashion that will appeal to a wide range of readers.

After a lucid introduction to the scope and limitations of modern corpus work, including research on frequency, phraseology, and collocation, Dr Hunston defines some of the basic issues surrounding the construction and evaluation of corpora in chapter 2. These include questions concerning the size, content, representativeness, and stability of corpora over time, and such matters as the relative merits of corpora designed as collections of texts and as collections of language samples, in turn reflecting how and for what purposes corpora are investigated. Subsequent chapters offer detailed coverage of methods of analysis in corpus linguistics, and of applications of corpus-based research in a variety of domains – most centrally in the design of syllabi and materials for language teaching, in English for specific purposes, and language testing, but also in dictionary work, the study of ideology and culture, translation, stylistics, forensic linguistics, and the provision of on-line assistance for writers in well-defined technical domains. Key terms and concepts are clearly explained, copious examples of corpus research are presented succinctly, and statistical analyses are handled in such a way as to be easily comprehensible to expert and non-expert alike.

Corpora in Applied Linguistics should be of great value to language teachers, syllabus designers, materials writers, and language testers, as well as to applied linguists involved in the kinds of work mentioned above. Offering an overview and searching analysis of the current state-of-the-art in applied corpus work, and based on years of first-hand experience in language teaching and corpus research, Dr Hunston's book is a most welcome and valuable addition to the *Cambridge Applied Linguistics Series.*

Michael H. Long
Jack C. Richards

Acknowledgements

Most of the corpus examples in this book are taken from the Bank of English. I would like to thank Collins Dictionaries and the University of Birmingham for permission to use and quote from this corpus. I would also like to acknowledge the contribution of colleagues and students at the University of Birmingham, whose insights into the uses of corpora have informed my own understanding.

1   *Introduction to a corpus in use*

What this book is about

It is no exaggeration to say that corpora, and the study of corpora, have revolutionised the study of language, and of the applications of language, over the last few decades. The improved accessibility of computers has changed corpus study from a subject for specialists only to something that is open to all. The aim of this book is to introduce students of applied linguistics to corpus investigation. Its topic is, for the most part, studies that have been carried out on corpora in English, and much of the focus of the book relates to corpora used in English language teaching. Other applications, however, such as translation and investigations of ideology, are also included. Unfortunately, the large amount of work that has been carried out on languages other than English is not covered by this book.

Although the book deals with a range of issues, there are two themes that run consistently through it. One is the effect of corpus studies upon theories of language and how languages should be described. Corpora allow researchers not only to count categories in traditional approaches to language but also to observe categories and phenomena that have not been noticed before. The other major theme is a critical approach to the methods used in investigating corpora, and a comparison between them. Corpus findings can be seductive, and it is important to be aware of the possible pitfalls in their production.

This book is intended for people who are interested in how language, more specifically English, works, and how a knowledge about language can be applied in certain real-life contexts. It is expected that the reader will wish to carry out corpus investigations for him or herself and will need to become acquainted with the range of research that has been carried out in the field.

After this introductory chapter, chapter 2 introduces some issues around corpus design and purpose, chapters 3 and 4 describe the methods used to investigate corpora, and introduce the main concepts about language that will be used in the rest of the book. Chapter 5 describes the various applications of corpora other than language teaching. Chapters 6, 7 and 8 deal with English language teaching, chapter 6 considering new, corpus-based views of language that are relevant to teachers and chapters 7 and 8 describing some of the ways that corpora are currently influencing trends in language teaching and learning. Chapter 9 concludes the book.

Before continuing, it is worth asking two questions about the title of this book: what is a corpus? and what is applied linguistics?

A corpus is defined in terms of both its form and its purpose. Linguists have always used the word *corpus* to describe a collection of naturally occurring examples of language, consisting of anything from a few sentences to a set of written texts or tape recordings, which have been collected for linguistic study. More recently, the word has been reserved for collections of texts (or parts of text) that are stored and accessed electronically. Because computers can hold and process large amounts of information, electronic corpora are usually larger than the small, paper-based collections previously used to study aspects of language. A corpus is planned, though chance may play a part in the text collection, and it is designed for some linguistic purpose. The specific purpose of the design determines the selection of texts, and the aim is other than to preserve the texts themselves because they have intrinsic value. This differentiates a corpus from a library or an electronic archive. The corpus is stored in such a way that it can be studied non-linearly, and both quantitatively and qualitatively. The purpose is not simply to access the texts in order to read them, which again distinguishes the corpus from the library and the archive.

The field of applied linguistics itself has undergone something of a revolution over the last few decades. Once, it was almost synonymous with language teaching but now it covers any application of language to the solution of real-life problems. As has often been said (e.g. Widdowson 1979; 2000), the difference between linguistics and applied linguistics is not simply that one deals with theory and the other with applications of those theories. Rather, applied linguistics has tended to develop language theories of its own, ones that are more relevant to the questions applied linguistics seeks to answer than are those developed by theoretical linguistics. Increasingly, corpora are adding to the development of those applied views of language.

The rest of this chapter will give an overview of what a corpus can do and how corpora are used in applied linguistics. This is followed by an account of the main types of corpora and an introduction to some of the terminology used in this book. The chapter concludes with a discussion of the advantages and limitations of using corpora in language study.

What a corpus can do

Strictly speaking, a corpus by itself can do nothing at all, being nothing other than a store of used language. Corpus access software, however, can re-arrange that store so that observations of various kinds can be made. If a corpus represents, very roughly and partially, a speaker's experience of language, the access software re-orders that experience so that it can be examined in ways that are usually impossible. A corpus does not contain new information about language, but the software offers us a new perspective on the familiar. Most readily available software packages process data from a corpus in three ways: showing frequency, phraseology, and collocation. Each of these will be exemplified in this section.

Frequency

The words in a corpus can be arranged in order of their frequency in that corpus. This is most interesting when corpora are compared in terms of their frequency lists. Table 1.1 shows the top 50 words in a corpus of politics dissertations compared with a comparable corpus of materials science dissertations (data from Charles, in preparation) and with the 1998 Bank of English corpus (data from Sinclair 1999).

In all three corpora, grammar words are more frequent than lexical words; indeed, the words *the, of, to, and, a* and *in* occupy the top six places in each corpus. The only lexical word which comes into the top 50 words of the general Bank of English corpus is *said* (at number 36). The lexical words in the other corpora reflect their subject matter, e.g. *surface* (34), *energy* (37), *electron* (48) and *particles* (50) in materials science, and *international* (21), *policy* (28), *states* (29) and *socialization* (50) in politics. There are more such words in the materials science list than in the politics list. One reason for this might be that in materials science the prose is more dense, with more lexical words occurring together without grammar words between them (cf Halliday and Martin 1993: 76–77), as in *electron probe microanalyser, electron spin resonance dating techniques* and *high electron mobility transistor*. Another reason might be that in materials science the vocabulary is less wide than in politics, so that fewer words appear more frequently. One of the notable features of the grammar words in the lists is that *this* occurs much higher up the materials science list (8) and the politics list (13) than the general corpus list (28). *This* is often used to summarise what has been said before, as in *'mind' and 'mental' processes are now respectable concepts in psychology . . . This is important not only*

Table 1.1. Word frequency comparisons across corpora

	General corpus	Materials science	Politics
1	THE	THE	THE
2	OF	OF	OF
3	TO	AND	TO
4	AND	IN	AND
5	A	TO	IN
6	IN	A	A
7	THAT	IS	THAT
8	S	THIS	IS
9	IS	P	AS
10	IT	THAT	WAS
11	FOR	FOR	FOR
12	I	BE	IT
13	WAS	AS	THIS
14	ON	HEAD	P
15	HE	ARE	ON
16	WITH	WITH	BE
17	AS	IT	BY
18	YOU	BY	WHICH
19	BE	ON	S
20	AT	WAS	NOT
21	BY	AT	INTERNATIONAL
22	BUT	WHICH	WITH
23	HAVE	FROM	AN
24	ARE	FIGURE	QUOTE
25	HIS	AN	ARE
26	FROM	NOT	FROM
27	THEY	HAS	WERE
28	THIS	WERE	POLICY
29	NOT	CAN	STATES
30	HAD	THESE	BUT
31	HAS	BEEN	STATE
32	AN	HAVE	WOULD
33	WE	OR	OR
34	N'T	SURFACE	ITS
35	OR	USED	MAZZINI
36	SAID	C	THEIR
37	ONE	ENERGY	HEAD
38	THERE	TEMPERATURE	AT
39	WILL	ALSO	HAD
40	THEIR	WILL	HAVE
41	WHICH	CONTRAST	MORE
42	SHE	TWO	BRITAIN
43	WERE	FIELD	THEY

Table 1.1 (*cont.*)

	General corpus	Materials science	Politics
44	ALL	SAMPLE	THESE
45	BEEN	MATERIAL	HE
46	WHO	CURRENT	BETWEEN
47	HER	BETWEEN	HIS
48	WOULD	ELECTRON	US
49	UP	HOWEVER	THAN
50	IF	PARTICLES	SOCIALIZATION

Note: In the corpora from which this table is derived, 'C' and 'P' are symbols and abbreviations, such as the abbreviation for *centigrade*. 'P' is sometimes also the code marking a new paragraph. 'S' is usually the 's' following an apostrophe, as in John'*s* or she'*s*.

for psychologists, but for society in general, where *This* summarises the preceding sentence. However, this use is more common in written argument, and therefore in academic prose, than in speech or in writing that is more speech-like. Other words associated more with speech and informal writing than with formal writing, such as *I, but* and *n't* occur in the general corpus list but not in the other two.

Frequency lists from corpora can be useful for identifying possible differences between the corpora that can then be studied in more detail. Another approach is to look at the frequency of given words, compared across corpora. Table 1.2 shows the number of occurrences of *must, have to, incredibly* and *surprisingly* in three corpora from the Bank of English: a corpus of books published in Britain, a corpus of *The Times* newspaper, and a corpus of spoken British English. Because the three corpora are of different sizes, a comparison of actual frequencies would not be useful, so the figures for occurrences per million words are given. For example, the *Times* corpus is nearly 21 million words. There are about 9,600 occurrences of the word *must* in that corpus, giving a frequency per million of just over 460.

Table 1.2 can be used to compare *must* with *have to*, and *incredibly* with *surprisingly*. Whereas the books corpus and the *Times* corpus use *must* in preference to *have to*, the spoken corpus shows the reverse trend, suggesting that *have to* is less formal than *must*. Similarly, *surprisingly* is found less frequently in the spoken corpus than in the other two, whilst for *incredibly* the reverse is true. This suggests that *incredibly* is a less formal word than *surprisingly*. Whilst this appeal to 'formality' may offer partial insight, a more satisfactory explanation can be found by looking at the words more closely.

Table 1.2. Frequencies of *must*, *have to*, *incredibly* and *surprisingly* across corpora (per million words)

	Books	*Times*	Spoken
must	683	460	363
have to	419	371	802
Total	1102	831	1165
incredibly	8	10	15
surprisingly	25	29	4
Total	33	39	19

In the three corpora mentioned, *incredibly* is used almost exclusively before an adjective or adverb, the most significant being *difficult, well, important, hard, complex* and *strong*. Here are some examples of typical uses:

Well I mean now as I'm unemployed with fairly specialist skills erm I find it incredibly difficult to find work that is suitable. (spoken corpus)

Why on earth was she standing here blubbing like a baby at her age? She should be proud at this moment. Noora had done incredibly well to get this far in so short a time. (books corpus)

But I was fascinated by it all to find out how this incredibly important woman operates, what she's really like, how she thinks, the whole upstairs-downstairs thing. (*Times* corpus)

The word *surprisingly* shares some of this behaviour: the words *good, little, large, few, well* and *strong* appear significantly frequently after it in the three corpora mentioned, as exemplified here:

The reason motorcycles have become popular inner-city transport owes much to the machines and the protective clothing now on the market. The machines are powerful, stylish and comfortable, and their aerodynamics give surprisingly good weather protection. (*Times* corpus)

As a society we are ill-informed about epilepsy, often finding it shocking and something we would prefer not to be exposed to rather than an illness. The sufferers often receive surprisingly little support either within their family or from colleagues, employers or friends. (books corpus)

I'm going to write some recommendation as to . . . how to publicize it if people don't know about it . . . Erm and so far erm surprisingly few people know about it. Erm I'd have thought more would know but they don't. (spoken corpus)

Looking at these examples it seems that *surprisingly* is used to mean 'contrary to expectation' whereas *incredibly* is used as a strong version of 'very'. This goes some way to explaining why *incredibly* is more frequent in spoken English than in written. The adverb *surprisingly* also has a use which *incredibly* does not have. As well as being followed by an adjective or adverb, it is also followed significantly often by a word that is the beginning of a clause, such as *he, the* or *it*. It is also often preceded by *not, perhaps* or *hardly*. This indicates that *surprisingly* is used to modify a clause as well as to modify an adjective or adverb, as in these examples:

Woan, now 28 . . . was rejected in his teens by Everton, indulged in non-league football with Runcorn until he was 22, and studied by day to be a chartered surveyor. <u>Not surprisingly</u>, he reads books more than most footballers do, and his recent favourite was *Extraordinary Power* by Joseph Finder. (*Times* corpus)

There was another shop just around the corner where I had to catch a second bus to Clapton and there, <u>hardly surprisingly</u>, the news that Sandown had indeed fallen victim to the elements was received with much regret. (books corpus)

Now having said that you then have the opposite problem that by being exhaustive everybody goes to sleep or throws the thing in the bin erm and <u>not surprisingly</u> it has been found that the first two or three items are attended to considerably more than the three hundred and thirtieth. (spoken corpus: from a seminar on survey techniques)

Although this use of an adverb to modify a clause does occur in some registers of spoken English, as the last example above shows, it is a feature not associated with colloquial speech. This adds another reason for the difference in frequency among the corpora.

Another example of differences in frequency is the words *man, woman, husband* and *wife*. Table 1.3 shows the frequencies (i.e. the number of occurrences per million words) in the same three corpora, and the total frequency across those three corpora.

The totals show that *man* occurs more frequently than *woman*, and it is therefore unexpected that *wife* should occur more frequently than *husband*. The most likely interpretation is that women are relatively more frequently referred to in relation to the person they are married to than men are. This seems to be confirmed by a more detailed investigation of the *Times* corpus, in which the phrase *husband of* occurs 53 times (2.5 times per million words) whereas the corresponding *wife of* occurs 299 times (14.3 times per million words). A typical instance is the description of a woman as *a top US model and wife of Gregory Peck's son*, illustrating (twice!) how

Table 1.3. Frequencies of *man, woman, husband* and *wife* across corpora (per million words)

	Books	*Times*	Spoken	Total
man	980	583	285	1848
woman	456	208	137	801
husband	163	140	92	395
wife	216	224	83	523

less famous people tend to be described in terms of their more famous relatives. Although the equivalent *husband of* is used in those cases where the wife is more famous, the frequency figures indicate that it is less usual for a woman to be more noteworthy than her husband.

The spoken corpus, however, reverses the trend apparent in the books and *Times* corpora. In that corpus, *husband* is more frequent than *wife*, just as *man* is more frequent than *woman*. In both cases the most frequent phrases are with possessive determiners: *my husband, his wife* and so on. Although *wife of* is fairly frequent (28 instances) and much more frequent than *husband of* (only 8 instances), this form of the possessive is less significant than in the *Times* corpus. In the *Times*, 6% of the instances of *wife* comprise the phrase *wife of*, whereas in the spoken corpus the figure is 1.6%. It seems, then, that one explanation for the discrepancy in figures between *husband* and *wife* is accounted for by the tendency to relate 'unknown' people to 'known' ones, a tendency which occurs in some registers much more than in others. This tendency in published written discourse might be argued to perpetuate discrimination against women.

More sophisticated work on comparative frequencies between registers has been undertaken by Biber and his colleagues (e.g. Biber 1988; Biber et al 1998; Biber et al 1999; see also Mindt 2000 and Leech et al 2001). They use software which counts not only words but also categories of linguistic item. One example among many is their calculation of the distribution of present and past tenses across four registers: 'conversation', 'fiction', 'news' and 'academic' (Biber et al 1999: 456). They note that in their conversation and academic corpora, present tense occurs more frequently than past tense. In the fiction corpus, the opposite is the case, with past tense preferred to present tense. In the news corpus, the figures are roughly equal. These findings may be seen in the context of Halliday's (1993) calculation that in the Bank of English, present and past tenses are found in roughly equal proportions. Common sense suggests that it is reasonable to extrapolate from these findings a statement about English as a whole. Each register has its own ratio of present and past, but overall the figures balance out, and a 50:50 proportion is maintained. However, Biber et al's findings also sound a warning in interpreting Halliday's figures. If the proportion of present to past is dependent on register, then the proportion in a large corpus will in turn depend on the balance of registers within that corpus. Too much fiction, for example, will bias the figures towards past tense. As will be discussed in chapter 2, however, this is a far from simple matter to resolve. How much fiction would be 'too much'? As we have no idea how to calculate proportions for 'English as a whole', we have equally no idea what would constitute a corpus that truly reflected English.

Phraseology

Most people access a corpus through a concordancing program. Concordance lines bring together many instances of use of a word or phrase, allowing the user to observe regularities in use that tend to remain unobserved when the same words or phrases are met in their normal contexts. (Sinclair and Coulthard 1975 used the term *latent patterning* to refer to this phenomenon.) It is through concordances, then, that phraseology is observed.

As much of chapter 3 of this book will consider phraseology in some detail, it will be dealt with only briefly here. One point of interest is the way that phraseology can be used as an alternative view of phenomena that teachers of English are frequently called upon to explain. For example, learners often confuse adjectives such as *interested* and *interesting*, and find that explanations of the different meanings do not make the choice more accessible in spontaneous speech. Below are 23 lines each of the words *interested* and *interesting* (selected at random from the Bank of English).

Interested
       and the surrounding areas who are interested in water sports. Rural
         than Barbados. If you are interested in wild-life, Tobago is heaven,
           The YOA claims to be interested in lobbying on issues, but it
      irony in that, whereas I'm more interested in the musical arrangements ad
       like bigger speakers. I'm more interested in playing videos. I've got a
  work or whatever that you might be interested in speakers.
 the new test. MORTIMER: We've been interested in looking at alternative methods
      by around half a dozen firms interested in acquiring its Welsh business.
  over a Labour Party which was less interested in evangelism than it was in the
  on radon, but they tend to be more interested in measuring it once it escapes

and from the outside and – I was interested in something somebody said about
(another ambiguity), became interested in African cash-crops, that it
to say, you're going to say she's interested in my money. I expected a
all his readings, he appeared more interested in developing independent grown-
those maps their due, it is more interested in reconstructing the maps etched
users and the medical company interested in the product. Even when venture
and what then?" Yes, he is interested in moving towards contemporary
that the Woodland Trust charity is interested in maintaining woodlands and we
in case of emergency and may be interested in a car kit for hands-free
on the work of Henry Miller first interested me in the subject. And now I am
know?' I do. Not to interfere. I'm interested.' OK. Do you want to come now?'
make decisions. Insurers are interested too; they want to use such
consultants have been interested you know in various systems. And

Interesting

Yeah. Yeah. But there's this interesting annual variation and erm I
rights legislation. Now this is interesting, Bob. Here's one that you would
trusted her." In one of the most interesting chapters of this biography,
Sunshine Sprint runners, but one interesting entry yesterday was the Glenn
Heal. Well, it's been an interesting few days for the Liberal
game." He might have added an interesting historical fact: The last Series
or in auto accidents. It's a very interesting idea because that could largely
image of the object. What is interesting is that it is not necessary to
ll mature into something big and interesting like REM, won't the music
conservation of some biologically interesting niches could also be brought
yard bet on Foyt, just to make it interesting. 'Not Andretti?' Tucker asked.
I learned a lot about geology, met interesting people and went home with a good
antiques, appropriate fabrics and interesting pictures. (There are no bar-
249), but this was hardly the most interesting point in his view. The
to be Master of Wine, argue an interesting proposition: 'At dollar 180,
the Republicans. It should be an interesting ride. When liberals were
just as things have started to get interesting, the film comes to an abrupt
curse which says, 'May you live in interesting times.' Well, here I am – living
e the game away but erm phoo er be interesting to see how people fall on that
Unidentified Man 1: It's interesting to – to know, but it doesn't
and style; it would be interesting to see what this McAllister pup
that has started to produce really interesting wines, especially whites, at &
Oh yes. That's very interesting yeah. If he didn't get

What these lines show is that, overwhelmingly, *interested* is used in the phrase *interested in*, and the pattern 'someone is interested in something' is exceptionally frequent. By contrast, *interesting* is nearly always used before a noun, in the pattern 'an interesting thing'. Significant exceptions to this include 'What is interesting is . . .' and 'It's interesting to see . . .' The minimal pair that might be represented by 'the boy is interested' and 'the boy is interesting' occurs comparatively rarely (though it must be remembered that 23 lines are only a small proportion of the total). The focus of what is to be taught, therefore, shifts from the confusable pair *interested* and *interesting* to the phrases 'someone is interested in something', 'an interesting thing', 'what is interesting is' and 'it is interesting to see', which are, hopefully, different enough to be less easily confused.

A similar approach is taken by Kennedy (1991) in his study of *between* and *through*. After pointing out that reference books have difficulty in expressing the differences between these words, Kennedy adopts a phraseological approach. He notes that *between* is frequently found after nouns such as *difference, distinction, gap, contrast, conflict* and *quarrel*, as well as *relationship, agreement, comparison, meeting, contact* and *correlation*, whereas *through* is more frequently found after verbs such as *go, pass, come, run, fall* and *lead*. These and other observations enable him to provide a profile of each word (1991: 106–107) that relates each aspect of meaning to typical phraseologies. Kennedy is also able to assign frequencies to the different meanings, or 'semantic functions'. Approximately a quarter of the instances of *between* in the Lancaster-Oslo-Bergen (LOB) corpus have a 'location' meaning (e.g. *the channel between Africa and Sicily; earnings between £5 and £6 a week*) whilst about the same proportion of the instances of *through* have an 'instrumental' meaning (e.g. *I should have met him through Robert Graves; evidence obtained through the examination of stones*).

Phraseology of this kind can be an extremely subtle phenomenon. Below are all the instances of the phrase *GRASP the point* from the Bank of English, with the lines numbered for reference. (Note: here and henceforward, capitals are used to indicate all the forms of a verb. For example, *GRASP* means *grasp, grasps, grasping* and *grasped*.)

```
1        in Free, where Teenotchy tries to grasp the point and the structure of
2            accident will help the islanders grasp the point. Racing: Guardian's
3         Please, all of you out there, try to grasp the point. We do not want
4       the Independent on Sunday. I fail to grasp the point of newspapers' divided
5     wonderful. People are able at last to grasp the point of it now that the
6          some scholars were beginning to grasp the point, most shared the
7    Beginning. When you want readers to grasp the point of a paragraph right
8              is likely to be his failure to grasp the point made by his former pri
9       incompetent, often envious, rarely grasp the point of any given book, if
10     always supposing the latter has yet grasped the point – and has responded
11     of it now. He doesn't seem to have grasped the point of the project.
12     me, I'd kill him." But when they had grasped the point of it, they became
13     this hornet's nest. Giovanni Benelli grasped the point at once. He saw Worl
14        genes in the cell. Once we have grasped the point about genes working
15      members – if they hadn't already grasped the point – that 'money has be
16        Belatedly, Yasser Arafat has grasped the point that his people in
17          team do not seem to have grasped the point about these jokes:
18     if not all communication that one grasps the point of what someone is
```

A simple observation here is that *point* is frequently followed by *of* (lines 4, 5, 7, 9, 11, 12, 18). Less obvious, perhaps, is what comes before *GRASP*. In most cases, there is either an indication of something not being done (lines 4, 8, 9, 11, 17) or an indication of something difficult being achieved (lines 1, 2, 3, 5, 6, 7, 10, 15, 16). Even when a line appears to be a counter-example, as in line 13, a look at more co-text indicates that 'grasping the point' is problematic even here: in this case, Benelli is contrasted with another person who fails to grasp the point. This subtlety of usage is difficult to intuit, and is observable only when a lot of evidence is seen together so that the pattern emerges.

Collocation

The final example of how the data in corpora can be manipulated is the calculation of collocation. This will be examined in more detail in chapter 4; here it is sufficient to note that collocation is the statistical tendency of words to co-occur. A list of the collocates of a given word can yield similar information to that provided by concordance lines, with the difference that more information can be processed more accurately by the statistical operations of the computer than can be dealt with by the human observer.

For example, collocates of the word *shed* include: *light, tear/s, garden, jobs, blood, cents, image, pounds, staff, skin* and *clothes*. Only when it collocates with *garden* is the word *shed* a noun; in all other cases it is a verb. Its meaning is something like 'lose' or 'give', but the precise meaning of each phrase depends on the collocate:

shed light (on) means 'illuminate', usually metaphorically;
shed tears means 'cry' (literally) or 'be sorrowful' (crying metaphorical tears);
shed blood means 'suffer' or 'die', either literally or metaphorically;
shed jobs and *shed staff* mean 'get rid of people';
shed pounds means 'lose weight';
in *shed skin* and *shed clothes*, *shed* means 'remove';
shed cents is used to indicate that shares or a currency become reduced in value;
shed image means a deliberate changing of how one is perceived.

Collocation can indicate pairs of lexical items, such as *shed + tears*, or the association between a lexical word and its frequent grammatical environment.[1] For example, the word *head* has the following lexical collocates:

---

[1] The collocation between a lexical word and a grammatical one is frequently termed 'colligation'.

SHAKE, injuries and *SHOOT,* in which *head* indicates a part of the body (as in *shook her head; head injuries; was shot in the head,* for example);

state, office, former and *department,* in which *head* indicates a person in charge;

and these grammatical collocates:

possessives such as *his, her, my* and *your;*
of, used in phrases such as *head of department;*
over, used in phrases such as *HIT/BEAT someone over the head, HOLD something over someone's head, GO over one's head* and *LOSE one's head over someone;*
on, as in *HIT someone on the head, PUT something on one's head, MEET something head on,* and *TURN something on its head;*
back, as in *back of the head, head back* and *PUT/THROW one's head back;*
off, as in *head off a problem, CUT someone's head off* and *head off towards somewhere.*

The various phraseologies of *head,* together with the meanings associated with these phraseologies, are indicated by these collocates.

What corpora are used for

Corpora nowadays have a diverse range of uses, which will be discussed more fully in chapters 5, 7 and 8, but some are summarised here:

- For language teaching, corpora can give information about how a language works that may not be accessible to native speaker intuition, such as the detailed phraseology mentioned above. In addition, the relative frequency of different features can be calculated. According to Mindt (2000), for example, nearly all the future time reference in conversational English is indicated by *will* or other modals. The phrase *BE going to* accounts for about 10% of future time reference, and the present progressive less than 5%. Information such as this is important for syllabus and materials design.
- Increasingly, language classroom teachers are encouraging students to explore corpora for themselves (see, for example, Burnard and McEnery eds. 2000), allowing them to observe nuances of usage and to make comparisons between languages.
- Translators use comparable corpora to compare the use of apparent translation equivalents in two languages, and parallel

corpora to see how words and phrases have been translated in the past. As an example in chapter 5 shows, for example, the English word *still* can translate or be translated by the French *toujours* or *encore*, or by expressions with *couramment* or the verb *continuer.* Sometimes when an English sentence includes the word *still* the parallel French sentence has no translation equivalent at all, but when *toujours* and *encore* are present in the French sentence, the English parallel sentence always contains *still.*

- General corpora can be used to establish norms of frequency and usage against which individual texts can be measured. This has applications for work in stylistics and in clinical and forensic linguistics.
- Corpora are used also to investigate cultural attitudes expressed through language (e.g. Stubbs 1996; Teubert 2000) and as a resource for critical discourse studies (e.g. Krishnamurthy 1996; Caldas-Coulthard and Moon 1999; Fairclough 2000).

Types of corpora

A corpus is always designed for a particular purpose, and the type of corpus will depend on its purpose. Here are some commonly used corpus types:

- **Specialised corpus.** A corpus of texts of a particular type, such as newspaper editorials, geography textbooks, academic articles in a particular subject, lectures, casual conversations, essays written by students etc. It aims to be representative of a given type of text. It is used to investigate a particular type of language. Researchers often collect their own specialised corpora to reflect the kind of language they want to investigate. There is no limit to the degree of specialisation involved, but the parameters are set to limit the kind of texts included. For example, a corpus might be restricted to a time frame, consisting of texts from a particular century, or to a social setting, such as conversations taking place in a bookshop, or to a given topic, such as newspaper articles dealing with the European Union. Some well-known specialised corpora include the 5 million word Cambridge and Nottingham Corpus of Discourse in English (CANCODE) (informal registers of British English) and the Michigan Corpus of Academic Spoken English (MICASE) (spoken registers in a US academic setting).
- **General corpus.** A corpus of texts of many types. It may include written or spoken language, or both, and may include texts produced in one country or many. It is unlikely to be representative

of any particular 'whole', but will include as wide a spread of texts as possible. A general corpus is usually much larger than a specialised corpus. It may be used to produce reference materials for language learning or translation, and it is often used as a baseline in comparison with more specialised corpora. Because of this second function it is also sometimes called a **reference corpus**. Well-known general corpora include the British National Corpus (100 million words) and the Bank of English (400 million words in January 2001),[2] both of which comprise a range of sub-corpora from different sources. Much earlier general corpora were the LOB corpus, consisting of written British English, and the Brown corpus, consisting of written American English, both compiled in the 1960s and comprising 1 million words each.

- **Comparable corpora.** Two (or more) corpora in different languages (e.g. English and Spanish) or in different varieties of a language (e.g. Indian English and Canadian English). They are designed along the same lines, for example they will contain the same proportions of newspaper texts, novels, casual conversation, and so on. Comparable corpora of varieties of the same language can be used to compare those varieties. Comparable corpora of different languages can be used by translators and by learners to identify differences and equivalences in each language. The ICE corpora (International Corpus of English) are comparable corpora of 1 million words each of different varieties of English.
- **Parallel corpora.** Two (or more) corpora in different languages, each containing texts that have been translated from one language into the other (e.g. a novel in English that has been translated into Spanish, and one in Spanish that has been translated into English) or texts that have been produced simultaneously in two or more languages (e.g. European Union regulations, which are published in all the official languages of the EU). They can be used by translators and by learners to find potential equivalent expressions in each language and to investigate differences between languages.
- **Learner corpus.** A collection of texts – essays, for example – produced by learners of a language. The purpose of this corpus is to identify in what respects learners differ from each other and from the language of native speakers, for which a comparable corpus of native-speaker texts is required. There are a number of learner corpora around the world, of which the best known is the

---

[2] The Bank of English has increased in size progressively since its inception in the 1980s. Some of the studies in this book were done on the 323 million word corpus; others on the 400 million word one.

International Corpus of Learner English (ICLE). This is in fact a collection of corpora of 20,000 words each, each one comprising essays written by learners of English from a particular language background (French, Swedish, German etc). There is a comparable corpus of essays written by native speakers of English: the Louvain Corpus of Native English Essays (LOCNESS).

- **Pedagogic corpus.** A corpus consisting of all the language a learner has been exposed to. For most learners, their pedagogic corpus does not exist in physical form. If a teacher or researcher does decide to collect a pedagogic corpus, it can consist of all the course books, readers etc a learner has used, plus any tapes etc they have heard. The term 'pedagogic corpus' is used by D. Willis (1993). A pedagogic corpus can be used to collect together for the learner all instances of a word or phrase they have come across in different contexts, for the purpose of raising awareness. It can also be compared with a corpus of naturally occurring English to check that the learner is being presented with language that is natural-sounding and useful.
- **Historical or diachronic corpus.** A corpus of texts from different periods of time. It is used to trace the development of aspects of a language over time. Perhaps the best-known historical corpus of English is the Helsinki Corpus, which consists of texts from 700 to 1700 and comprises 1.5 million words.
- **Monitor corpus.** A corpus designed to track current changes in a language. A monitor corpus is added to annually, monthly or even daily, so it rapidly increases in size. However, the proportion of text types in the corpus remains constant, so that each year (or month or day) is directly comparable with every other.

Issues in the design and purpose of corpora are discussed in chapter 2.

Some key terms

The literature on corpora makes use of a certain amount of technical terminology. It may be helpful to explain a few of the most essential terms here. Eight terms will be explained: *type, token, hapax, lemma, word-form, tag, parse* and *annotate*.

'Type', 'token' and 'hapax'

How many words are there in the following paragraph (taken from Simpson and Montgomery 1995: 140)?

What elements make up a narrative? Providing an answer to this question has become one of the central challenges for a stylistics of prose fiction. Much work in modern narrative stylistics seeks to isolate the various units which combine to form a novel or short story and to explain how these narrative units are interconnected. Having identified the basic units in this way, the next task is to specify which type of stylistic model is best suited to the study of which particular unit.

In one sense, there are 84 words. That is, there are 84 sequences of letters separated by spaces or punctuation. This is the figure that the word-count function of a word-processing program gives. In other words, there are 84 **tokens**.

However, many of these words occur more than once:

a	occurs 3 times
narrative	occurs 3 times
to	occurs 6 times
this	occurs 2 times
of	occurs 4 times
the	occurs 5 times
in	occurs 2 times
stylistics	occurs 2 times
units	occurs 3 times
which	occurs 3 times
is	occurs 2 times

Counting each repeated item once only, so that only different words are counted, gives a total of 60 items. Using the terminology, there are 60 **types**. The words that occur only once are called **hapax legomena** or **hapaxes**.

The short sample paragraph, therefore, comprises a corpus of 84 tokens and 60 types, including 33 hapaxes. In a very small corpus like this, the ratio of types to tokens might be expected to be high as in this example. In a larger corpus, there will be relatively more tokens for each type, as there is more repetition of individual words in longer texts (Biber et al 1999: 53).

'Lemma' and 'word-form'

There is a further factor to be taken into account when dealing with 'words' in a corpus. In the paragraph about narrative quoted above, for example, it could be argued that *unit* and *units* are in a sense the 'same word', in that one is simply the plural form of the other. We might say, then, that *unit* and *units* are two **word-forms** belonging to the same **lemma**: *UNIT*. In the same way, *eat, eats, eating, ate* and *eaten* are word-forms belonging to the lemma *EAT*. There is some debate as to whether two word-forms belong to the same lemma if they belong to different word-classes (for example, do the adjective *stylistic* and the noun *stylistics* in the above paragraph belong to the same lemma or not?). To a large extent the notion of lemma is a convenience, so what is to be counted in a lemma depends on what use the idea is to be put to. Often, for example, it is useful to see what prepositions follow an adjective by getting all instances of the adjective lemma only. In this book, unless otherwise stated, word-forms will be said to belong to the same lemma only if they belong to the same word-class. Thus, *quick*, *quicker* and *quickest* belong to the lemma *QUICK*, but *quickly* will not be said to belong to the same lemma.

'Tag', 'parse' and 'annotate'

These terms refer to procedures that are carried out to add information to the words in a corpus. The additions may be made automatically (i.e. by a computer program alone) or manually (i.e. by a human being working with the computer program). Adding information automatically is a fast and easily repeated process, but often of limited accuracy; adding information manually is a relatively slow process, and needs to be repeated if the corpus is changed or enlarged, but the results are more accurate.[3] Speed and accuracy are two of the key issues in the addition of information to a corpus.

The term **tagging** is normally used to refer to the addition of a code to each word in a corpus, indicating the part of speech. It is feasible to tag a corpus automatically, and such tagging will be reasonably, but not entirely accurate. For a small corpus it is possible to edit the tags to obtain a higher degree of accuracy; for a very large corpus, this is not normally practical.

Tags are useful as components of word searches. Someone wishing to investigate a word such as *work*, for example, may wish to look at the nouns separately from the verbs. A tagger allows these to be searched for independently. In addition, a tagger may be used to make calculations of proportions of word use. For example, Granger and Rayson (1998) compare native and non-native corpora and

---

[3] For the purposes of this discussion, 'accurate' means 'what a competent human analyst would decide'. The issue of accuracy is not this simple, however. Human analysts make mistakes if they are tired or bored; computers do not become tired, and in that sense they are 'more accurate'. Sometimes even the notion of 'accuracy' itself is misleading. For example, both human beings and computers may argue about whether *circle* in *circle line* is a noun or an adjective.

report that the non-native speakers use more determiners, pronouns and adverbs than native speakers do, but fewer conjunctions, prepositions and nouns. A possible explanation for this is that the native speakers use more complex and abstract noun phrases than the non-native speakers do. As another example, it is possible to count the number of nouns, verbs, and so on, in a corpus as a whole, or to calculate whether a particular word is more frequently used as a noun or a verb in a given register. In the *New Scientist* corpus of the Bank of English, the verb *WORK* occurs 926 times per million words, and the noun occurs 654 times. In the spoken corpus, the verb occurs 1,060 times per million words, and noun 572 times. Although in both corpora the verb is more frequent than the noun, the noun is relatively less frequently used in the spoken corpus than in the *New Scientist* corpus. Looking at the collocations of the noun *WORK* in each case suggests differences in meaning too. The most significant collocates in the *New Scientist* are the possessives, especially in the phrases *their work* (i.e. the investigations of a group of scientists) and *the work of*. In other words, a frequent meaning of the noun *WORK* is scientific discovery. Another frequent meaning is to describe what non-human entities, such as bacteria, do. In the spoken corpus, significant collocates include *of work* (as in *loads of work, sort of work*) and *at work*. The most frequent meaning of the noun *WORK* is 'job'. The meaning of *WORK* (noun) in the *New Scientist* is more central in terms of the topic of that magazine than the meaning of the noun in the spoken corpus is, and this perhaps explains why the noun is relatively more frequent in the *New Scientist* corpus.

Corpus **parsing** is the analysis of text into constituents, such as clauses and groups. A parsed corpus can be used to count with great accuracy the number of different structures in a corpus.

Parsing can be done automatically, but the resulting output is often not very accurate. Accuracy can be improved by 'training' the automatic parser, that is, by setting up the parser to learn from past examples. In that case, a small corpus is parsed and edited manually and the resulting output is used to train the automatic parser (Leech and Eyes 1997). Parsers of this level of sophistication have been developed by Leech and his colleagues at Lancaster University and, though the process is somewhat cumbersome, a high level of accuracy is achieved. Where total accuracy is required, however, for example where the parsed text is being used to teach human learners how to do grammatical parsing, manual editing is still needed (McEnery et al 1997).

A superordinate term for tagging and parsing is **annotation**. 'Annotation' is also used to describe other kinds of information that can be added to a corpus. Again, Lancaster University leads this field, and numerous interesting examples can be found in Garside et al (eds. 1997). Annotation in this more limited sense is often done manually. Typical examples include: the annotation of a spoken corpus for intonation; annotation for anaphora, which identifies the cohesive item and its referent; and annotation of various means of representing speech and thought in written text. Annotation of this kind essentially uses the computer to keep track of very lengthy manual analyses, so that the statistics from these analyses can more easily be calculated. (See chapter 4 for further examples of corpus annotation.)

Why corpora? Why not?

At the end of this introductory chapter, it is worth returning to the central question of why corpora are important for applied linguists, and also to consider their limitations. Corpora are often described as a tool, and the development of corpora has been likened to the invention of telescopes in the history of astronomy (Stubbs 1996: 231). It might be more proper to say that corpora are a way of collecting and storing data, and that it is the corpus access programs – presenting concordance lines and calculating frequencies – that are the tools. Stubbs (1999) points out that, just as it is ridiculous to criticise a telescope for not being a microscope, so it is pointless to criticise corpora for not allowing some methods of investigation. They are invaluable for doing what they do, and what they do not do must be done in another way.

A corpus essentially tells us what language is like, and the main argument in favour of using a corpus is that it is a more reliable guide to language use than native speaker intuition is. Although a native speaker has experience of very much more language than is contained in even the largest corpus, much of that experience remains hidden from introspection (although see Cook 2001). For example, native-speaker language teachers are often unable to say why a particular phrasing is to be preferred in a particular context to another, and the consequent rather lame rationale 'it just sounds better' is a source of irritation to learners.

Intuition is a poor guide to at least four aspects of language: collocation, frequency, prosody and phraseology. Examples of each of these are given below.

Judgements about collocations. Some collocations are easy to intuit (*play* – *game*, for example), others are more difficult. Granger (1998a) points out that some adverbs collocate with particular adjectives. She mentions 'stereotyped combinations such as *acutely* *aware, keenly felt, painfully clear, readily available, vitally important'* which learners of English tend not to use (1998: 150), presumably because no course writer has had the accuracy of intuition to be aware of them. Johansson (1993: 46) adds several more common combinations, including *broadly comparable, comparatively new/ small, deadly dull, deeply concerned, desperately worried, diametrically opposite, eminently respectable, equally good/important, exceptionally cheap/high, extremely difficult, fairly accurate/certain/ small/wide.* It is difficult for the native speaker to be conscious of these combinations, and others like them, without corpus evidence.

Judgements about frequency. It is almost impossible to be conscious of the relative frequency of words, phrases and structures except in very general terms (anyone might guess that *take* is a more frequent verb than *disseminate,* but it is difficult to guess whether *fare* or *fantasy* is more frequent).[4] Halliday (1993: 3) points out that whereas people do have some intuitions about the frequency of lexis (*go* is more frequent than *walk,* which is more frequent than *stroll*), they are unlikely to have intuitions about the frequency of grammatical categories, and may even resist information about these.

Semantic prosody and pragmatic meaning. Channell (2000) makes the point very strongly that many instances of pragmatic meaning are beyond the reach of intuition. For example, she notes that the phrase *par for the course* is used not only to comment that something frequently happens, but also to evaluate that event negatively. Native speakers of English often react with surprise to information of this kind and sometimes attempt to find alternative explanations for it, such as a bias in the corpus. Often, though, the reaction is of surprised recognition – 'of course that's true, why didn't I think of it before?'.

Details of phraseology. Although native speakers can often recognise if a phraseology is unusual, articulating the nature of the atypicality may be more difficult. One example may be taken from Owen (1996). Owen notes that the Bank of English corpus has several examples of *require/s* followed by a passive to-infinitive clause, even though such a construction, as in *Further experiments require to be done,* seems wrong to Owen's native-speaker intuition. A closer look at phraseology resolves the problem. Although *REQUIRE to be* is found in the Bank of English, and fairly frequently, the past participle that follows is usually that of a verb with a specific meaning, not a general verb such as *do.* There are plenty of examples of the type *These roses require to be pruned each*

---

[4] In fact, *fare* occurs about 4,000 times in the Bank of English; *fantasy* about 10,000 times.

spring but very few indeed of *require to be done* (only 3 out of 302). Thus Owen's intuitions are backed up by the evidence of the corpus, but on phraseological rather than grammatical grounds. (See chapter 7 for more details of this argument.)

Although an over-reliance on intuition can be criticised, it would be incorrect to argue that intuition is not important. Indeed, it is an essential tool for extrapolating important generalisations from a mass of specific information in a corpus. An example can be taken from Sripicharn (1998). Looking in the Bank of English for examples of the verb and noun CONTACT, Sripicharn noticed that not only was the noun followed by *with* whereas the verb was not (the expected finding), but in addition that the verb was typically used with 'official' persons – an office, a newspaper etc (e.g. *Contact your local travel agent*) – whereas the noun was chosen when the person was a family member or friend (e.g. *She had no contact with her father*). Sripicharn intuitively realised that the difference between the two kinds of nouns (*travel agent* and *father*) was important.

Having argued for the benefits of corpora to the study of language, it is as well to consider also the limitations of a corpus. These might be summarised as follows:

1 A corpus will not give information about whether something is possible or not, only whether it is frequent or not. Descriptions of English are moving towards a concentration on the typical and away from notions of well-formedness (Sinclair 1991: 17; Biber et al 1998: 3), but questions of the type – 'Can I say this?' – still need to be answered. To give a specific example, is the verb *EXPIRE* used with the preposition *of*, by analogy with *DIE of* (e.g. *died of heart disease*)? The Bank of English shows us that *EXPIRE of* is rare: 5 lines out of 3,519 lines for *EXPIRE* (0.1%), compared with *DIE of*, which has 5,259 lines out of 85,511 lines for *DIE* (6%). It is also rare in comparison with *EXPIRE from* (12 lines). Further-more, of the 5 lines of *EXPIRE of*, three are jokey, non-serious.[5] All this is useful information, but it does not actually answer the question as to whether *EXPIRE of* is acceptable English. Native-speaker intuition has to answer that question.

2 A corpus can show nothing more than its own contents. Although it may (justifiably) claim to be representative, all attempts to draw

---

[5] This example of a non-serious use is from a review of a film about poverty and revolution: *You know it will all end in tears, of course, with a lorry load of cast members either* <u>expiring of</u> *starvation, consumption or falling under the sharp heel of capitalism spurned.*

generalisations from a corpus are in fact extrapolations. A statement about evidence in a corpus is a statement about that corpus, not about the language or register of which the corpus is a sample. Thus conclusions about language drawn from a corpus have to be treated as deductions, not as facts.

3 A corpus can offer evidence but cannot give information. For example, what does the phrase *something of a* mean before a noun, as in *something of a surprise*? It might be supposed to be a 'downtoner': *something of a surprise* is a small surprise. Comparing *COME as something of a surprise* with *COME as a surprise* in the Bank of English affirms this supposition to some extent, in that adjectives such as *total, complete* and *big* occur before *surprise* but not in the phrase *something of a surprise*. Apart from that, however, there are no real clues as to the meaning of *something of a surprise* in the concordance lines. The corpus simply offers the researcher plenty of examples; only intuition can interpret them.

4 Perhaps most seriously a corpus presents language out of its context. The work of Kress and van Leeuwen (Kress and van Leeuwen 1994; Kress 1994), for example, depends upon a text being encountered in its visual and social context (or, more properly, the text consists not of the words alone but of the spatial context in which the words appear). A corpus (as corpora are currently conceived) cannot show this. Equally significant is the issue of spoken data, in that transcription can never represent intonation, kinesics ('body language'), and other paralinguistic information entirely accurately. Even if the issue of visual and intonational features is ignored, it remains true that a corpus masks some of the features of the texts in it by presenting concordance lines, in which the structure of the original is lost. These factors all show the need for a corpus to be one tool among many in the study of language.

Conclusion

This chapter has introduced some of the basic concepts that are important when using corpora in applied linguistics. Some of the possible uses of corpora have been demonstrated, along with arguments for the usefulness of corpora in describing how a language works and what language can show about the context in which it is used. Some of the limitations of corpus use have also been mentioned. The next three chapters will discuss in more detail the issues and methods in compiling and investigating corpora.

Note on sources of examples

Unless otherwise indicated, the examples, concordance lines and statistical information in this book come from the Bank of English corpus. Some of the concordance lines include codes used in that corpus, although many have been edited to exclude unnecessary codes. Examples of codes include:

<p>	start paragraph
</p>	end paragraph
<h>	start headline
</h>	end headline
<FO1>	female speaker number 1
<MO2>	male speaker number 2
<MOX>	unidentified male speaker

The concordancing program used ('Lookup') sometimes leaves incomplete words at the beginning or end of a concordance line.

2 The corpus as object: Design and purpose

As corpora have become larger and more diverse, and as they are more frequently used to make definitive statements about language, issues of how they are designed have become more important. Four aspects of corpus design are discussed in this chapter: size, content, representativeness and permanence. The chapter also summarises some types of corpus investigation, each of which treats the corpus as a different kind of object.

Issues in corpus design

Size

As computer technology has advanced since the 1960s, so it has become feasible to store and access corpora of ever-increasing size. Whereas the LOB Corpus and Brown Corpus seemed as big as anyone would ever want, at the time, nowadays 1 million words is fairly small in terms of corpora. The British National Corpus is 100 million words; the Bank of English is currently about 400 million. CANCODE is 5 million words. The feasible size of a corpus is not limited so much by the capacity of a computer to store it, as by the speed and efficiency of the access software. If, for example, counting the number of past and present tense forms of the verb *BE* in a given corpus takes longer than a few minutes, the researcher may prefer to use a smaller corpus whose results might be considered to be just as reliable but on which the software would work much more speedily.

Sheer quantity of information can be overwhelming for the observer. In the Bank of English corpus, for example, a search for the word *point* gives almost 143,000 hits. Few researchers can obtain useful information simply by looking at so many concordance lines. One solution is to use a smaller corpus, which will give less data. Another is to keep the large corpus, but to use software which will make a selection of data from the whole, either by selecting at random a proportion of the total concordance lines, or by identifying and allowing selection of the most significant collocates, or other significant features. In this way, the data from a very large corpus can be reduced to a manageable scale whilst retaining the advantages of coverage of the large corpus.

The question of corpus size can be a contentious one. There are many arguments to support the view that a small corpus *can* be valuable under certain circumstances. Carter and McCarthy (1995: 143), for example, argue that for the purposes of studying grammar in spoken language a relatively small corpus is sufficient (because grammar words tend to be very frequent). Some kinds of corpus investigation that depend on the manual annotation of the corpus are also, necessarily, restricted in terms of the size of the corpus that can feasibly be annotated. Similarly, many commercially available concordance software packages restrict the size of the corpus they can be used with (see Biber et al 1998: 285–286 for details). Someone aiming to build a balanced corpus may restrict the amount of data from one source in order to match data from another source (for example, the amount of written data may be kept smaller than it need be because it is difficult to obtain large amounts of spoken data).

A more extreme view is that for some purposes there is an *optimum* corpus size that should not be exceeded even if practical considerations would allow it, that is, that a relatively small corpus is not just sufficient but also necessary. However, this argument usually refers to the difficulties of processing large amounts of information about very frequent words, as discussed above (e.g. Carter and McCarthy 1995: 143). The opposing view would be that it is preferable to select from a large amount of data than to restrict the amount of data available (Sinclair 1992).

Arguments about optimum corpus size tend to be academic for most people. Most corpus users simply make use of as much data as is available, without worrying too much about what is not available. As well as the very large, general corpora designed to assist in writing dictionaries and other reference books, there are thousands of smaller corpora around the world, some comprising only a few thousand words and designed for a particular piece of research.

Content

It is a truism that a corpus is neither good nor bad in itself, but suited or not suited to a particular purpose. Decisions about what should go into a corpus are based on what the corpus is going to be used for, but also about what is available. A researcher who wishes to study academic articles in History, for example, may plan to build a corpus consisting simply of published articles. Even with such a straight-forward design plan, however, a number of issues will have to be resolved, such as:

- Will the articles come from one journal, or from a range of journals? How will the journal(s) be selected?
- Will the articles chosen be restricted to those apparently written by native speakers of the target language, or not?
- Will articles other than research articles, such as book reviews, be included?
- If the articles are to be stored electronically, and copyright clearance is required, which publishers are willing to give permission for their articles to be used?
- If the articles are required in electronic form, which publishers are willing to make electronic versions of their journals available?

To the first three of these questions, there are no 'right' answers. The best choice in each case will depend on the precise purpose of the research. The last two questions refer to purely pragmatic issues, but these may in the end affect the design of the corpus more profoundly than the first three.

Publishers' policies are not the only issues affecting availability for corpora. Parallel corpora, for example, are composed of texts that are translations of each other. They can make use only of texts that have been translated between the two languages involved. Other issues of selection come second to the question of what translations exist. Using unpublished material in a corpus does not obviate the issue of availability. For example, a researcher wishing to study student writing may ask students to submit electronic versions of their essays to assist in this work. If this submission is voluntary, the researcher will collect only the essays whose authors are willing for their essays to be used.

For some purposes, corpus design is scarcely an issue. For example, if a corpus is being used to encourage learners to investigate language data for themselves, the precise contents of that corpus may be relatively unimportant. Any collection of newspapers written in the target form of the language, for example, will be adequate for some investigation purposes, even if the newspapers do not represent all aspects of language use (see, for example, Dodd 1997). Where the corpus is being taken as representative of a language or a language variety, the notion of design and balance is very important. This will be considered separately below.

Balance and representativeness

Corpora are very often intended to be representative of a particular kind of language. If the object of study is academic prose, or casual conversation, or the language of newspapers, or American English, for example, an attempt must be made to build a corpus that is representative of the whole. (See Kennedy 1991: 52; Crowdy 1993; Burnard ed. 1995 for discussions of representativeness in the British National Corpus.) Usually, this involves breaking the whole down into component parts and aiming to include equal amounts of data from each of the parts. For example, under 'the language of newspapers', it may be decided to include a range of newspaper types (broadsheet and tabloid, for instance) and a range of article types (hard news, human interest, editorials, letters, sports, business, advertisements and so on). A balanced corpus might be said to consist of equal numbers of words in each category: broadsheet hard news; tabloid hard news; broadsheet human interest; tabloid human interest and so on. This notion of balance is, however, open to question. It might be argued that broadsheet newspapers contain more words, on average, than tabloids, and that therefore the corpus should contain more from the broadsheets than from the tabloids. Alternatively, it might be argued that tabloids are read by more people than broadsheets and that therefore they should comprise a larger part of the corpus. If the broadsheets contain more hard news and editorial than the tabloids, and the tabloids contain more human interest and sports news, should the proportions in the corpus be adjusted accordingly? In the case of newspapers, the solution may be to include all issues of a selection of publications from a given week, month or year. This will allow the proportions to determine themselves. It does mean, however, that more data will probably be gathered from one type of publication than another. Similar problems with relation to the collection of academic prose or casual conversation, for example, are not open to so easy a solution. The problem is that 'being representative' inevitably involves knowing what the character of the 'whole' is. Where the proportions of that character are unknowable, attempts to be representative tend to rest on little more than guesswork.

The problem of representation and balance becomes more difficult when the corpus is supposed to represent a regional variety of English (Singapore English, or British English, or Australian English), with all its complexity of internal variation. In practice, the way that this is done depends on the purpose of the corpus. The International Corpus of English (ICE), for example, exists to facilitate comparison between regional varieties. To enable this to be done, the compilers of each regional corpus were given precise instructions as to how much of what kinds of language (newspapers, literature, conversation etc) to include, irrespective of the internal make-up of their own variety. The Bank of English is designed as a resource for writers of dictionaries and other reference books for learners of English. It is assumed that learners will expect to find standard English described in such books, and as a result there is no attempt to represent regional or social varieties of spoken English in it. There is in fact a good deal of non-standard spoken language in the BoE, but it is not possible to use this corpus to compare, say, the English spoken in Bristol with the English spoken in Newcastle. The British National Corpus, on the other hand, is designed to represent the different varieties of spoken English within Britain, and to allow comparisons to be made, although only between very broadly identified groups, such as 'south' and 'north' (Rayson et al 1997).

Spoken language exists in unknowable quantities and in an unknowable range of varieties. How, then, is a corpus builder to 'represent' the diversity in a meaningful way? One approach is to make a list of variables, as discussed above, taking into account age, gender, social class and home town of each speaker, as well as settings or genres, such as casual conversation, service encounter, radio broadcast, classroom, office and so on. Roughly equal amounts of data can then be collected under each heading. This will give a reasonable spread of registers, but it is important to remember that we do not know how balanced or representative the resulting corpus is. For example, we do not know how much weight should be given to 'service encounters' as opposed to 'office talk', and so on, or, indeed, how many and which genres should be included. After all, no definitive list of spoken genres exists. An alternative is to include whatever data is available, covering as many different settings and genres as possible, but without attempting to balance the corpus between the types. The advantage of this is that no data has to be wasted, as conversations between male speakers, for example, do not have to be discarded because no conversations of an equivalent kind between female speakers have been obtained. The hope is that once the corpus is of a substantial size the relevant figures can be checked and efforts made to collect data from under-represented groups, so that balance, where it is possible, is achieved after the corpus is (partially) complete, rather than from the outset. The disadvantage is that even where there is adequate information on the relevant groups in the population as a whole (for example, there are roughly equal numbers of women and men) the corpus may be biased towards one group or the other. The books in the original Cobuild corpus, for example, consisted of 49 written by men and only 15 written by women (Renouf 1987: 33).

The real question as regards representativeness is how the balance of a corpus should be taken into account when interpreting data from that corpus. De Beaugrande (1999), for example, reports that the Bank of English (the 211 million word version) contained 11 instances of *did not/didn't mean to kill*, whereas the British National Corpus contained only 2 instances. A reviewer of de Beaugrande's paper (1999: 258) apparently commented that this discrepancy might arise because the Bank of English contains proportionally more journalistic prose than the British National Corpus does. It is not possible to reconstruct from de Beaugrande's note what the full import of the reviewer's comment was. It is most likely to be a warning: 'Don't assume that *didn't mean to kill* is typical in English as a whole, because it is generally only found in newspapers.' This is true: of the 23 instances of *did not/didn't mean to kill* in the current Bank of English, four occur in books and all the others in newspapers. On the other hand, this does not substantially affect de Beaugrande's point, which is that *didn't mean to* often has a pragmatic meaning of apology rather than being a straightforward statement of fact, *I didn't mean to kill him* being only one instance of this, if a dramatic one. Corpus design is less important here than, where necessary, paying attention to the distribution of a phrase across sub-corpora. This can be done by looking at comparative frequencies, even where sub-corpora are of unequal sizes. For example, the phrase *didn't mean to* (followed by any verb) is found most frequently in books (about 3 times per million words), then in spoken English (1.3 times per million words), then in journalism (below once per million words). The relative frequency of *did not mean to kill* in journalism is explained by the large number of reports of court cases in that register.

Permanence

One aspect of representativeness that is sometimes overlooked is the diachronic aspect. Any corpus that is not regularly updated rapidly becomes unrepresentative, in the sense that it no longer represents the language as currently written or spoken. A monitor corpus, which is added to very frequently, clearly has temporal representativeness as a key aspect of its design. It is usually, however, impossible to maintain a monitor corpus that also includes texts of many different types, as some are just too expensive or time-consuming to collect on a regular basis. On the other hand, the easy availability of newspaper material makes it feasible to build a monitor corpus that can be enlarged and updated annually, weekly, or even daily (for an account of monitor corpora see Sinclair 1991: 23–26). Such a corpus does not represent all kinds of language use, but can be used to keep track of changes in the language appearing in newspapers. There is some evidence (Hundt and Mair 1999) that newspapers, although they have their own style, are a good source of general information about language change, as they incorporate changes more quickly than other kinds of discourse do. A monitor corpus comprising only newspaper data sacrifices 'what is desirable' (adding to a general corpus from all of its component registers every year) to 'what is feasible' (developing a corpus that is restricted in terms of register but expansive in size and in currency).[1]

A monitor corpus is an object in constant flux, something that is transient and fleeting. The other side of the coin is a corpus which is a permanent artefact, a definitive and fixed representation of a language variety. Permanence is significant when a corpus has symbolic value. For many minority languages, the establishment of a corpus serves to assert identity and importance, rather as writing a dictionary of the language has always done. For example, the TRACTOR archive (a resource produced by the Trans-European Language Resources Infrastructure research project) contains corpora of languages from newly independent European countries, such as Estonian, Latvian, Lithuanian, Slovenian, Ukrainian and Uzbek, as well as the more widely spoken languages, such as English, French and Spanish (http://www.telri.de). In the Netherlands, a corpus of Dutch from the eighth to the twenty-first century is sponsored by the Dutch and Belgian governments (Kruyt 2000). The motivation behind the financing of such a project is political as well as linguistic.

A corpus, once compiled, can assist in other language-maintenance projects such as the preparation of descriptions of the vocabulary, grammar and pragmatic usage of contemporary native speakers. Ahmed and Davies (1997: 158), who have compiled corpora of Welsh, refer to these products of corpus research as 'an infrastructure for promoting Welsh as a language'. They note that the preparation of 'term banks' (lists of technical terms from science and technology in the target language) is particularly important to the maintenance

---

[1] I am indebted to conversations with Professor Wolfgang Teubert for the development of this idea.

of a minority language such as Welsh, and give details of how this can be done using a corpus as a resource.[2]

The issue of permanence raises the question of what kind of object a corpus is. At extreme ends of the spectrum, it is a permanent, definitive record of a language, or a fluctuating trace of change. Further, different views about the nature of a corpus as an object will be considered in the next section.

Corpus, text and language

Another basic distinction that needs to be made is between a corpus as a collection of texts and a corpus as a collection of samples of language (Scott 2000). In terms of how the corpus is designed, this is a fairly simple distinction: a corpus may consist of whole texts or of extracts from texts. The distinction goes beyond this, however, to how a corpus is investigated, and for what purpose. Below are some examples of studies, each of which takes a different approach to what a corpus is.

The corpus as a collection of texts I

For a study of *thank you* as a conversational closing, Aston (1995) has collected two corpora consisting of 'naturally occurring service encounters between assistants and customers' in bookshops in Britain and in Italy (Aston 1995: 64). There are 160 English encounters and 181 Italian ones. Fifty-three per cent of the English encounters include an expression of thanks, while 70% of the Italian ones do. Of the English thanks, 94% are produced by the customer, while 85% of the Italian ones are (1995: 66). Through close examination of the encounters with thanks, Aston gives an account of how and why thanking is employed, arguing that its use goes far beyond a simple politeness token and that 'thanking can be seen as motivated to a large extent by concerns of conversational management, where there is a need to ratify referential and/or role alignment' (1995: 78). For example, he cites examples from the corpus where a customer needs

---

[2] An issue of current importance is the status of sign languages, such as British Sign Language, which is at the time of writing not recognised as a language by the British government. A corpus of sign language presents particular challenges, as the language does not have sounds that can be represented by letters. However, building a corpus of BSL, which would necessitate annotating a video corpus with transcription symbols (see, for example, Brien et al 1992: xvii–xxiii), would aid the cause of those pressing to have BSL officially recognised.

to check that he/she has understood the assistant's information correctly. Once the problem of possible misunderstanding has been settled, the customer typically uses thanking in acknowledgement (1995: 70).

The research that Aston reports in this article uses methods which essentially belong to conversation analysis. Although the corpus may be stored electronically, the only part of the method that could use corpus search techniques is the identification of which of the candidate dialogues include thanking and therefore form part of this study. In this particular paper, then (though not in his other work), Aston uses an electronic corpus simply as a convenient way to store a collection of texts. (For other work on thanking and other routines, see Aijmer 1996.)

More recently, studies have combined techniques of conversation analysis with the possibilities of annotation that corpora provide. For example, Barth (1999) discusses examples of the concessive relation in spoken English. She argues that there is a 'cardinal' concessive pattern consisting of (X) a statement, (X') a positive reference to that statement, (Y) a counter-argument; the pattern may occur in the canonical order or with variation. This is illustrated in the following two examples (heavily adapted and simplified from Barth 1999, with intonation coding omitted):

Code	Dialogue	Explanatory gloss
(1)		
(X)	S: and it was it was like the norm. Everybody knew that that was really a sacred thing to a certain extent	[in the 1940s, everyone knew that sexual abstinence was the norm]
(X')	D: right	[agree that everybody knew that]
(Y)	and nobody did it though	[people did not practise sexual abstinence]
(2)		
(X)	R: but when we look at . . . your inner circle of advisors we see white men only	[the government employs only (white) men]
(Y)	B: you can look all around and you'll see first class strong women	[the government employs women]
(X')	Uh Jim Baker's a man yeah I agree . . .	[one top advisor is a man]
(Y)	but look around who's . . . around with him there	[the others are women]

Like Aston, Barth uses the corpus as a convenient way of storing texts, with the additional advantage that selected features can be tagged. The annotation is, however, carried out entirely by hand.

According to Barth, the concession sequences are identified by the presence of connectors such as *but* and *though*, by paralinguistic cues such as intonation, and by contextual cues, that is 'world knowledge'. Unfortunately, neither connectors nor particular intonation patterns can reliably identify only these sequences in a corpus. Items such as *but* and *though* signal other forms of contrast, for example. The 'world knowledge' in the above examples seems to consist of the recognition of contrasts, such as that between *everybody knew that* and *nobody did it* and that between *men* and *women*, and the recognition of class membership, e.g. *Jim Baker* belongs to the class of *inner circle of advisors*. Selecting and balancing such items requires human input and cannot be automated. Because of this, Barth's work illustrates some of the problems involved in developing the use of corpora for the investigation of pragmatic features of language.

Like Aston, then, Barth uses the computer to facilitate work which could feasibly, if less conveniently, be done on paper. The corpus assists but does not drive methods of discourse analysis.

The corpus as a collection of texts II

Channell (2000) uses the Bank of English corpus to study the uses of a variety of words and phrases, such as *fat, right-on, off the beaten track, in the sticks* and *par for the course*. With respect to *par for the course*, she argues that speakers use the phrase to indicate not only that a situation is negatively evaluated, but also to confirm 'affiliation' – the sharing of experience (Channell 2000: 48–49). Using a method of examination that is not dissimilar to Aston's, she shows the detailed interaction management that is achieved by use of this phrase.

Like Aston, then, Channell uses the corpus as a collection of texts, employing search techniques to find her target phrases but then viewing the dialogue as a whole and examining it in ways that would be just as appropriate using paper and pencil as using a computer. Such a method is of course unavoidable when items with a clear discourse function, such as *thank you* or *par for the course*, are being studied. The difference between the two studies lies in corpus design. Aston uses a corpus that has been designed to investigate service encounters in order to carry out such an investigation. It would not be possible, however, to design a corpus to include instances of *par for the course*. Instead, Channell uses a corpus collected for other purposes to find examples of the item she wishes to study. If the corpus did not contain this phrase she would not study it; indeed, she would probably use such negative evidence to argue that the phrase is not significant enough to be worth study.[3]

The corpus as a collection of words in context: qualitative

Barlow's (1996) study is concerned only with the immediate environment of each word rather than with the discourse in which it occurs (unlike Aston's study, above). Barlow examines reflexive pronouns such as *myself* and observes the most frequent verbs with which they co-occur. The verbs co-occurring most significantly with *myself* are: *FIND, SEE, TELL, ASK, LET, MAKE, STOP, BRING, GET, GIVE, CONSIDER, FEEL, ENJOY* and *HELP*. This observation suggests that *myself* is not most usefully considered as an item in a paradigm with other pronouns (Barlow notes that *I could not bring myself to watch the race* is nothing like *I could not bring him to watch the race*) but as something that occurs as an element in a number of phrases, each with its own meaning. Echoing Francis et al (1996: 62–68), Barlow also argues that the tendency to be followed by a reflexive is an important aspect of the behaviour of a number of less frequent verbs (Barlow, 1996: 12–13).

Barlow's work is a typical example of its kind. He begins with a word (although he takes a category – reflexive pronouns – he treats each lexical instance as a separate item) and examines its immediate context, comparing what is found with what intuition or grammatical theory would predict. The role of the word in the larger discourse is not commented on, except insofar as it is observable from the immediate context. As far as Barlow is concerned, then, the corpus could consist only of the word *myself* and its immediate co-texts. From the collocational information found, conclusions are drawn regarding the way that language can and should be described.

The corpus as a collection of words in context: quantitative

Mason's (1999) study also begins with a single word and ends with a theoretical conclusion, but the study is entirely quantitative and the conclusions drawn about language are statistical in nature. Here we are very far removed from the individual discourses that make up the

---

[3] It appears that corpora as collections are being used increasingly by linguists of various kinds. For example, Gomez-Gonzalez (1998) finds and analyses instances of extended multiple themes in a corpus, and He and Kennedy (1999) use a prosodically tagged corpus to find and categorise successful turn-bidding.

corpus in question. Like Barlow, Mason looks at the words occurring in the immediate environment of the target (node) word, but unlike Barlow he is not primarily interested in what those words are, only how many types there are in relation to the total number of concordance lines used. A low number of types means that the node word exerts a strong influence, a high number means that it exerts a weak influence. If the number of types at each point in relation to the node (one word before, two words before, one word after, two words after and so on) is calculated, it is possible to see where the node word exerts its influence. With the word *of*, for example (Mason 1999: 271), the number of types immediately before *of* is much less than that immediately after. This shows that *of* exerts more of an influence on the words it follows than on the words that follow it. Mason also shows that this influence extends to words up to four places to the left of *of*. If types of lexical items are replaced by types of word-class tag (so that all nouns count as the same thing), a similar pattern of the grammatical behaviour of a word is shown. Mason uses his study to suggest that the span used for calculating collocation (usually +/− 4) should vary according to the patterning of each word.

Mason's study thus has implications for how statistics are applied to corpora. For the purposes of this interpretation, the words that make up a corpus are simply symbols, without meaning or significance. At the same time, however, Mason interprets his findings in terms of actual phrases such as *the best of*.

The corpus as a collection of categories

Aarts and Granger (1998) use a version of a group of learner corpora that is tagged to show parts of speech. The frequency of various sequences of tags in those corpora, such as 'preposition + article + noun' or 'article + adjective + noun', is then calculated. Like Mason's study, then, they treat the corpus as a collection of symbols, without meaning. In this case, the symbols are not individual words, but word-class categories. The corpora are compared in terms of the most frequent tag sequences.

Work of this kind is very abstract, but can immediately be related to specific phraseologies, as will be demonstrated in chapter 8. The abstract categories are used to produce statistical measurements, which give a starting point for less abstract explanations.

Conclusion

This chapter has briefly introduced some of the tensions that might exist when answering the question: what kind of object is a corpus? In corpus design, the criteria of size, balance and contemporaneousness are in tension with one another. In terms of use, a corpus may be constructed and/or used as a collection of individual texts, or as a collection of words in context, or as a collection of categories. Each of these implies an object of a different kind.

3 Methods in corpus linguistics: Interpreting concordance lines

Introduction

This chapter is the first of two that present some of the most commonly used methods and approaches in corpus linguistics. Producing concordance lines is perhaps the most basic way of processing corpus information, and most corpus users rely heavily on concordances and their interpretation. This is particularly true for those who are using a corpus in day-to-day teaching or translation, for whom an intuitive response to data may be more immediately useful than a more statistical approach. For this reason, concordance lines have a chapter to themselves in this book.

This chapter offers a number of examples of corpus searches, each one illustrating one or more points about the methodology of finding and interpreting concordance lines, and about the kind of findings that emerge from such study. In this chapter, a number of topics are addressed, which might be summarised as follows:

1 What kind of searches are useful in finding out about how English works? Examples are given of searches for a single word-form (e.g. *point*), for a lemma (e.g. *CONDEMN*), or for a series of words (e.g. *on* ADJECTIVE *terms with*). Sometimes a search is designed to show not the words searched for but a concept that often co-occurs with it (e.g. *what would* co-occurring with expressions of hypotheticality). In some of the examples given, a series of searches has to be conducted, because a single search cannot give the required data in manageable form (e.g. a very frequent word such as *point*). In some cases, more context than single concordance lines is required to allow conclusions about regularity to be drawn (e.g. *I must admit*).

2 How can concordance lines be presented in an accessible way? Examples are given of sets of lines which are unsorted, and lines which are sorted alphabetically. Concordance lines are also shown in groups which have been selected and organised to illustrate a particular behaviour.

3 What are concordance lines useful for? Although this topic will be taken up in much greater depth in chapters 5 to 8, this chapter does suggest some of the main types of information that can be

gained from concordance lines, and what this might be used for. The main use that is illustrated in this chapter is examining the meaning and behaviour of individual lexical items, and the pragmatic meaning of given phrases.

4 What do we see in concordance lines? or, Why are concordance lines worth looking at? These questions as they stand are perhaps a little disingenuous, and may be re-phrased as: What view of language does this chapter want to put across? and What general assumptions about language investigation are made in offering concordance lines as a source of information? The view of language taken in this chapter is in accord with that described in more depth in chapter 6, which prioritises lexis and stresses the association between pattern and meaning (both lexical and pragmatic). Examples are chosen that illustrate this view, illustrating general and detailed patterns of lexis, word meaning and pattern, and semantic prosody and pragmatic meaning. Additional assumptions are that observed language is a more valid object of study than intuition, that it matters how frequently a linguistic item occurs, and that a corpus can produce results that can be extrapolated to a more general category of language.

The chapter begins with an introductory section showing what concordance lines look like and how their presentation can influence their interpretation. The chapter then moves on to ask what is observable from concordance lines, and to show how searches can be adapted to cope with a lot of data. From there we look at information gained from more context than the simple concordance line, and probes are used. The final section summarises some of the issues raised in the chapter.

Concordances are an example of what I refer to as 'word-based' methods of investigating corpora. Chapter 4 will compare these methods with 'category-based' methods and consider the advantages and disadvantages of each.

Searches, concordance lines and their presentation

A concordancer is a program that searches a corpus for a selected word or phrase and presents every instance of that word or phrase in the centre of the computer screen, with the words that come before and after it to the left and right. The selected word, appearing in the centre of the screen, is known as the **node word**. Here are 15 randomly-selected concordance lines for the word *critical* (from the 1999 Bank of English corpus):

attack on ground targets will be critical to success in any Gulf conflict,
for parents is to children to be critical. Some ways to encourage
benefit by adopting a more self-critical and experimental approach.
These films have a self-critical subtext and a depth of
within Afghan society. Arney is critical of the lack of political
The Daily Telegraph remains critical of Syria and Iran. It says as on
guard who insists on a literary-critical seminar correct me if I'm wrong,
DeConcini's letter is even more critical. The committee said that even
claim to having helped, through his critical writing, to save figurative
this certainly might be a critical clue. Physical relaxation may just
But a more considered view, highly critical of Eden, was expressed among both
that colonial possessions were of critical importance for advanced or
a mental health professional is critical to the success of the therapy. In
nearly a century later. Led at this critical juncture by a man with vision and
the chief inspector's view may be critical in determining its future

It is helpful to sort these lines so that the lines that are like each other in some way appear next to each other. Below are the same lines sorted so that the words immediately before (to the left of) *critical* are in alphabetical order. The words that the corpus user is likely to focus on are printed in bold.

this certainly might be **a critical clue**. Physical relaxation may just
attack on ground targets will **be critical** to success in any Gulf conflict,
for parents is to children to **be critical**. Some ways to encourage
the chief inspector's view may **be critical** in determining its future
But a more considered view, **highly critical** of Eden, was expressed among both
claim to having helped, through **his critical writing**, to save figurative
within Afghan society. Arney **is critical** of the lack of political
of a mental health professional **is critical** to the success of the therapy. In
guard who insists on a **literary-critical** seminar correct me if I'm wrong,
DeConcini's letter is even **more critical**. The committee said that even
that colonial possessions were **of critical importance** for advanced or
THE DAILY TELEGRAPH **remains critical** of Syria and Iran. It says as on
benefit by adopting a more **self-critical** and experimental approach.
These films have a **self-critical** subtext and a depth of
nearly a century later. Led at **this critical juncture** by a man with vision and

This organisation highlights the fact that *critical* often follows a form of the verb *BE* (*be* or *is*) and sometimes follows a determiner (*a*, *his* or *this*) in a noun group. It is sometimes used in compounds such as *self-critical*, and it sometimes follows a grading adverb (*highly*, *more*). Here are the same lines again, this time sorted so that the words immediately after (to the right of) *critical* are in alphabetical order. Again, the words the user is likely to focus on are in bold.

benefit by adopting a more **self-critical and** experimental approach.
this certainly might be a **critical clue**. Physical relaxation may just
that colonial possessions were of **critical importance** for advanced or
the chief inspector's view may be **critical in** determining its future
nearly a century later. Led at this **critical juncture** by a man with vision and

within Afghan society. Arney is **critical of** the lack of political
THE DAILY TELEGRAPH remains **critical of** Syria and Iran. It says as on
But a more considered view, highly **critical of** Eden, was expressed among both
guard who insists on a **literary-critical seminar** correct me if I'm wrong,
for parents is to children is to be critical. Some ways to encourage
These films have a self-critical subtext and a depth of
DeConcini's letter is even more critical. The committee said that even
attack on ground targets will be **critical to** success in any Gulf conflict,
of a mental health professional is **critical to** the success of the therapy. In
claim to having helped, through his **critical writing**, to save figurative

Sorting the lines this way highlights the fact that *critical* is sometimes followed by *of*, *to* and *in*. A different meaning of *critical* is associated with each preposition: *be critical of* is associated with the 'negative opinion' meaning of *critical*, whereas *be critical to* and *be critical in* are associated with the 'important' meaning. The lines also show, again, that *critical* is sometimes followed by a noun. The most frequent meaning in that case (as in *critical clue, critical importance* and *critical juncture*) is the 'important' meaning. (*Critical writing* is another meaning.)

Even in these few lines, then, we begin to see something of how the word *critical* behaves. It is both an attributive adjective (occurring before a noun) and a predicative one (occurring after a link verb), though on the evidence of these lines the predicative use is slightly more frequent. The adjective is followed by certain prepositions, of which *of* and *to* appear to be the most frequent. Each of the behaviours of *critical* is associated more closely with one meaning than another, according to the evidence of these lines. When used attributively, *critical* is likely to mean 'important', as it does also in the phrase *be critical to*. The meaning of 'negative opinion' is associated with the phrase *be critical of*.

The lines for *critical* were selected using simply the word *critical* as the search-word. Most concordancers allow the researcher to make more specific searches, with various permutations. For example, you may be able to search for a phrase, or for specific word-classes. Below are some lines selected with the search '*on* followed by an adjective, followed by *terms*, followed by *with*', which show the kind of adjective that is used in this phrase. The lines have been sorted so that the adjectives appear in alphabetical order.

family when she is known to be on **bad** terms with some of them. And it is hard
a case of erm trying to be on **equal** terms with everybody else Yes.
older than she was, she felt on **equal** terms with him. Anyway, it's all
on they will have to beg on **equal** terms with the rest of the poor world for
team even if they're not on **familiar** terms with them. They've brought
Mr Botha is said to be on **friendly** terms with Mr Mandela. Nevertheless his
republics while staying on **friendly** terms with the resourceful but hard-

the Georgians, who were on **friendly** terms with the Germans, the Armenians had
information. Moutet was on **good** terms with the porters and cleaners in
though she wanted to live on **good** terms with the former Dutch colony, whose
t write to me; I want to stay on **good** terms with my postman. Write to Pete
any reason. He left the pub on **good** terms with everybody. He even borrowed
dreams in which I'm on **intimate** terms with the Queen. Woody Allen is
months in disguise and on **intimate** terms with nomads and pilgrims – not
more important to be on **reasonable** terms with the Israelis than to

These adjectives can be grouped according to meaning: *familiar,*
friendly and *intimate* indicate a degree of closeness; *good, reasonable*
and *bad* indicate whether or not the two groups like each other;
equal indicates a similarity in status. Thus, three aspects of a relationship – closeness, symmetry and affect (liking or disliking) – can be
indicated by the phrase *on* + adjective + *terms* + *with*.

What is observable from concordance lines?

In this section the main types of observation that can be made about
concordance lines are exemplified. They are presented under the
following headings: observing the 'central and typical', observing
meaning distinctions, observing meaning and pattern, and observing
detail.

Observing the 'central and typical'

Linguistic description of the kind that has been traditional since the
1950s focuses on distinctions between what 'can' and 'cannot' be
said in a particular language, with little regard for whether what is
possible frequently or rarely occurs in practice. Corpora cannot be
used to determine what is impossible in a language, as they do not
offer negative evidence, and they cannot really even be used to
determine what is possible, as a corpus may well contain utterances
which any speaker of a language would reject as 'incorrect' (e.g. *I'm*
just sort of showing you perhaps some dishes which are more
healthier than others). In Swan's (1994) terms, there is no 'demarcation' between the correct and the incorrect. In place of demarcation,
a corpus offers information that a native speaker cannot replicate: an
indication of 'central and typical' usage (Hanks 1987: 124–125;
Sinclair 1987a: 108, 114; Sinclair 1991: 17).

The terms 'central' and 'typical' are often used synonymously, but
it is useful also to make a distinction between them in order to
illustrate different types of centrality/typicality. 'Typical' might be
used to describe the most frequent meanings or collocates or
phraseology of an individual word or phrase. To illustrate typicality,

here are ten randomly selected concordance lines for the phrase *recipe for*:

1   and making merry are a sure-fire recipe for long-term damage to the mind
2   Tuigamala and you could have the recipe for a World Cup surprise or two.
3   On the face of it, it should be a recipe for easy success. A female singer-
4   Civil Aviation Authority are not a recipe for failure but a time-bomb for
5   not as a dangerous Treasury-view recipe for prolonged slump, but as a
6   rally in Edinburgh: 'It's a recipe for constitutional chaos. The
7   massacre was no part of their recipe for government. Because of this
8   demand for efficiency savings was a recipe for disaster in education.
9   to good material, and you have a recipe for serious success. But it's not a
10   or cucumber. A favourite Welsh recipe for salmon trout (or sewin, as it

From the evidence of these lines, the typical meaning of *recipe for* is metaphoric rather than literal (only line 10 is an exception to this). Furthermore, the nouns following *for* are slightly more frequently negative (*damage* 1, *failure* 4, *slump* 5, *chaos* 6, *disaster* 8) than they are positive (*surprise* 2, *success* 3 and 9) or neutral (*government* 7). When the phrase is metaphoric, it most frequently follows the verb *BE* and the determiner *a* (lines 1, 3, 4, 6, 8); most exceptions to this (lines 2, 7, 9) are positive or neutral rather than negative. Thus, although the phrase *recipe for* has a range of meanings, collocates and grammatical co-texts, its typical use is in the sequence 'something *is a recipe for* something bad'. A typical example would be, *Eating, drinking and making merry are a sure-fire recipe for long-term damage to the mind and body* (line 1). This example does not show all the ways that the phrase can be used, but it combines all the most frequent features.

The concept of 'centrality' can be applied to categories of things rather than to individual words. For example, the present progressive in English can indicate the present (e.g. *she's working at the moment*), the future (e.g. *she's taking an exam tomorrow*), or no specific time (*she's always making mistakes*). As Mindt (2000: 262) shows, however, the future and 'timeless' uses are relatively infrequent, making the reference to present time the central use of the present progressive. A central adjective might be one that occurs both attributively (*rich man*) and predicatively (*he was rich*), whereas an adjective such as *asleep* occurs only predicatively, and so is not central. In the *recipe for* example, words such as *damage* and *failure* form the class of nouns that centrally follow the phrase, whereas *government* is less central.

Although speakers of a language may have intuitions about typicality, these intuitions do not always accord with evidence of frequency. Barlow (1996) and Shortall (1999) use the term 'prototypical' to indicate a usage which is commonly felt to be typical but which is not necessarily most frequent. They suggest that English teaching course books tend to present usage which is prototypical in this sense but not typical in the sense of 'most frequently occurring'. One example of this is comparatives. A prototypical (if out of date) example might be *The USSR is larger than China* (Hsia et al 1989: 178), in which the comparative adjective *larger* is followed by *than*. From a sample of 100 lines of *larger* from the Bank of English, however, only 17 included *than*. In most lines, the adjective is followed by a noun, as in *a much larger plan* or *their larger but poorer northern neighbours*, where the comparison is implicit. A truly typical example would be as in the following:

> In some cultures such as Britain and America, women architects and engineers are seldom found. Yet in others, such as Egypt and Eastern Europe, they form a far <u>larger</u> proportion of these professions. (British non-fiction book)

Here the two parts of the comparison are present, but not in the same sentence.

As noted in chapter 2, Barlow (1996) has made similar observations with relation to the use of reflexive pronouns such as *herself*, noting that coursebook writers often present these pronouns contrastively, setting *be proud of oneself* in opposition to *be proud of one's child*, for example. Hsia et al (1989: 222) ask students to produce sentences such as *I saw myself in the mirror*; *He hit himself with the hammer*; *We dried ourselves with the towel*. Barlow notes that in fact the reflexives have phraseologies which are quite distinct from those associated with other pronouns. For example, the most frequently used verb is *FIND*, and *found myself by the sea* has a very different meaning from *found him by the sea*. In addition, the other verbs with which reflexives co-occur most frequently are those indicating thoughts and speech, such as *SEE, IMAGINE, VISUALISE, CONSIDER* and *ASK* (Barlow 1996: 9), rather than the verbs of physical action represented by *he hit himself* and so on.

The psychologically prototypical is not necessarily to be ignored in language teaching. Learners may find it difficult to grasp the meaning of comparatives unless they are first presented with examples in which two items are compared explicitly. Also, usages which are non-central and non-typical do still exist and cannot be omitted from the learner's repertoire. Knowing what is central and typical in frequency terms, however, can indicate what the bulk of examples that a learner is exposed to should be like.

In chapter 6 the notion of typicality will be related to the idiom principle and to the reduction of ambiguity in English. Ambiguous utterances, such as *Time flies*, are sometimes used to illustrate parsing techniques, or to make jokes. (It can mean either 'we perceive time to pass quickly' or 'use a stop-watch to time how quickly flies move'.) In practice, however, the first meaning is the most typical. Of 52 instances in the Bank of English, 51 had the temporal meaning, and the exception was part of a discussion about parsing. A speaker of English hearing *Time flies* does not need to work out which meaning is the most likely in a given context: typicality encourages the hearer to assume only one meaning unless the context makes that impossible.

Observing meaning distinctions

Many words have meanings that are similar, and yet the words are not able to be substituted one for the other. Dictionaries, which deal with words separately rather than comparatively, can be of little help, but observing typical usages of near-synonyms can clarify differences in meaning. Corpus investigations that distinguish between near-synonyms include those by Kennedy (1991; and see chapter 1) and Partington (1998: 33–46).

Partington's study focuses on what he calls 'semi-grammatical' words, that is, words which by themselves carry only a general meaning. The examples he gives are the intensifying adjectives *sheer, pure, complete, utter* and *absolute*. He points out that dictionaries tend to define these words in similar ways, and even give them as synonyms of each other. The *Collins COBUILD English Dictionary* (CCED), for example, suggests that *complete* and *pure* are synonyms of *sheer*; the *Longman Dictionary of Contemporary English* (LDOCE) gives *pure* as a synonym of *sheer*; the earlier *Collins COBUILD English Language Dictionary* (CCELD) gives *absolute* as a superordinate of *sheer*. In spite of this apparent similarity in meaning, the typical collocates of each adjective differ to quite a considerable degree. For example, *sheer* is used with nouns of degree or magnitude (*sheer weight, sheer number*), often in the pattern *the sheer* N *of* N (*the sheer weight of noise, the sheer scale of the shelling*). The other adjectives do not collocate with these nouns. In addition, *sheer* alone is often used in expressions indicating causality (*through sheer insistence; out of sheer cussedness; by sheer hard work; because of sheer hard work; his sheer integrity got him though; his enthusiasm and sheer hard work meant that things moved quickly*) (1998: 36). *Complete* is used with nouns indicating absence (*complete ban*), change (*complete revamping*), and destruction (*complete collapse*), often in the pattern *the complete* N *of* N (*the complete absence of perspective*) (1998: 43). *Absolute* is used with what Partington

(1998: 45–46) calls 'hyperbolic' nouns, such as *chaos, disgrace, genius, godsend*, whereas the other adjectives are not.

Observing meaning and pattern

One theme that has emerged from all the examples above is that the meaning of a word is closely associated with its co-text. That is, although ambiguity is possible, for the most part the meanings of words are distinguished by the patterns or phraseologies in which they typically occur. To illustrate this, it is common to divide concordance lines into sets, each set exemplifying one meaning. The first example given here is of a noun: *initiative*. This noun has three distinct meanings, shown here in three sets of concordance lines.

Set 1

```
                    a practising GP. 'That makes this initiative attractive to all parties. We all
          said it will announce a new Punjab initiative in the next few days to deal with
                  Giuliani's latest law-and-order initiative is aimed at New York's drink –
                        a need for a new national initiative on immunization – one that
          capital that he can use. And every initiative that a president undertakes,
          continual latecomers as part of an initiative that has produced dramatic
                    education. He said the initiative was aimed at remedying Britain's
```

Here *initiative* is a count noun meaning 'something that someone (usually a government agency or other institution) starts to try to solve a problem'.

Set 2

```
          I would be expected to take the initiative and tell players to sit back and
              should refrain from taking the initiative in these matters. According to so
                      only if France takes the initiative is there a chance of success at
          elsewhere, women have seized the initiative. We've come a long way from the
                  has his best chance to seize the initiative – or at least go some way down
          pocket before saying, 'Losing the initiative can be disastrous.' It never
                  then veto, thereby losing the initiative in its efforts to isolate Iraq.
```

Here the phrase *the initiative* is used with verbs meaning 'take' or 'lose'. 'Take the initiative' means 'start something and so gain an advantage over a competitor' while 'lose the initiative' means 'fail to start something and so allow a competitor to gain an advantage'.

Set 3

```
          that the president must show more initiative and leadership on domestic
              think and not to act on their own initiative. Only the elite are encouraged to
                      had the imagination or initiative to read books that were not on
          cult. Greater enthusiasm and more initiative, together with the expansion of
          encourage them to use their own initiative when learning. The modern
                  the road and showed a lot of initiative'. 'She used to sit on my lounge
          failing, however, was his lack of initiative and leadership in dealing with
```

Here the meaning is 'the quality of being able to do things without being told'. Only the possessive (e.g. *their, his*) is used as a determiner; in most cases there is no determiner.

In short, the word *initiative* does not have one meaning but several. Distinguishing between the meanings is a matter of distinguishing between patterns of usage. *An initiative* or *a government initiative* indicates the first meaning. *TAKE/LOSE the initiative* indicates the second meaning. *A lot of initiative* indicates the third meaning. Meaning and phraseology are indistinguishable, and the concordance lines show both.

The second example is a verb: *CONDEMN*. Again, there are several different meanings, and the concordance lines are grouped so that each set illustrates one meaning.

'criticise'
> should be welcomed rather than **condemned** and the most enlightened – not
> s action, saying it totally **condemned any steps** violating the right of
> a Western-style democracy, which he **condemned as 'bourgeois liberalism'**. But
> The Fable of the Bees **was tried and condemned as a public nuisance** by the Grand
> leader, Jean-Marie le Pen while **condemning the desecration as ignoble**
> involved in the talks yesterday, **condemned the incident as 'the dangerous**

'pass sentence'
> one that sixteen years later **would condemn him to death** on even more
> people who a few days before **had condemned him to death**. Ironically, the
> secret recesses of his own mind and **condemned them to deportation**. Even if he

'sentenced to death'
> advisory committee, although **the condemned man** had no right that he should
> Then he would turn to face **the condemned man**: 'You who have sinned against
> the death sentences of many of **the condemned prisoners**, it urges that the

'make something bad happen'
> in restricting uniforms and **condemning people to wear tattered clothes**
> Many fear Fuerstenberg's past **will condemn it to being a ghost town**, trapped
> Four decades ago, Asia seemed **condemned to poverty**. Half of Japan's
> an in-person this decade and **who is condemned to the social wilderness**. Out

As expected, each meaning is clearly associated with a particular pattern. The 'criticise' meaning, for example, is associated with the patterns 'condemn something' and 'condemn something *as* something'. On the other hand, 'condemn someone *to* something' is used with both the 'make something bad happen' and the 'pass sentence' meanings, suggesting that one may be a metaphoric extension of the other. The pattern 'condemn someone to do something' (or the passive 'be condemned to do something') always indicates that the 'something' is bad or undesirable. This is true even when 'something' is not bad on the surface. In the following example, *a life of nursery nursing* may not seem to be a terrible fate to many people, but the phrase *condemn her to* indicates that Elaine would see it in this way.

In Britain, despite a bad choice of school – 'my parents didn't know the system' – and a careers teacher who tried to condemn her to a life of nursery nursing, Elaine got together enough qualifications to go to teacher training college.

In each of the examples above, the corpus search specified an individual word. The association between meaning and pattern of use was illustrated by words with several meanings. The other side of the coin – that words with similar meanings tend to share patterns – can be illustrated by searching for a phrase and noting the words that frequently occur within it. This will be illustrated with the phrase or pattern '*it* followed by *BE* followed by an adjective, followed by a that-clause', as in *it is apparent that fate intervened*. Below are 45 lines, randomly selected, that illustrate the pattern.

```
           Constable Jones, Mr Casey said. It is apparent that fate intervened th
              Elegance being a key factor, it was appropriate that Joanne
         evening of a change of plan. It was clear that Mr Chernomyrdin did
      I can tell you.' From his tone it was clear that Dick Ryle had had
                pessimism and quiescence. It is clear that the Nobel Laureate's
       to discredit UN forces. By now it was clear that both the Croats and
            in Mecca to perform the haj. It is clear that the revolution in mas
           Union of Students said that it is crucial that universities give a
            o add the fateful words: 'But it is essential that we end it in such
      dgate Valley Country Park, and it was fitting that two of the city's
         t result might become positive. It is important that social workers
             health clinic, or any hospital. It is important that the woman
      ewn up is not so important; but it is important that North Korea should
               impossible. At the same time it is inevitable that those at home,
           rs to Stick Letters. I suppose it was inevitable that this passionate
      im to act so out of character? It was ironic that Penelope's insistence
      co-operation, however he said it was likely that Germany would have t
      ucing three different products, it is likely that management will be
         s and the quality of your life. It is likely that you will exhibit all
          lethal muscle wasting disease. It is likely that any child with this
         joyment of this exquisite poem, it is necessary that the reader should
            a camera attached and working. It is obvious that the chance of a
      zing in wonderment about them. It was obvious that they believed they
      h it had been contracted here, it was obvious that that was not what
                  And we asked them and it was overwhelming that the the the
              nt parts of every relationship. It is possible that your partner's mil
         emplate for building proteins – it is possible that the FraX protein h
      xchange transactions in London. It is revealing that the Socialists who
         st the end of the year. Indeed it was significant that the Jakarta
               euthanasia is a guess at best. It is surprising that, following an
         others. Some doctors have said it is suspicious that the pills named
         r as simple as presented. While it is true that vertical integration
           in the Old Testament, because it is true that it has been used for
            the PPI after Sturzo's exile, it was true that he had 'no experience
      Europeans are two-thirds wrong. It is true that the Turks are Muslims,
         e will require a high-wire act. It is true that Malcolm Rifkind, the
```

e were absolutely amazed and if it is **true** that St George's Hall has
him, but he couldn't help it. It was **typical** that Robyn would have
said: 'In a civilised society, it is **unacceptable** that women are
in this Year of Remembrance. It is **unfortunate** that the article made
i-government protests. He said it was **unfortunate** that a number of
re foreign policy picture, that it is **unfortunate** that we cannot have
its policy on public debate. It is **unlikely** that the second and third
recent work has suggested that it is **unlikely** that family boundary
to testify. In retrospect, it is **unlikely** that a US court would

The adjectives that appear in these lines are: *apparent, appropriate, clear, crucial, essential, fitting, important, inevitable, ironic, likely, necessary, obvious, overwhelming, possible, revealing, significant, surprising, suspicious, true, typical, unacceptable, unfortunate* and *unlikely.* Some of these adjectives occur several times, others only once or twice: a larger sample of concordance lines would show more examples of all these adjectives, together with others. As noted by Francis (1993; see also Francis et al 1998: 480–484), the adjectives all indicate an evaluation or judgement, specifically judgements of likelihood (*inevitable, likely, possible, unlikely*), clarity (*apparent, clear, obvious*), necessity (*crucial, essential, important, necessary*), significance (*revealing, significant*), goodness or badness (*appropriate, fitting, suspicious, unacceptable, unfortunate*), as well as a few other kinds of judgement (*ironic, overwhelming, surprising, true, typical*).

A variation on this approach is the concept of 'frames'. Frames are sequences of, usually, three words in which the first and last are fixed but the middle word is not. Renouf and Sinclair (1991), for example, list the following frames from a small corpus (10 million words of written English; 1 million words of spoken English):

a . . . of e.g. *a lot of, a kind of, a number of, a couple, of, a matter of, a sort of, a series of;*
an . . . of e.g. *an act of, an example of, an average of, an expression of, an air of, an element of;*
be . . . to e.g. *be able to, be allowed to, be expected to, be said to, be put to, be made to;*
too . . . to e.g. *too late to, too much to, too young to, too easy to, too small to, too close to;*
for . . . of e.g. *for most of, for all of, for one of, for fear of, for both of, for some of, for lack of;*
had . . . of e.g. *had enough of, had plenty of, had thought of, had heard of, had one of, had died of;*
many . . . of e.g. *many thousands of, many years of, many kinds of, many parts of, many millions of.*

Each of these frames is frequent in the corpus used, much more frequent than any one of the triplets formed by it. For example, in Renouf and Sinclair's corpus there are 3,830 occurrences of *a . . . of* but only 1,322 occurrences of the most frequent triplet with this frame – *a lot of* – and only 174 occurrences of the twentieth most frequent triplet – *a quarter of*. In other words, the frame as a whole has a numerical significance to the corpus which far outweighs the significance of any one of the triplets. Not only that, but the frame is significant to each word which occurs as the middle item in it. Of all the instances of *lot* in the corpus, 53% of them are in the triplet *a lot of*.

When the triplets formed by each frame are examined, it is found that the middle words are not a random selection, but belong to particular meaning groups. For example, the words that are found most frequently with *many . . . of* in Renouf and Sinclair's corpus fall into these groups:

words indicating numbers: e.g. *thousands, millions, hundreds*
words indicating a type or aspect: e.g. *kinds, ways, aspects, types, varieties*
words indicating a length of time: e.g. *years, hours*
words indicating a group of people or things: e.g. *members, examples, species.*

Frames are particularly useful because programs can be written to identify them automatically, without the researcher knowing or guessing in advance what they will be. They show part of what is typical in a corpus and, because they incorporate variation, they are much more frequent than fixed phrases are. Frames and patterns are an alternative to the very general statements made by most grammars and the very specific statements that can be made about the collocations of each individual word in a language. Because of this, they might be a good starting point for organising the way that language is presented to learners. Frames are particularly useful when looking at a specialised corpus, and can be used as the basis for investigating the language of a discipline (Luzon Marco 2000). Chapter 6 considers this point further. Corpus-based work on frames has been carried out on languages other than English; Butler (1998), for example, considers frames in Spanish.

Observing detail

So far we have seen how concordances can be used to give very general ideas about the ways that words behave and the meanings that can be associated with patterns. Any work with concordances, however, tends to lead to more specific observations about the behaviour of individual words. For example, the nouns *advice* and *ANSWER*, among others, are often followed by *as to* and a clause beginning with a wh- word. In the case of each of these nouns, however, more detail can be added to this patterning. For example, *advice as to* often follows a verb indicating 'getting', 'giving', 'wanting' or 'offering'. The following are ten randomly selected concordance lines, with the relevant words underlined.

women, had surreptitiously asked his advice as to whether the Orthodox Church
meeting was invalid. I'm seeking advice as to my remedies in relation to
Instead of providing medical advice as to why this may have occurred,
Metropolitan Opera, in order to get advice as to where I should be sent in
Erm I'd like some advice as to how Key Stage Four would er
though there was no practicable advice as to how this could be done
of food allergies you should take advice as to the best way of altering your
with water and said I would need his advice as to how to cut around his ears
picnics, petty economies, wholesome advice as to how to succeed in life, and
Youthfully dispensing criticism and advice as to how they could and should do

ANSWER as to tends to follow the same kind of verb, underlined below. In addition, it often follows a phrase indicating either that a clear answer is not available, or that to give a clear answer is difficult or unexpected, as shown in bold below.

1   Picasso. There is **no definitive** answer as to who was the greatest," said
2   readers who can <u>give</u> us a persuasive answer as to why the narrator is male or
3   t want to wait fourteen days for an answer as to whether they can get a
4   that lawyers **could not <u>give</u> a clear** answer as to what would happen if the Bil
5   means. There can only be one answer as to where Croatia could possibly
6   waving his hands to **demand** an answer as to whether Labour would join a
7   Well, I **can't give** you **an exact** answer as to what he has. Reporter 5:
8   But **no one really has a concrete** answer as to why the incidence is
9   will one day <u>present</u> us with the answer as to what chemical change takes
10   seemed disturbed. He **even had** an answer as to why no scientific publicatio
11   reason why there must be a single answer as to the relative effects of
12   not only for a cure, but also for answers as to why we suffer from such hig
13   searchers hope to <u>find</u> some of the answers as to why the virus is
14   President, to **demand** of him **clear** answers as to how the plan stood. Leonida
15   re hampered by the **lack** of medical answers as to why many miscarriages

For some lines, a short concordance line is not sufficient to show the negativity and it is necessary to obtain more co-text. Two examples from these lines are:

3 The public **don't want to wait** fourteen days for an **answer as to whether** they can get a mortgage on a house.

9 It may well be that science or medical research will one day present us with the **answer as to what** chemical change takes place in the body of the alcoholic . . . But, to date, **no answer has been forthcoming.**

This suggests that *answer as to* is part of a phrase which might be expressed as '[negative] [clear] *answer as to* [wh-word]'. The precise wording is not fixed, but it is constrained within limits. As we shall see in chapter 6, a great deal of English is made up of sequences of this type, and it raises a problem as to how the phraseology is to be described in a useful way. The sequence '[negative] [clear] *answer as to* [wh-word]' may well apply to only this noun, which makes it useless as a generalisation. A more general expression '[get] NOUN *as to* [wh-word]' could be applied to *advice* and *answer*, but would miss some of the essential detail.

Coping with a lot of data: using phraseology

One of the problems brought about by the increasing size of corpora is that searches for frequent words will yield too much data to be interpretable in the form of concordance lines. A corpus-user can probably cope with looking at, at any one time, about 100 lines for general patterns and about 30 lines for detailed patterns. If the word under investigation is a frequent one, such a small number of lines will not show all the patterning, and slightly different methods may be employed. Sinclair (1999) advocates selecting 30 random lines, and noting the patterns in them, then selecting a different 30, noting the new patterns, then another 30 and so on, until further selections of 30 lines no longer yield anything new. An adaptation of this method is 'hypothesis testing', in which a small selection of lines is used as a basis for a set of hypotheses about patterns. Other searches are then employed to test those hypotheses and form new ones. This method will be demonstrated using two frequent nouns: *SUG-GESTION* and *point*.

Suggestion

To begin, here are 20 random concordance lines for the noun *SUGGESTION*, sorted one to the right of the node-word:

```
           insistence always that it was his suggestion; and if it turned out to be a
                 Island, and Lady Stallard. Suggestions are being sought by the Histor
              there's never a shortage of suggestions as to what's on in town and we
                and controversial field. The Suggestions for Further Reading list severa
          and find a centre that will hold. Suggestions for Discussion. Why does Russell
           style book awaits the liveliest suggestion for the name of the place and the
          reasons', although there were suggestions he was unhappy with the safety
        to the House of Lords; there is a suggestion legal advisers to the Guinness
                   he was hoping I would fail. My suggestions never got past his desk. He
             Hailsham said. Responding to the suggestion of removing the remaining
```

letter and style. Erm the suggestion of how you write it past
signed.' Andrew was angered at suggestions that he resigned because he had
George Hannaford rejected a suggestion that the Government delay the
QUEENSLAND Softball officials' suggestion that Ballymore should be the
of an ankle injury. There were suggestions that midfielder Todd Viney would
party programme, and agreed to his suggestion that the party should hold a
since the war, has rejected suggestions that there should be a
nor did I ever hear the slightest suggestion that we should do otherwise
have been interrogated. Another suggestion that something was going on. The
has never been any suggestion that his action is anything other

These lines show that *SUGGESTION* is frequently followed by a finite clause, either introduced by *that* or not. It is also followed by *as to, for* and *of*. To investigate this behaviour further, another 50 lines are selected, but this time the lines in which *SUGGESTION* is followed by a finite clause are deleted (as no further evidence is needed for this), as are lines in which *SUGGESTION* simply behaves as an ordinary noun, as in *My suggestions never got past his desk*. The remaining lines are as follows:

to us. One key reflection: many suggestions for classic Hollywood and
and find a centre that will hold. Suggestions for Discussion. Why does Russe
Hailsham said. Responding to the suggestion of removing the remaining
advertising. Send information and suggestions of relevant book/articles to
quite the contrary. So no suggestion of a coup? The word was floating
dispute at Wapping. There were suggestions of organised violence on the
became the Royal Arsenal at the suggestion of George III, when he paid a
a helping hand? The panel's suggestion of giving the authorities power
hour, if you like, so there's no suggestion of office harassment. Presumably
said. He smiled at her with no suggestion of patronization, no sense of
himself from the cautious suggestion of the Treasury's post-crash
travel is bearing fruit. Our suggestion to run weekday trains every 20
down the dust; there was even a suggestion to pipe seawater from Brighton
General Shintaro Abe. The clear suggestion was that they had decided to

These lines confirm that *SUGGESTION* is frequently followed by *of*. There are two lines in which it is followed by *for*, but no lines in which it is followed by *as to*. On the other hand, a new pattern seems to be emerging, in which the noun is followed by a to-infinitive clause (*a suggestion to pipe seawater*). There is also a variation of the that-clause, in which the clause follows a link verb (*The clear suggestion was that they had decided . . .*). The behaviours of *SUGGESTION* for which there has not been much evidence so far can now be tested using searches for individual combinations of words: *SUGGESTION for*, *SUGGESTION to*, and *SUGGESTION as to*.

First, *SUGGESTION for* occurs over 1,000 times in the Bank of English corpus, confirming the hypothesis that *for* is a significant part of the way *SUGGESTION* behaves. Below is a random selection from these lines for illustration:

Thames TV has rejected this suggestion for its annual amateur tournament
for the arms clampdown and the suggestion for the meeting came from the
There have been numerous suggestions for clarifying decision-making
the home throughout the year, with suggestions for scented indoor plants,
He was also doubtful of Italian suggestions for merging the organisation
polish a telescope mirror, and add suggestions for building an observatory from
a variety of imaginal devices and suggestions for pain control. Before you
repair strategies? What other suggestions for repairing a relationship by
confusing passages, and offer suggestions for revision. Together, through
union and in come tentative suggestions for institutional reforms to

We might further note that *suggestions* is more frequent than
suggestion in this pattern, and that *for* is as likely to be followed by a
present participle (*for repairing a relationship*) as by a noun (*for pain
control*).

Next, a search for *SUGGESTION to* followed by the base form of
a verb yields just over 200 lines. These lines need interpreting,
however. In some cases, the to-infinitive clause is dependent on a
word other than *SUGGESTION*. For example, *suggestion* sometimes
follows *HAVE* (e.g. *I have a simple suggestion to make*) and
exemplifies one of the ways that *HAVE* behaves (e.g. *have a book to
read*). In terms of the specific behaviour of *SUGGESTION*, then,
these lines can be discounted. Of the remaining lines, some are like
these:

NTUC after he accepted the NTUC's suggestion to contest in the presidential
of my friends the post-hypnotic suggestion to freeze at my command.
officials say they oppose American suggestions to include European countries
Hongkong Bank has blithely ignored suggestions to release it, which seems a

In these lines, the to-infinitive clause explains what the suggestion
is. For example, someone in the NTUC said, 'I think you should
contest in the presidential election', or something like that. Therefore,
the to-infinitive clause is an important part of the behaviour of
SUGGESTION. In the following lines, however, the meaning is
different, and the to-infinitive clause means something like 'in order
to':

the rescue with 30 sanity-saving suggestions to make this summer a holiday
listener may also have ideas and suggestions to help you get started
turned down some of the dafter suggestions to save coal

These clauses do not tell us what the suggestion is, but what it
does. For example, no-one said 'I think you should make this
summer a holiday to remember', or anything like that. In fact, we do
not know (yet) what the thirty suggestions are, only what they are
designed to achieve. The conclusion is that *SUGGESTION* does
have a pattern in which it is followed by a to-infinitive, but that
pattern is not exemplified by all 200 lines of *SUGGESTION to*.

Finally, there are almost seventy examples in the Bank of English of *SUGGESTION* followed by *as to*. In nearly every case, *as to* is followed by a clause beginning with a wh-word (*what, where, how, why, when, who, which*), as in these examples:

> had asked for constructive suggestions as to how the tax could be
> There have been suggestions as to how this difficulty might
> of unemployment, while giving suggestions as to how to deal with the
> fracas and the navel. Any suggestions as to what prevented this from
> Croll asked Salter if he had any suggestions as to where Brady might be
> this power play to counter Chris's suggestion as to why the car isn't starting

Thus, concordance lines can be selected to test hypotheses, so that the corpus-user does not need to examine every one of thousands of lines to obtain a reasonably accurate picture of how a word behaves. The same method will be used to describe the behaviour of an even more frequent noun: *point*.

Point

The noun *point* is an extremely frequent word in English: the Bank of English corpus has almost 100,000 instances. (It is also a word that, like many other frequent words, finds its way into very few lists of vocabulary.) Below are a mere 20 randomly selected concordance lines to illustrate the wide variety of ways the word is used. The phraseology of *point* is highlighted by bold type.

1	Kinnock as the 'big idea' **selling point** of Labour's next election
2	They told him they were **on the point of passing** a vote of no confidence
3	has attacked the document **point by point**. In part it says Primac has
4	nvesting in the burgeoning **Kangaroo Point** residential precinct. Mr Dick
5	ll not be entirely finished **at this point**, and therefore be prepared for
6	you. Thank you for **making the point**. Nice to talk to you. Bye.
7	Mm. **There's no point in us trying** to make a cooker in
8	the military Commanders **made the point that** there was a limit to the civil
9	Commonwealth.' To **underline that point**, he said that France was ready to
10	lish the black comedy. Even **at the point at which** the Entrance Hall was
11	rnals. On the face of it, he **has a point**: it is difficult to find, difficult
12	in fact, is at perhaps **the weakest point in** its 10-year history in office.
13	u appear to have reached **a turning-point in** your life, but that implies that
14	for the lorry. Fortunately **at this point** a group of children came walking
15	your training skill from the group **point of view**. There will also be open-
16	me, but that wasn't the point. **The point was to** make him yearn for her, to
17	d charge a 'reasonable' fee. **A key point in** the debate will be determining
18	greater Cincinnati area **prove the point**. In rich Indian Hill, for example,
19	f the 19th century, resigning on **a point of principle** in 1867, there have
20	successive win. But Barcelona, **a point behind**, showed the kind of form

Each of the phraseologies noticed here can be used as the starting point for other searches. The search may be based on what comes before *point* (*a point, the point, no point* and so on) or what comes after *point* (*point of, point in* and so on), or it might be based on a word-class ('possessive followed by *point*' or 'present participle followed by *point*'). Each search throws up new patterns or phrases, and each phrase illustrates a different meaning of the word *point*. Some of these are picked out in Table 3.1.

Point is also found in the sample lines to indicate the name of a place (line 4), and to indicate a way of scoring in a game (line 20). It is also used with *this* or *that* to refer back to something that has been said before (line 9).

Thus a small number of lines can be used to form hypotheses as to what might be important to the word *point*. Further corpus searches refine the patterns, and these can be grouped in terms of what they mean. Again, this is a way of investigating a very frequent word without being faced by thousands of lines at once.

Using a wider context: observing hidden meaning

I must admit

In the discussion of *answer as to* above, it was mentioned that a larger context than a concordance line is sometimes needed to find out about patterning. This is often the case when subtle meanings and usages are being observed. For example, Channell (2000) investigates the phrase *par for the course*, which in general terms means 'this kind of thing is to be expected'. She points out that it is used to comment on events which are negatively evaluated, not on events that are desirable.[1] Illustration of this can be given in concordance lines:

> Grumbles and counter-grumbles are par for the course and the chances are
> police and harassment by landlords are par for the course for students.
> a transformation, the odd set-back is par for the course. The Yarlotts'
> This sort of gush is rapidly becoming par for the course for this review, but
> and 24th are dates when obstacles seem par for the course, and perhaps a

She goes on to point out that, in spoken English, the phrase is often used by one speaker apparently to express solidarity with another speaker who is reporting a frustrating, annoying or inconvenient event. This can only be observed by looking at an extended piece of discourse. In the following example from Channell (ibid: 48), speaker

---

[1] The original meaning of the phrase *par for the course* is 'the number of strokes needed by a good player to complete a golf course'. The phrase is therefore used to indicate a notional standard, not to evaluate as good or bad. It is only the metaphorical extension of this meaning that carries the evaluative prosody.

Table 3.1. Phrases with *point*

Phrase	Comment
selling point (line 1); *turning-point* (line 13)	There are numerous other phrases on the same pattern, such as *boiling point, breaking point, freezing point, melting point, rallying point, starting point, sticking point, talking point*. Each has its own meaning.
on the point of -ing (line 2)	Usually follows a form of the verb *BE*. The meaning might be expressed as 'be about to do something'.
point by point (line 3)	This means 'taking each thing that is said in turn'.
at this point/ at the point at which (lines 5, 10, 14)	Other similar phrases are: *at a point (where); at one point; at that point; at no point*. The meaning might be expressed as 'at some place in a sequence of events or at some place in a discourse'. A similar meaning is expressed by the phrases *there comes a point (when); REACH/ GET/up to a point where; REACH/BE near the point where/when*.
MAKE the point (that) (lines 6, 8)	Other similar phrases are: *MAKE your point; my point is (that . . .)*. The meaning might be expressed as 'the most important thing you want to say'. There is also a phrase *MAKE a point of* -ing, which indicates that someone does something deliberately.
there's no point in someone -ing (line 7)	Other similar phrases are: *there's no point in* -ing, and *there's no point* -ing. The meaning might be expressed as 'it is not worth doing something'.
HAVE a point (line 11)	This is used to mean something like 'I can agree with (part of) what you say'.
weak/key point in (lines 12, 17)	This means 'the part of the argument that is ineffectual/ important'.
the point BE to . . . (line 16)	Another similar phrase is: *the point (of something) is that . . .* It is used to indicate 'the reason that something is done' or 'the most important aspect of something that is said or done'.
from someone's point of view (line 15)	The phrase *point of view* is very frequent, with or without *from*. It is used with a possessive: either 'someone's point of view' or 'the point of view of someone'. Also with the possessive are phrases such as *see your point* and *take your point*, which indicate that what someone says is understood or accepted.
PROVE the point (line 18)	This is also used with *a* or a possessive instead of *the*. The meaning is 'make one believe what has been said'. The phrase *MISS the point* indicates that what has been said has not been understood.
a point of principle (line 19)	There are numerous other phrases on the same pattern, such as: *point of order, point of reference, point of departure, point of law, point of honour*. Each of these has its own meaning.

F is telling speaker G about problems he is having in printing a computer file. Speaker G expresses fellow-feeling with *it's par for the course for today.*

F: . . . bombs the machine when you go to print. Soon as you hit er 'Okay' that's it. [laughs] Terminal. So erm I can only think there's something in the file that's doing it.
G: Oh shit. Well it's par for the course for today I think.
F: Is it. Oh dear. [laughs]
G: It's been a real shit day.

The two phenomena – looking at extended context, and observing the subtle meaning of a phrase – can be illustrated by the phrase *I must admit* in a corpus of spoken English (Hunston 1993b).[2] Here are some random examples (some codes indicating pauses and other features of spoken language have been omitted; speaker change is indicated by 'M1:', 'F2:' and so on).

> a life of its own. M1: Well I must admit I do like the admire the honesty of
> as white as sheet and I and I must admit all the experience I've had it did up
> ever done that? I haven't I must admit I've never quite gone that far.
> I? Or do I? F2: No. No. I must admit you look better from the front than
> I've very grateful for that. I must admit I hadn't thought that one through
> M1: No I haven't read it I must admit. M2: Oh well wait a minute I
> ekends would be. Well though I must admit I wasn't taking a lot of them. I
> keen on the teaching bit and I must admit I actually. But my mum is very keen
> u see we've let things slide I must admit. F: I can't think M: Er and
> M: Yeah. M2: You know I must admit I'm you know mm very lax when it

To understand how the phrase is used, the observer tries to establish a pattern from the different instances of the phrase. In many cases, to do this, more co-text for each line needs to be seen. What the following lines have in common is that the speaker uses *I must admit* when saying something that is uncomplimentary, either about the hearer or about a third party:

it's not a very complimentary saying **I must admit**, but it reminds me of Leicester women
they weren't very helpful **I must admit**
I really hate the Leicester accent **I must admit**
I didn't used to listen to you [your radio show] **I must admit**
My esteem of [name] though has dropped somewhat **I must admit**

In the following examples, what is said is not uncomplimentary, but looking at a larger co-text shows that what the speaker says or implies contradicts what a previous speaker has said.

[2] This work uses the spoken corpus from the Bank of English. Phrases such as *I must say* and *must admit/confess* account for a surprisingly large number of the instances of *must* in that corpus.

[Speaker 1 complains that it is impossible to phone some people because they are using a fax machine on the same number]
Speaker 2: I thought people had different numbers for their faxes **I must admit**

Speaker 1: It's a printed bit okay called Financial Development Models for Recent and . . .
Speaker 2: For oh er yeah. Financial Developments for er and recent financial Developments. Although **I must admit** I thought they'd changed the titles.

[Speaker 1 believes that her daughter must pay tax on a bank account even though she has no income and does not pay income tax.]
Speaker 2: Well I am rather puzzled by that little rule there **I must admit** because as an individual she will be entitled to her personal allowance . . .

Speaker 1: They have a market on a Thursday don't they. Is it Thursday?
Speaker 2: I didn't know it was a regular occurrence **I must admit**.
Speaker 1: Yeah.
Speaker 2: Well I didn't go in the Guild this lunchtime.
Speaker 1: Every fortnight.
[Speaker 1 implies that the market is held every week. Speaker 2 indicates that he doesn't believe this. Speaker 1 changes her claim: the market is held every two weeks.]

In the following lines, the speaker says something that is potentially embarrassing to him or herself, not to the hearer:

M1: Never been up there **must admit**. M2: Haven't you?
Of course **I must admit** that I had my own prejudices.
I've been sitting here in the studio **I must admit** sneezing my head off.
there were young people round there er mainly males **I must admit** who'd had a few drinks. [this is a male speaker]

In the following example, the speaker uses *I must admit* when saying something negative about a book which on the whole he has enjoyed:

. . . towards the end of the book **I must admit** it does go rather fanciful and he travelled abroad and slew dragons and things like that . . . But er up until that time it was rather a rather interesting story.

The common theme in all these examples is the need for a speaker to protect their own face or that of their hearer (Brown and Levinson 1987). The phrase *I must admit*, suggesting that the speaker is reluctant to say something and only does so under duress, is used in mitigation when 'face' is threatened. In the examples where what is said is uncomplimentary to the hearer or to someone else, and where the hearer is contradicted, it is the hearer's face that is threatened. In those examples where the speaker's utterance is uncomplimentary to him or herself, or where something is said that is contradictory to the speaker's main argument, the speaker's own face is threatened.

To test this theory it is necessary to consider an apparent counter-example. In the next example, a previous speaker has spoken at some length about her dislike of hearing swear-words in public. This speaker gives an opinion which appears to be in agreement with what the previous speaker has said:

I must admit I don't like to hear bad language in the street.

This use appears to be incompatible with the generalisation that *I must admit* mitigates a threat to face. However, it is possible to argue that a threat to face is being implied by the use of the phrase itself. The most likely explanation is that this utterance contradicts the general line of the speaker's opinion, as in the 'dragon story' example above. The speaker may dislike hearing bad language in the street, but may not object to it in other contexts. The speaker does not actually say this, thereby not contradicting the previous speaker, but maintains his integrity by implying a measure of disparity between their opinions. It is not possible to prove or disprove this hypothesis, but at least this possible explanation of an apparent counter-example means that the general theory is not necessarily falsified.

SIT through

The final example in this chapter is the phrasal verb *SIT through*. This verb demonstrates what is sometimes called **semantic prosody** (Sinclair 1991; Louw 1993; 1997; and see also chapter 6). To illustrate this, here are 15 randomly selected lines for the base form *sit* followed by *through*:

```
1          a long battle with deja vu, as we sit through the 30th anniversaries of
2      for anyone who can't be bothered to sit through a hundred-minute feature to
3         who asked singles and couples to sit through Danish X-rated films. If
4      e business meeting. Not only did she sit through it, she sat next to some men
5    Anyone who was unfortunate enough to sit through every ball of the Texaco
6       enitalia. He claims he was forced to sit through the lecture because the
7     to go to where we would be forced to sit through endless hours of speeches
8     has now been made. They have had to sit through two hours of a court
9        a compromise. I wouldn't have to sit through the actual ceremony, but on
10      lander who is at present having to sit through a 180-day waiting period?
11        for say. And instead of having to sit through something that actually you
12     switch videos and make his players sit through the Wales match in Cardiff
13     tochastic; also sometimes murder to sit through. Post, by Bjork
14      Are Tory backbenchers prepared to sit through the summer nights for a bill
15        even idle curiosity is no reason to sit through this sad dud. If you haven't
```

Sit through is often preceded by *to*, as most base forms of verbs are. More importantly, it often follows *have to* (lines 9, 10, 11) or an expression indicating that pressure has been exerted (lines 6, 7, 12) or an expression indicating that someone does not want to do something (lines 2, 5, 8, 13, 15). In other words, in 11 out of the 15 lines, there is evidence that the experience being undergone is unpleasant in some way. It might be argued that this is because the verb-form chosen is *sit*, which as a base-form often follows modals and other expressions with a modal-like meaning. To test the hypothesis, then, here are a further 20 lines of *SIT through*, using all the forms of the verb except *sit*:

1   nth, never mind the year, but having sat through 90 harrowing minutes, I can
2   Van de Velde) and Andrew and we sat through a few videos and they showed
3   with it. So the prospect of sitting through a 3- to 4-hour history of
4   that I don't generally get while sitting through a movie. Simon: Tell
5   trial places on their clients. Sitting through a six-month trial as a
6   ggled simultaneously yesterday as he sat through a screening of the low-
7   already released five titles). Sitting through an hour and 20 minutes of
8   heading. He later revealed that he sat through boring public zoning
9   Red Sea, Moses-style. Those who've sat through Cecil B de Mille's epic film
10   but his patience was remarkable. He sat through endless negotiating sessions
11   Wayne-Katharine Hepburn classic. I sat through it twice and then came home
12   nnel should pay its viewers for sitting through live coverage of England
13   nsen: You know, Dan, you and I have sat through many a summit together and –
14   UN representative, Abdul Al-Anbari, sat through the half-hour speech, and
15   Mr Goldman Sr and his family had sat through the courtroom proceedings in
16   by Domican. Domican, who has sat through the hearing, survived a mach
17   went to church with his parents and sat through the service and the sermon,
18   in the MGM commissary, he not only sat through the following speech but
19   our home grown industry and having sat through this delightful, acid, piece
20   Yes we we went and sat through to the bitter end you see.

In many of these lines, *SIT through* is followed by an indication of a specific length of time (lines 1, 3, 5, 7, 14) or by an indication that the length of time is judged to be uncomfortably long (lines 8, 10, 20). In line 12, the indication of tedium comes before the verb. Looking at more context indicates a sense of discomfort in the following lines also:

6 Lewis squirmed and giggled simultaneously yesterday as he sat through a screening . . .
15 Mr Goldman Sr and his family had sat through the courtroom proceedings in silent, dignified anguish.

In two thirds of the lines for *sit through*, and in over half the lines for *sat/sits/sitting through*, there is clear evidence that use of *SIT through* implies boredom or discomfort. In most of the other lines, although there is no evidence, the 'boring or uncomfortable' interpretation is a reasonable possibility. Line 19 is a rare but clear exception to this generalisation. As a counter-example it cannot be dealt with in the same way as the counter-example to the rule about *I must admit* discussed above. In that case, the apparent counter-example was shown in fact to comply with the rule. In this case, it has to be said that the suggested 'hidden meaning' of *SIT through* can be overridden by the rest of the context. The connotation applies only in cases where the context does not contradict it. To summarise, *SIT through* might be said to carry connotations of 'boredom', amassed through the typical contexts in which the phrase is used. The connotations hold unless there is very clear evidence to the contrary, as in line 19. Typicality is crucial here – the connotation cannot be observed by examining one or two instances of the phrase, but depends on its most frequent contexts.[3]

Using probes

In the examples given in this chapter so far, a search for a word or phrase has been used to gain more information about that word or phrase. It is possible, however, to use searches to find sets of words or expressions that cannot easily otherwise be called to mind. These searches are known as 'probes'. For example, to find how men and women are typically evaluated, the sequence *something/nothing* + adjective + *about/in* + *him/her* can be used to find lists of adjectives that are used to describe a male or female person.[4] Here are some sample concordance lines for illustration, with lists taken from a larger set of concordances below:

Male person

has charm in spades but there's nothing boyish about him. He is a real
the gravel drive, someone would say something candid about him, provoking
t changed. Now I knew there was something different about him, something
on many occasions. But there was something equivocal about him, a reserve, a
to each of us. As Cayce spoke, something familiar about him beckoned to
all my life. There was nothing funny about him.' Go on.
I was playing him I had to find something likeable in him' Trevor says.
who knew him would think there's something odd about him, he does something
able to support her. There was something panicky about him that confused
his opinion all the time. There was something reassuring about him. She wasn't
it and I began to think there was something special about him. I told his
so certain that there was something suspicious about him, some
all his ineffable niceness there is something unyielding about him. Bleasdale

*absurd, arresting, attractive, big, boyish, candid, childlike, danger-
ous, decent, Dickensian, different, disturbing, electric, endearing,
equivocal, familiar, fantastic, fascinating, funny, good, heroic, im-*

---

[3] But speakers may be alerted to the presence of connotation or semantic prosody by a single example that exploits or mis-uses it (see Louw 1993; 1997). I became aware of the 'hidden meaning' of *SIT through* when someone mentioned 'sitting through' a talk I had given! As this was said in my hearing, I prefer to assume that the speaker was mistaken in her use of the phrase, rather than that she was really saying that my talk was boring.

[4] The concordance lines with *her* have to be edited, as they will include examples such as *she has found something strange about her husband.*

patient, indefatigable, indefinable, inspiring, insubordinate, human, likeable, masculine, Napoleonic, odd, pagan, panicky, pathetic, peculiar, positive, reassuring, remarkable, remote, reptilian, robotic, sad, saintly, scary, sexy, sinister, special, strange, suspicious, sympathetic, terrible, theatrical, uncanny, unreal, unyielding, wild, womanly, wonderful, wrong

Female person

```
         her for a beautiful chair. There's something decadent about her, don't you
    sings her songs. They know there's something different about her and they'll
         an apple, he sees a nun. There is something familiar about her. Does Sophia
if nothing had happened. There was something odd about her, but what was it?
      s true,' Emily conceded, 'there is something peculiar about her.' Large had
           t bear to see her. There was something sacred about her, and we were
    for a while but I knew there was something special about her. I just drove
Park and meets a young girl with something strange about her. At the end of
realized this. There was certainly something stricken about her and it had
      about nineteen and there was something vulnerable about her. She
 loves him. He is her sort. There is something wild about her. They fit
```

appealing, bad, dark, decadent, different, disconcerting, earthy, endearing, exotic, extraordinary, familiar, insolent, kittenish, objectionable, obsessive, odd, pathetic, peculiar, poignant, professional, pure, repellent, sacred, special, strange, stricken, unknowable, Victorian, voluptuous, vulnerable, wild

Among these adjectives are ones that might be expected, including:

- Adjectives focusing on the construal of age and sexuality: *boyish, childlike, masculine, womanly* (examples found in the male list only).
- Adjectives focusing on sexual attractiveness or behaviour: *sexy* (male list); *earthy, kittenish, voluptuous, pure* (female list).
- Adjectives focusing on the person's effect on others' feelings: *arresting, attractive, endearing, fascinating, inspiring, likeable, reassuring*; and *disturbing, scary, sinister, pathetic* (male list); *appealing, endearing, poignant, vulnerable*; and *disconcerting, objectionable, pathetic, repellent* (female list).
- Adjectives indicating positive or negative moral values: *candid, decent, heroic, saintly, sympathetic* (male list); *bad, dark, decadent* (female list).
- Adjectives indicating the person's feelings or behaviour: *insubordinate, panicky, sad, unyielding* (male list); *insolent, obsessive, professional, stricken* (female list).

In addition to these, a surprisingly large number of adjectives indicate that someone fits into, or more often does not fit into, human society in general. These include:

- *Human, reptilian* and *robotic* (male list only).
- Indicators of a difference that is humorous or frightening: *absurd, dangerous, fantastic, suspicious* (and *disturbing, scary, sinister*) (male list only).
- Indicators of simple sameness or difference or, most revealingly, a difficulty in interpreting the person concerned: *familiar, odd, peculiar, special, strange, unreal, wild* (male list); *different, exotic, extraordinary, familiar, odd, peculiar, special, strange, unknowable, wild* (female list).

As well as evaluating people in terms of their moral and psychological characteristics, therefore, it seems that we evaluate them surprisingly often in terms of how much like other people they are, and with how much confidence we are able to understand them. Using the probe reminds us of the range of possibilities. (The differences between the 'male' and 'female' lists are of course striking, and deserving of further study.)

In a slightly different vein, a probe such as *what would* can be used to collect ways of expressing possible or hypothetical events other than with an *if*-clause or a *when*-clause (Tim Johns, personal communication). Here are some examples from a corpus of issues of the *New Scientist* magazine:

A second form of evidence [for glaciation] comes from sediments left behind as ice moved across the land. They often fill in what would <u>otherwise</u> be hollows. (= if glaciation had not occurred)

If migrating birds rely heavily on the direction of the Earth's magnetic field for navigation, what would happen <u>in the event of</u> the Earth's magnetic field reversing. (= if the Earth's magnetic field reversed)

The mind boggles about what would happen to California's agriculture, <u>should</u> global warming tip the local climate towards another drought. (= if global warming tipped the local climate towards another drought)

A jellyfish is more than 99 per cent water. <u>Bury</u> it for a few hundred million years beneath a pile of sand some 5 kilometres thick, and what would be left? (= if you buried it for a few hundred million years beneath a pile of sand)

<u>Suppose</u> someone gave you a large quantity of separated isotope, what would happen? (= if someone gave you a large quantity of separated isotope)

<u>Faced</u> with a charging Tyrannosaurus rex, what would be the best way to stop it? (= if you were faced with a charging Tyrannosaurus rex)

Such a search might be useful to a teacher or translator wishing to find alternative ways of expressing hypotheticality.

Issues in accessing and interpreting concordance lines

In this chapter, the techniques needed to access and interpret concordance lines have been discussed. There has been an emphasis on:

- the variation in the kind of search that is possible, using the word, the lemma or the phrase as a target;
- with some searches, the need to edit the lines to separate the target phrase from others that the search has found;
- the need to sort lines to make the patterning in them more visible;
- the fact that it is often necessary to look at only part of each line in a set of concordance lines in order to identify patterning;
- conversely, the need sometimes to look at more co-text than a short concordance line can show;
- the need to tackle a large amount of data by looking at successive groups of a small number of lines, forming and testing hypotheses;
- the need to concentrate on evidence for the 'central and typical';
- conversely, the need to consider counter-examples which apparently fail to support the hypothesis being developed. A more careful study might show either that the apparent counter-example actually supports the hypothesis, or that the hypothesis has to be amended.

Concordance lines present information; they do not interpret it. Interpretation requires the insight and intuition of the observer. For example, in the discussion of *suggestion* above, it was noted that the sequence *suggestion to* has at least three possible meanings. In one, the to-infinitive clause is in apposition to, and is dependent on, the noun *suggestion* (as in *their suggestion to contest the election*); in another the to-infinitive clause means 'in order to' (as in *suggestions to save coal*); in the third the to-infinitive clause 'belongs to' the verb preceding *suggestion* (as in *have a suggestion to make*). The distinctions, particularly between the first two, cannot be made automatically: human judgement is needed. To some extent, this is a disadvantage, as it complicates statistical work on corpora. The enormous benefit, however, is that the human eye can perceive features of language that were hitherto unguessed-at.

One type of corpus interpretation, then, involves distinguishing between categories, such as types of clauses. Another type involves making generalisations about the association between the way a word is used and its meaning. This generalisation may be straightforward, as in the CONDEMN example above, or it may involve features less open to demonstration, as in the *par for the course* and *I must admit* examples.

Of particular interest, and difficulty, are cases where evidence from a corpus is used to make statements about 'the way the world is' (see also chapter 5 on this point). For example, there are roughly twice as many instances of *left-handed* as *right-handed* in the Bank of English corpus. What is the reason for this? One possible explanation is that there are more left-handed people in the world than right-handed people, but we know that this is not so. Another explanation is that left-handed people are considered to have a higher status than right-handed people, and therefore to be more worth talking about. Most left-handers would argue that this does not accord with their daily experience. A third possibility is that right-handedness is considered to be 'the norm' and left-handedness is 'deviant', and that deviance is more often mentioned than normality. Looking at the lines themselves suggests that this is the most likely interpretation, but it is important to recognise that this is an interpretation of evidence, not 'fact'.

4 *Methods in corpus linguistics: Beyond the concordance line*

Concordance lines are a useful tool for investigating corpora, but their use is limited by the ability of the human observer to process information. Assessments of frequency and significance are difficult to make impressionistically, particularly in the case of very frequent words. Also, they are not particularly useful in collecting information about categories of things, such as ways of expressing future time, or the frequency of nominalisations, as opposed to words. In this chapter we look at methods of investigating corpora that go beyond concordance lines. These include statistical calculations of collocation and corpus annotation.

As suggested above, a distinction is made in this chapter between methods which are based on individual words and those which are based on categories. The final section in this chapter discusses the implications of the two approaches, making the point that what is at issue is not only methodology, but the theoretical presuppositions that lead to that methodology. Essentially, the word-based and the category-based approaches are used to answer different sets of questions, and may be evaluated in terms of the perceived usefulness of the questions. I shall stress that what is important is that anyone who uses commercially produced programs for exploiting corpora, or who reads about work in this area, should be aware of the assumptions behind the work, and the alternatives available.

Frequency and key-word lists

A frequency list is simply a list of all the types in a corpus together with the number of occurrences of each type. The list can be displayed in frequency order, in alphabetical order, or in the order of the first occurrence of the type in the corpus (Barnbrook 1996: 43–64). As suggested in chapter 1, comparing the frequency lists for two corpora can give interesting information about the differences between the texts comprising each one. This is particularly useful when specialised corpora are being compared. Kennedy (1998: 101–2; 105–6) mentions two such studies. A comparison between a corpus of Economics texts and one of general academic English shows the words *price, cost, demand, curve, firm, supply, quantity, margin* and *economy* among those which are frequently found in the Economics corpus but not in the general one (Sutarsyah et al 1994). Thus the lexis peculiar to Economics is identified. Similarly, Johansson (1981) compares a corpus of academic texts and one of fiction, finding *constants*, *axis*, *equations* and *oxides* among the most frequent nouns in the academic corpus, while *mister*, *sofa*, *wallet* and *cheek* are the corresponding nouns in the fiction corpus. Similar comparisons for verbs, adjectives and adverbs are also carried out.

Words which are significantly more frequent in one corpus than another are sometimes known as **keywords**. The corpus investigation package *Wordsmith Tools* (Scott 1996) includes a program which automatically compares two corpora – usually a smaller, more specialised, one and a larger, more general, one – and lists the keywords for the more specialised corpus. It can therefore be used, for example, to list the significantly different lexis between a small set of newspaper articles and a corpus of newspaper texts. Many researchers find 'keywords' a useful starting point in investigating a specialised corpus: Gledhill (1995; 1996), for example, uses the program to identify the items which are significantly frequent in different sections of a research article (see chapter 8 for more details of Gledhill's work). Tribble (2000) compares a corpus of romantic fiction with a general corpus and identifies features occurring in the fiction texts which are more typical of spoken than written English. These include *I* and *you* and proper nouns. Also *the* and *of* are negative keywords, that is, they are significantly less frequent in the target corpus than in the general one. Both words are frequent in complex noun phrases. As Scott (2000) points out, keywords can be lexical items which reflect the topic of a particular text, but they can also be grammatical words which convey more subtle information.

Collocation

Collocation is the tendency of words to be biased in the way they co-occur. For example, the word *toys* co-occurs with *children* more frequently than with *women* or *men*. This collocation might be said to be motivated, in that there is a logical explanation for it (toys belong to children, on the whole, rather than to adults). Other collocations, such as *strong tea* but *powerful car* (Halliday 1976: 73) appear to be unmotivated. Collocation may be observed informally in any instance of language, but it is more reliable to measure it statistically, and for this a corpus is essential. It can be considered as the tendency of two words to co-occur, or as the tendency of one word to attract another.

Measurements of collocation

Any program which calculates collocation takes a **node word** and counts the instances of all words occurring within a particular **span**, for example, four words to the left of the node word and four words to the right.[1] To give an idea of what this means, the following concordance lines show a 4:4 span of the node word *gaze*. The words included in the span are in bold.

> by Philippe **Halsman, in which the gaze of the elderly Duke** of Windsor
> de, **muscular head and penetrating gaze, Licks is a big** puppy, giving hugs
> one below the **other and if my gaze happens to flick downwards** at nearly
> sat down in a **chair to wait, her gaze moving round the shop.** Rose had
> our way and **men and women would gaze closely upon me, too.** Would they
> a **break for it. The other nurse's gaze switched to something over** my
> r with a **fortune in diamonds. His gaze returned to Rick's** gun, steady on
> rity?' **Kadredin fixed his bulbous gaze on Burnell and rubbed** a long pale
> de **was she on? Forcing himself to gaze over the balcony's** edge, Joe scanned
> esh water, a **brand-new life." Her gaze was curiously fixed and bright,**
> scape. Time **and again in Ulysses' Gaze, Theo Angelopoulos renews** his

Note that this particular count of 4:4 ignores punctuation marks but counts *'s* as a separate word. The count ignores sentence boundaries. Some of the words co-occurring with *gaze* here might be supposed to do so by chance (*wait . . . gaze, life . . . gaze*, for example), whilst others (*penetrating gaze, my/her/his gaze*) might be said to be 'meaningful'. The reason for obtaining large quantities of data to calculate collocation is that the chance collocations will be shown to be insignificant overall when compared with the meaningful ones.

These lines include both the noun and the verb *gaze*, but it is possible of course to restrict the search to one of these, and to choose only the word-form *gaze* or the lemma *GAZE*. For the purposes of illustration, I shall select all instances of the noun *gaze* (the plural is not found in the corpus) from the Bank of English. There are 2,864 lines. The collocations program then calculates the frequency of each item in a 4:4 span, giving these as the fifteen most frequent collocates:

the	1,511
his	822
her	628
's	442
on	333
he	277
from	228

[1] See Mason (1999) for a critique of the notion of a single span used for any word.

with	225
she	213
my	177
under	154
their	140
public	109
fixed	102
then	86

The words at the top of this list are all grammatical words. The high frequency of determiners (*the* and the possessives *his, her, my* and *their*) is to be expected when the word concerned is a noun. The prepositions *on, from, with* and *under* occur because of phrases such as *turn one's gaze on, away from the gaze of, with a firm gaze* and *under the watchful gaze of.* Of the two lexical words in this list, *public* occurs in the phrase *public gaze* and *fixed* is used in expressions such as *fixed his gaze on* and *her gaze was fixed on.*

The problem with a list of raw frequencies, such as this one, is that it is impossible to attach a precise degree of importance to any of the figures in it. Is it significant, for example, that *his* occurs near the top of this list, or might this word occur with any noun? As a way of answering questions such as these it is possible to calculate the significance of each co-occurrence. Three of the most commonly used measures of significance are: Mutual Information (MI) score, t-score, and z-score.[2] Useful discussions of these can be found in Clear 1993; Stubbs 1995; Barnbrook 1996: 87–101; McEnery and Wilson 1996: 71–73; Biber et al 1998: 265–268; Oakes 1998. I will concentrate on t-score and MI-score, for which brief definitions are given below, adapted from Barnbrook (1996: 97–100). Both depend on two calculations: how many instances of the co-occurring word are found in the designated span of the node word (the Observed), and how many instances might be expected in that span, given the frequency of the co-occurring word in the corpus as a whole (the Expected). In addition, the t-score uses a calculation of standard deviation, which takes into account the probability of co-occurrence of the node and its collocate and the number of tokens in the designated span in all lines.

- The t-score is calculated by subtracting Expected from Observed and dividing the result by the standard deviation.
- The MI-score is the Observed divided by the Expected, converted to a base-2 logarithm.

---

[2] In terms of how they are calculated, t-score and z-score are most similar, but in terms of output, z-score and MI-score are most similar.

The examples given below are based on the collocations programs which are part of the 'Lookup' package available with the Bank of English corpus. Other packages use slightly different methods of calculation, so it is not easy to make direct comparisons between them, but the general principles are the same.

Very generally, an MI-score indicates the strength of a collocation. It compares the actual co-occurrence of the two items with their expected co-occurrence if the words in the corpus used were to occur in totally random order.[3] In other words, the MI-score measures the amount of non-randomness present when two words co-occur. An MI-score of 3 or higher can be taken to be significant. Some examples of collocations with high MI-scores in the Bank of English are: *ballpoint + pen* (an MI-score of 11.6); *distinctly + unenthusiastic* (12.7); *kith + kin* (18.1); *hardly + surprising* (7.8). The 15 collocates of *gaze* with the highest MI-scores are:

angelopoulos	12.1
gorgon	10.7
ronaldson	10.6
averts	10.2
vlahov	10.1
unblinking	9.4
unflinching	9.4
basks	9.2
unseeing	9.2
ulysses	9.1
averted	8.9
unfocused	8.8
baleful	8.7
unwavering	8.5
watchful	8.2

The figures show the MI-scores obtained using the software specified. Some of these words appear on this list because there is a high degree of co-occurrence in a particular text or a particular part of the corpus. For example, reviews of the film *Ulysses Gaze*, directed

---

[3] Burrows (1992) and Stubbs (1995) point out that utter randomness is a somewhat bizarre notion when applied to language. Even aside from their collocational behaviour, words do not occur randomly. For example, a noun such as *girl* could conceivably follow a determiner (*a, the, every* and so on) or an adjective (*green, smooth, pretty* and so on), but is unlikely, grammatically, to follow a pronoun (*he, she, I* and so on) or an adverb (*very, fairly* and so on). Thus, if the significance of, say, *pretty* as a collocate of *girl* is to be calculated, the expected co-occurrence if distribution were random should take into account only the grammatically possible co-occurrences, not the impossible ones. The problem with putting this into practice lies in the difficulty of determining the 'grammar only' probabilities.

by Angelopoulos, account for the presence of *ulysses* and *angelo-poulos* in the list. Accounts of a poem *The Gaze of the Gorgon* accounts for *gorgon*. Two reporters named *Ronaldson* and *Gaze* are frequently mentioned in the collection of Australian newspapers, which accounts for the presence of *ronaldson*. Also in the Australian newspapers, Andrew Vlahov and Andrew Gaze are mentioned together, accounting for *vlahov*. Other words, such as *baleful* and *unwavering*, are more generally associated with *gaze*, although they are not particularly frequent words. *Baleful* and *gaze* co-occur only 6 times, for example, but because *baleful* is an infrequent word, even such a low co-occurrence is significant. This example illustrates the fact that if a word occurs rarely, but in most of its few occurrences appears in the proximity of another word, the collocation between those words will obtain a high MI-score. MI, then, is a measure of how strongly two words seem to associate in a corpus, based on the independent relative frequency of the two words.

As the case of *baleful* and *gaze* shows, however, knowing the strength of the collocation is not always a reliable indication of meaningful association – we also need to know how much evidence there is for it, that is, how certain we can be that the collocation is the result of more than the vagaries of a particular corpus.[4] For this, the calculation of t-score, which takes the amount of evidence into account, can be used. A t-score of 2 or higher is normally taken to be significant. Examples of collocations with high t-scores in the Bank of English corpus include: *things + considered* (a t-score of 91.6); *could + hardly* (55.5); *argument + that* (54); *children + toy/s* (18.4). The following figures show the 15 collocates of *gaze* that have the highest t-scores.

his	25.2
her	22.9
under	11.3
my	10.8
she	10.5
's	10.5
fixed	10.0
on	9.5
public	9.4
from	8.6

---

[4] To illustrate this: imagine that you do a survey of 10 people, of whom 6 answer 'yes' to a particular question. You note that 60% of your sample answered 'yes'. But six people is a very small number, so you cannot be very certain of the reliability of this figure. Now suppose you do the same survey with 500 people, and 300 (60%) answer 'yes'. You would be much more confident about the reliability of this 60% figure.

eyes	8.6
turned	8.2
away	7.7
he	7.7
followed	7.1

This list is clearly different from the MI-score list, in that collocates depending on particular parts of the corpus do not appear, but it is also different from the raw frequency list. For example, the co-occurrence of *the* and *gaze* does not have a high t-score. Clearly, then, the appearance of *the* at the top of the frequency list came about to a large extent because *the* is such a frequent word, not because of its association with *gaze*. In the case of *his*, however, the t-score confirms that the collocation between this word and *gaze* is not due purely to the high frequency of *his* but to the lexical preferences of *gaze*. *His* and *gaze* do not have a high MI-score, because *his* also collocates with so many other things, but there is a lot of evidence for their co-occurrence, hence they have a high t-score.

The important differences between MI-score and t-score are:

- MI-score is a measure of strength of collocation; t-score is a measure of certainty of collocation. This is because:
- The value of an MI-score is not particularly dependent on the size of the corpus. For the t-score, however, corpus size is important, because the amount of evidence is being taken into account. The larger the corpus is, the more significant a large number of co-occurrences is. Here is an example of this difference. The Bank of English includes some (59) occurrences of the mis-spelling *suprising* [sic]. If the word *hardly* is taken as a node word, the collocate with the highest MI-score (8.0) is, surprisingly, this spelling of *suprising*. The correctly spelled *surprising* has a slightly lower MI-score (7.8), even though there are vastly more instances of *hardly surprising* (1,636) than there are of *hardly suprising* (9). This is because *suprising* co-occurs with *hardly* proportionally more often (15.2% of its total occurrences in the corpus) than *surprising* does (13.1% of total occurrences). When the amount of evidence is taken into account, *hardly surprising* remains a highly significant collocate (with a t-score of 40.2, taking *surprising* as the node word), whereas *hardly suprising*, for which there is much less evidence, has a t-score of only 2.9.
- Thus, MI-scores can be compared across corpora, even if the corpora are of different sizes, but absolute t-scores cannot be compared across corpora (though it is reasonable to compare t-score rankings) because the size of the corpus will affect the

t-score. For example, in the Bank of English the corpus consisting of editions of the *Times* is about twice the size as that consisting of editions of the *Economist*. The word *decided* occurs with roughly the same frequency in each (37.4 and 42.1 times per million words). The collocation of *decided* and *to* is very comparable in each corpus in terms of MI-score (4.2 and 3.9 respectively), but the t-score in the *Times* corpus is much higher: 45.0 as opposed to 28.6 in the *Economist* corpus. It would be reasonable to take the MI-score evidence and argue that the collocation *decided to* is stronger in the *Times* corpus than in the *Economist* corpus, but it would not be reasonable to make a similar argument from the t-scores. The *Times* figure is higher, not because the collocation is stronger but because the corpus is bigger. (In both corpora, *to* is the most frequent word occurring one to the right of *decided*.)

- Looking at the top collocates from the point of view of t-score tends to give information about the grammatical behaviour of a word. For example, the list above shows that *gaze* often co-occurs with a possessive. On the other hand, looking at the top collocates from the point of view of MI-score tends to give information about its lexical behaviour, but particularly about the more idiomatic ('fixed') co-occurrences. For example, in the lists above, the MI-score list highlights *unblinking/unflinching/unwavering gaze*.

- The collocates with the highest t-scores tend to be frequent words (whether or not they are grammatical words) that collocate with a variety of items. For example, *followed* collocates with *gaze* but also with other words. The collocates with the highest MI-scores tend to be less frequent words with restricted collocation. For example, *averts* is closely associated with *gaze* and with only a few other words, such as *danger*.

Calculations of MI-score and of t-score both have their uses, and both, of course, need to be interpreted carefully. As illustration of this, the following information was obtained by getting all instances from the Bank of English corpus of 'adverb followed by *significant*', and then obtaining information on the strength and certainty of collocation between the adverbs and *significant* (an idea inspired by Granger 1998a). The top collocates from the point of view of MI-score (the strongest collocates) are *radiologically, statistically, electorally, militarily* and *symbolically*. These words remind us that *significant* has specific meanings in different academic fields, and that the purpose of the adverb may be to tell us what kind of significance is meant in each instance. Although the collocates are strong, however, they are not all particularly certain. For example, *electorally signifi-*

cant occurs only five times in the whole corpus. The top collocates in terms of t-score (the most certain collocates) are *more, most, very, statistically, highly, not, particularly*. This is a less 'technical' list and tells us less about what *significance* 'means'. On the other hand, it does indicate that *significant* is often used in comparisons and which adverbs are most typically used with it. The presence of the phrase *statistically significant* in both lists shows us that it is important in all ways. It is a strong collocate, and a certain one.

A final point that needs to be made about calculations of collocation is that in some instances they may require a wider span than is commonly used. This is particularly true with respect to what might be called 'clause collocation', that is, the tendency of one kind of clause to co-occur with another. For example, clauses beginning with *I wonder* can be observed to co-occur reasonably frequently with clauses beginning with *because*, as in the following (spoken) examples, where *because* seems to mean 'the reason I mention this is . . .':

And <u>I wonder</u> who the writer of this is <u>because</u> it quite probably or quite possibly could have been Hansom much later on.

<u>I wonder</u> where it [postage price increase]'s going to stop John anyway <u>because</u> I don't think the service is that much better anyway John.

<u>I wonder</u> if you found this here <u>'cos</u> I did at Sheffield.

<u>I wonder</u> if the lady on the counter [has a bag] <u>cos</u> the print all comes off [the newspapers] doesn't it by the time you've taken them home.

To calculate the significance of the co-occurrence would require a very large span indeed, as there is little restriction on the length of the *I wonder* clause.[5]

The uses of collocational information

Collocational statistics can be helpful to the corpus user in summarising some of the information to be found in concordance lines, thereby allowing more instances of a word to be considered than is feasible with concordance lines. If a word has 10,000 occurrences in a corpus, it may be possible to look only at 500 concordance lines, but collocational software can make calculations using all 10,000 occurrences and so give information that is more reliable. When looking at concordance lines, it is reasonable to make a selection of

---

[5] I am grateful to the assistance of Jeremy Clear and Geoff Barnbrook while writing this account of collocation.

all the instances. When obtaining statistical information, however, the calculations should be made using all the available data.

One use of collocational information is to highlight the different meanings that a word has. For example, here are the collocates of the verb *LEAK*, showing the raw frequencies in the second column and the t-scores in the third:

the	3,456	19.8
out	454	17.3
from	568	16.4
document	246	15.5
information	252	15.2
report	242	14.8
documents	209	14.3
to	1,544	13.0
into	269	12.6
memo	153	12.3
confidential	138	11.7
press	149	11.6
details	145	11.6
letter	140	11.2
was	576	11.0
had	342	10.7
oil	120	10.3
news	126	10.0
water	122	9.9
a	1,256	9.8
gas	102	9.7
draft	88	9.2
roof	86	9.1
been	230	8.3

It can be seen immediately that some of these words are associated with the physical meaning of *LEAK*: *oil, water, gas, roof;* while others are associated with the metaphoric sense: *document/s, information, report, memo, confidential, press, details, letter, news* and *draft*. The list also suggests that prepositions and adverbs of direction (*out, from, to* and *into*) are important to the behaviour of *LEAK*. In short, the list of collocates gives a kind of semantic profile of the word involved. Stubbs (1995; 1996) uses this technique to establish, for example, that *CAUSE* is typically used with nouns indicating 'something bad' (*anxiety, concern, AIDS, cancer, problems, damage* and so on), and also to argue for the importance of certain words as diagnostics of cultural attitudes (1996: 176–181).

What the simple collocation list cannot show is the association of meaning and phraseology. For example, *LEAK* in the physical sense can have either the substance as subject (*the oil leaked out*) or the container as subject (*the tank leaked oil*). The metaphoric sense behaves in a similar way: *the news leaked out* and *he leaked the news*. However, the metaphoric sense has an additional pattern, with *to*, that the physical sense does not have, as in *he leaked the document to his boss* (presumably by analogy with *he gave the information to his boss*). This variation in pattern can be seen only from the concordance lines.

A somewhat different method of displaying collocational information can, however, be used to obtain clues as to the dominant phraseology of a word. This is something of a short-cut to the information that could be obtained from concordance lines. For example, here is some information about the words that occur one, two and three places to the left of the word *shoulder*. Each column is arranged in t-score order. The table shows that *his* is the most significant word immediately to the left of *shoulder*, while the most significant word occurring two places to the left is *over* and so on.

hand	over	his	shoulder
on	on	her	
looking	shoulder	my	
over	his	the	
back	off	s	
arm	from	right	
chip	neck	left	
him	your	a	
looked	with	your	
head	at	hard	
look	against	cold	
glanced	around	to	
slung	between	one	
her	touched	dislocated	
me	her	their	
with	dislocated	broken	

These columns suggest how phrases with *shoulder* are built up, though the concordance lines need to be checked to be sure of the phraseology. *Shoulder* often follows a possessive, or *right* and *left*, or occurs in a phrase such as *hard shoulder* or *cold shoulder*. Injuries to shoulders also contribute to collocations, as in *dislocated shoulder* and *broken shoulder*. The most significant words before *his/her/my/ the shoulder* are *over* and *on*. *Over* is used following a range of verbs: LOOK *over [his] shoulder*, GLANCE *over [his] shoulder*, *slung over [his] shoulder*. *On* occurs in the phrases *hand on [his] shoulder* and *chip on [his] shoulder*.

The collocates occurring to the right of *shoulder* also contribute to phraseology.

shoulder	and	shoulder
	injury	he
	–	cry
	length	the
	to	hair
	blades	she
	bag	his
	blade	burden
	pads	said
	at	apart
	he	and
	as	was
	height	her
	strap	saw
	she	responsibility
	straps	I
	I	arm
	holster	see
	high	blame

The first column suggests compounds, such as *shoulder-length, shoulder blade/s, shoulder bag, shoulder pads*. From the next column we get *shoulder to cry on* and *shoulder [the] burden/responsibility/ blame*.

Finally, collocations can be used to obtain a profile of the semantic field of a word. For example, a list of the collocates of *bribe* and *bribery*, taken together, can be grouped into semantic areas (Orpin 1997). These include:

• Words connected with wrong-doing: *allegations, scandal, corruption, alleged, fraud*;
• Words connected with money: *dollar, money, tax, pound*;
• Words connected with officialdom: *officials, police*;
• Words connected with sport: *players, referee*;
• Words connected with the legal process: *charges, trial, investigation, charged, accused, convicted, guilty*.

This grouping of words gives information not only about the meaning of the words *bribe* and *bribery*, but an insight into some of the cultural ramifications of the concept of 'bribery'. This will be discussed further in chapter 5.

Before leaving the topic of collocation information and fixed phrases, it is worth giving a warning about interpreting such information. It is tempting, when looking at a list of collocates, to draw conclusions about the overall frequency of compounds and phrases that may not be justified. For example, the list of right-collocates for *shoulder* showed that the compounds *shoulder blade(s)*, *shoulder bag(s)*, and *shoulder pad(s)* are significantly frequent uses of the noun *shoulder*. Although this is true, it is also the case that together these compounds comprise fewer than 5% of all occurrences of *shoulder*. A similar example can be found with the word *deaf*. Looking at the collocates suggests that the phrase *FALL on deaf ears* might be the most frequent use of *deaf* (because *on* is the most significant word to the left of *deaf* and *ears* is the most significant word to the right). The phrase is certainly an important one, with 355 occurrences in the Bank of English, but it accounts for only 10% of all occurrences in that corpus of *deaf*. The point is that calculations of collocation will always prioritise uses of a word that tend to be lexically fixed or restricted. Other uses, such as *deaf* as an attributive adjective, are less restricted lexically (*deaf actress/ adult/alcoholic/baby/babysitter/baker/boy/brother/caller/child/client/ co-worker* and so on) and so appear to be less significant when lists of collocations are being observed. It is therefore important to recognise the importance of highly significant collocations but not to mis-interpret information about them.

Tagging and parsing

Categories and annotation

Corpus **annotation** is the process of adding information to a corpus. As Leech (1997b: 2) points out, this information is designed to interpret the corpus linguistically, for example by indicating the word-class of each of the words in it. The term 'annotation' is used to cover tagging, parsing and other forms of annotation (for details, see below). Using annotations to explore a corpus is referred to here as a 'category-based' methodology, because the parts of a corpus – the words, or phonological units, or clauses etc – are placed into categories and those categories are used as the basis for corpus searches and statistical manipulations. This is in contrast to the 'word-based' methods described above.

Everyone would agree that some degree of annotation is a useful feature of a corpus, especially a large corpus. In addition, many people regard extensive annotation as an essential step in the exploitation of corpora. Leech (1997b: 2) says:

Corpus annotation is widely accepted as a crucial contribution to the benefit a corpus brings, since it enriches the corpus as a source of linguistic information for future research and development.

The idea that annotation adds value to a corpus, making it easier to retrieve information and increasing the range of investigations that can be done on the corpus will be illustrated below. It is not the concern of this book to teach the reader how to annotate a corpus, for which specific software is often necessary. Instead the types of annotation used and the uses to which they are put are discussed.

Before beginning the discussion of corpus annotation, however, it is worth pointing out that corpus investigations involving categories can be carried out on a non-annotated corpus, as Halliday (1993; see also Halliday and James 1993) and Stubbs (1996; see also Stubbs and Gerbig 1993) have shown. Halliday calculates the approximate proportions of positive and negative clauses (9:1) and of present and past clauses (5:5) in a fairly large unannotated corpus (the 18 million word Birmingham Corpus). Stubbs calculates the proportion of transitive and intransitive instances of ergative verbs (e.g. *John broke the vase* and *The vase broke*) in three corpora: one consisting of a Geography textbook, one consisting of an Ecology textbook, and the LOB corpus which is used for comparison.

Tagging

Tagging means allocating a part of speech (POS) label to each word in a corpus. For example, the word *light* is tagged as either a verb, a noun or an adjective each time it occurs in the corpus. The tag can be chosen to give general or specific information. For example, the word-form *being* in the verb phrase *is being considered* can be tagged as 'verb', or as 'present participle of a verb', or as 'present participle of the verb *be*', or as 'present participle of the verb *be* used as an auxiliary'. (Short codes are used to express the information, for example 'VVG' to mean 'present participle of a lexical verb'.) Details of how corpora are tagged may be found in Leech (1997b) and in Garside and Smith (1997).

As suggested in chapter 1, a tagged corpus has various uses. Looking at the concordance lines for a word with several senses can be made much simpler if the word-class can be specified. For example, 100 randomly selected lines of the lemma *LIGHT* included only 10 examples of the verb use. Investigating the verb is much easier if the search can specify that only verb instances of *LIGHT* are wanted.

The relative frequencies of different parts of speech for a specific word can be compared. Biber et al (1998: 31) quote the example of *DEAL*, whose frequencies in the LOB corpus are:

deal (singular common noun)	115
Deal (proper noun)	1
deals (plural common noun)	5
deal (base form of the verb)	66
dealing (present participle)	51
deals (third person singular form of the verb)	20
dealt (past tense of the verb)	14
dealt (past participle)	17

These figures suggest that the form *deal* is more frequently a noun than a verb, but that *deals* is more frequently a verb than a noun. Sinclair (1991: 46) gives a similar example using the lemma *DECLINE* from the early 20 million word Birmingham Corpus. He points out that *decline* is most frequently a noun but *declines* is most frequently a verb. Observations such as these indicate that it cannot be assumed that all forms of a lemma behave in the same way, though it has not been proven that they always behave differently either.

Often the collocations of a word depend on its word-class. For example, the most frequent collocates of the verb *LIGHT* in the Bank of English (in t-score order) are: *cigarette, came, fire, candle, candles*. The noun *LIGHT* has the collocates *red, green, bright, traffic, flashing*. The adjective *LIGHT* collocates with *dark, brown, blue, touch, very*.

More sophisticated uses can be made of a tagged corpus. Perhaps most significantly, total occurrences of word-classes in a particular corpus can be counted. Biber et al (1999) compare word-class occurrence in a number of corpora. A simplified version of their findings, comparing news reportage, conversation and academic prose, is shown in Table 4.1.

As the table shows, Biber et al find that nouns are most common in news and academic prose and least common in conversation. Verbs and adverbs are particularly common in conversation. In conversation, speakers use more pronouns than nouns. In news and academic prose they use more nouns than pronouns. Because nouns are often used with determiners and prepositions (as in *the end of the road*), a high frequency of nouns necessitates also a high frequency of determiners and prepositions. Similarly, because auxiliaries and particles co-occur with verbs, it is not surprising that conversation, with most verbs, also has the greatest number of auxiliaries and particles.

Table 4.1. The comparative frequency of word-classes in three corpora

	Conversation	News	Academic
More common	Pronouns	Nouns	Nouns
	Verbs	Determiners	Determiners
	Adverbs	Prepositions	Prepositions
	Auxiliaries		
	Particles		
Less common	Nouns	Pronouns	Pronouns
	Determiners	Verbs	Verbs
	Prepositions	Adverbs	Adverbs
		Auxiliaries	Auxiliaries
		Particles	Particles

(data derived from Biber et al 1999)

In addition, the word-classes, rather than the individual words, that collocate with a given item can be listed (see, for example, Mason 1999: 274). Finally, the frequency of sequences of tags can be calculated and corpora can be compared in this respect. Aarts and Granger (1998: 135), for example, find that non-native speakers writing in English differ from equivalent native-speaker writers in the sequences of tags that recur. Dutch, Finnish and French speakers writing in English all use fewer of the following tag sequences than native-speaker writers do:

preposition-article-noun (e.g. *in the morning*)
article-noun-preposition (e.g. *a debate on*)
noun-preposition-noun (e.g. *part of speech*)
noun-preposition-article (e.g. *concern for the*)

This suggests that the non-native writers do not use prepositions in a 'native-like' way. In turn, this suggests that the non-native writers are using fewer of the lengthy noun phrases that are essential to formal, particularly academic, writing in English (Halliday and Martin 1993).

Corpus tagging needs to be done automatically, that is, by a computer programmed to recognise parts of speech, otherwise the labour of adding tags by hand would outweigh the advantages of having them. Programs that assign tags (**taggers**) tend to work on a mixture of two principles: rules governing word-classes and probability. For example, if the word-form *light* follows the determiner *a*, it may be a noun or an adjective, but it is unlikely to be a verb. This is a rule. When applying the rules fails to identify the word-class, many taggers use probability, based on the overall frequency of the word and word-class. For example, if the program could not identify an instance of *deal* as a noun or a verb, it may assign the tag 'noun' because *deal* more frequently occurs as a noun than as a verb. (This would in itself increase the frequency of *deal* as a noun, thereby altering the measurement of probability that the program makes.)[6]

Automatic taggers are usually claimed to have an accuracy rate of over 90%. It is important when using a tagged corpus, however, to remember that the tagger may be wrong, and the human user's judgement is more reliable in individual cases. This is particularly so when a word is being used in an unusual way. Taggers work with some kind of lexicon or dictionary, which determines what parts of speech a given word is known to be (*light* is known to be a verb, a noun, and an adjective, for instance). No other tag can be assigned to that word. If the lexicon is wrong, the tagger cannot possibly be right. For example, the Bank of English tagger does not recognise that *sleaze* can be a verb (though it does recognise that *sleazed* is). In the somewhat odd phrase *trying to sleaze his way into our hearts again*, therefore, *sleaze* is tagged as a noun. A further point to note is that inaccuracies produced by a tagger are not usually spread evenly throughout a corpus. For example, few taggers will ever mis-tag a word such as *hamster*, which is only ever a noun, or a word such as *the*, which is only ever a determiner. All the mistakes a tagger makes, therefore, will be clustered around words which have several possible tags. Out of 20 lines of *light* which the Bank of English tagger classifies as 'noun', I identified three lines (15% of the total) which I would have tagged differently, one as a verb (*Symonds' big hits light up the Gabba*), one as an adjective (*light-skinned*) and one as an adverb (*light yellow*). Thus, a tagger with an accuracy rate of 96%, say, may be 100% accurate for many words, but only 70% accurate for some words.

The inaccuracy of automatic taggers will affect the reliability of statistics based on them. For this reason, some tagged corpora have the tags corrected manually once the automatic tagger has finished. A tagger can be instructed to suggest more than one tag, in cases of ambiguity, and the human researcher can then simply pick out the ambiguous cases and make a judgement as to the best tag (see, e.g., Biber et al 1998: 93).

---

[6] I am grateful to Cathy Rosario for pointing out to me the self-perpetuating feature of this type of tagging process.

Parsing

Parsing means analysing the sentences in a corpus into their constituent parts, that is, doing a grammatical analysis. The parser identifies boundaries of sentences, clauses and phrases and assigns labels to the parts identified, such as 'adverbial clause', 'nominal clause', 'relative clause,' 'adjective phrase' and 'prepositional phrase' (Leech and Eyes 1997: 38). For example, Leech and Eyes (1997: 51) demonstrate a parsed version of the sentence:

The victim's friends told police that Krueger drove into the quarry

in which:

- the whole is identified as a sentence;
- *the victim's friends* is identifed as a noun phrase, within which *the victim's* is identified as a genitive;
- *told police that Krueger drove into the quarry* is identified as a verb phrase;
- *police* is identified as a noun phrase;
- *that Krueger drove into the quarry* is identified as a nominal clause;
- *Krueger* is identified as a noun phrase;
- *drove into the quarry* is identified as a verb phrase;
- *into the quarry* is identified as a prepositional phrase;
- *the quarry* is identified as a noun phrase dependent on the preposition.

Although computer programs are written for parsing (**parsers**), it is difficult to make these work completely accurately, and parsed corpora are often edited by hand to achieve a greater degree of accuracy.[7] Some parsed corpora, such as the Polytechnic of Wales (PoW) corpus of children's spoken language, are the result of manual parsing by teams of researchers. Manual parsing is time-consuming, however, and only small corpora can be parsed in this way (the PoW corpus is 10,000 words). Even editing a corpus is expensive in person-hours, and the aim must be for a fully automatic parser. Automatic parsers make use of tagged corpora; in fact, one of the purposes of producing a tagged corpus is to pave the way for parsing.

Parsed corpora are the basis for much of the statistical work that has been done on different registers. In particular, Biber's work (e.g. Biber 1988; Biber et al 1998; Biber et al 1999; and see chapter 6) depends on parsed corpora. To give a brief example: Biber et al

---

[7] See Aarts et al 1998 for a discussion of accuracy in parsers.

(1998: 98–99) examine the use of *BEGIN* and *START* in two small sub-corpora from the Longman-Lancaster Corpus. The sub-corpora comprise fiction and academic prose respectively. The different ways that the verbs are used are identified (intransitive, followed by a noun group, followed by a to-clause, followed by an '-ing' clause) and the proportion of instances of each verb in each register used with each pattern are noted. Biber et al find that for each verb in each register one use predominates over the others:

- the intransitive use of *START* accounts for 64% of the uses of this verb in academic prose
- *BEGIN* followed by a to-clause accounts for 72% of the uses of this verb in fiction; only 4% of instances of *BEGIN* in fiction are followed by an '-ing' clause

Observations such as these can be explained with reference to the function of these uses in the register concerned. Biber et al suggest that the intransitive *START* is frequent in academic prose because it is used in sentences indicating the start of a process (e.g. *Blood loss started about the eighth day of infection . . .*), and this function is frequent in academic prose. Following this lead, it might be observed that the function of *BEGIN* followed by a to-clause in fiction is to describe the start of an action (e.g. *I began to move instinctively to my right*) or a reaction to events (e.g. *I began to feel uneasy*) – functions which are frequent in narrative. The preference for *BEGIN* plus to-clause over *BEGIN* plus '-ing' clause can be explained using information obtained from the collocations of *began* followed by a to-clause and by an '-ing clause'. The verbs most frequently following *began* in fiction are shown (t-score order) in Table 4.2.

What can be seen from the list in Table 4.2 is that whereas some groups of verbs, such as those indicating movement (*move, walk, fall, run; walking, moving, running, pacing, falling*), are used with both complementation patterns, the verbs indicating thought and feeling (*feel, think, wonder, realise*) are used in a to-clause only. In other words, phrases such as *began to feel, began to think* and so on have no '-ing' equivalent. What cannot be seen from the list alone is that where there are two equivalent expressions (e.g. *began to move, began moving*), the to-clause expression is always more frequent than the '-ing' expression.

A parsed corpus can be used to investigate this because all instances of the relevant use of the verb can be seen as concordance lines, and collocational statistics can be obtained. Without a parsed corpus it is easy to search the corpus for a verb followed by a to-clause or an '-ing' clause, but less easy to search for intransitive

Table 4.2. Words following *began* in fiction

began to	began -ing
feel	talking
move	walking
walk	moving
take	making
think	writing
speak	working
talk	taking
cry	speaking
wonder	looking
look	asking
make	reading
get	running
laugh	playing
see	pacing
fall	collecting
run	crying
realise	falling

verbs, for example. In general terms, this study demonstrates a useful synergy between word-based methods and category-based methods. The initial inquiry is word-based (*BEGIN* versus *START*), a parsed corpus is used to obtain the initial data, and word-based methods are used to explain the data in terms of function, collocation and preferred phraseology.

Before leaving the topic of parsing, it is worth mentioning one other use of a parsed corpus: to teach grammatical analysis to students (McEnery et al 1997). For this purpose, a parsed corpus that has been extensively edited by hand is used, to ensure complete accuracy. McEnery et al's results suggest that students who have practised analysis with a computer, using a parsed corpus, do better than equivalent students who have been taught by a human being. Certainly it seems likely that the absence of a human judge might do much to reduce the level of anxiety often associated with learning how to do grammatical analysis.

Other kinds of corpus annotation

As well as being a general term for tagging and parsing, **annotation** is used to describe other kinds of categorisation that may be performed on a corpus. Corpora can be annotated to give a wide range of information. Examples in addition to the types discussed in detail below include the annotation of a spoken corpus for prosodic features (Taylor 1996; Williams 1996) and the annotation of a corpus of learner English for types of error (Reppen 1994; Biber et al 1998). There are two types of annotation that are particularly interesting and potentially useful to applied linguists: annotation of anaphora and semantic annotation. In addition, the use of annotation to identify 'how meanings are made' has a great deal of potential. These areas will be discussed in more detail below.

Annotation of anaphora

One of the most important features of text is cohesion: the use of words and phrases in a text to refer to preceding or subsequent words and phrases (Halliday and Hasan 1976). Some cohesive items are used to summarise, label or encapsulate chunks of discourse, thus playing a role in the organisation of text (Francis 1994; Sinclair 1993). The term **anaphora** is used in schemes which annotate the cohesion in texts, with the term **anaphor** being used for the cohesive item (whether the direction of connection is forwards or backwards). Different systems of annotation can be used to analyse the anaphora in a text, but most do some or all of the following (Garside et al 1997):

- identify an anaphor and its antecedent (the word or phrase it refers to), or establish whether an antecedent is identifiable or not;
- categorise the antecedent (as nominal, clause etc);
- identify the direction of connection (forward or backward);
- identify the type of anaphor (reference, substitution etc);
- note the distance between an anaphor and its antecedent.

Perhaps the most interesting aspect of this is the linking of each anaphor with its antecedent. This involves allocating a number to each antecedent, with the same number being given to the anaphora that refer to it, as in this example (from Garside et al 1997: 72):

(1 *A man carrying a blue sports bag* 1) . . . *was arrested when* <REF=1 *he* . . .

(The left angle bracket indicates that the direction of connection is backwards; REF means 'reference'.)

In this way it is possible to track the development of a text, showing which people or things are referred to most frequently and how the text is progressively chunked, as in this example (ibid.) in which the precise extent of the antecedent is uncertain:

?(9 *It is true that governments can influence the outcome of the competitive process in various ways, and that particular business enterprises can be owned or backed by governments* 9)?, *but even when* <REF=9 *this is allowed for, it is not states that are generally the sole . . .*

The disadvantage of this kind of annotation is that it cannot be done automatically (though see Mitkov 1999 for an account of automated identification of anaphora) and the amount of text that can be coded in this way is therefore limited. On the other hand, this form of annotation raises exciting possibilities. It is possible to see what types of anaphor and antecedent most frequently occur in different registers, to see how anaphora typically change as a text progresses, and ultimately to provide an anaphoric profile of sets of texts from different registers.

Semantic annotation

Semantic annotation refers to the categorisation of words and phrases in a corpus in terms of a set of semantic fields (Thomas and Wilson 1996; Wilson and Thomas 1997). Each word or multi-word item (such as a phrasal verb or idiom) from a tagged corpus is matched against a lexicon in which the items are assigned to a semantic field, such as 'colour', 'power', 'education' or 'medicine'. Wilson and Thomas (1997: 61) provide an example of semantic annotation, using among others the sentence:

Joanna stubbed out her cigarette with unnecessary fierceness.

in which:

- *Joanna* is identified as a Personal Name;
- *stubbed out* is assigned to the class 'Object-Oriented Physical Activity' and the class 'Temperature';
- *cigarette* is assigned to the class 'Luxury Item';
- *unnecessary* is assigned to the class 'Causality/Chance';
- *fierceness* is assigned to the class 'Anger';
- *her* and *with* are identified as 'Low Content Words' and are not assigned to a semantic category.

The outcome is a string of annotations which can then form the basis of calculations which in turn provide an analysis of the content of each part of the corpus.

In an application of this method, Thomas and Wilson (1996) describe an analysis of interactions between doctors and patients in two clinics. Using the system of semantic classification devised, the computer calculates the most frequent meanings made by doctors, other health workers and patients. Thomas and Wilson compare two doctors (A and B) and find significant differences between them. Doctor A used far more discourse particles, first and second person pronouns, boosters and downtoners, suggesting that he might be perceived as more interactive and friendly. Doctor A also made more meanings than Doctor B in the categories of 'Start', 'Cause', 'Change', 'Power' and 'Treatment'. Examination of the transcripts suggested that this was because Doctor A spent more time explaining to patients what their treatment would be and what they could expect from it than Doctor B did. On the other hand, Doctor B used more technical terms, and was found to spend time explaining to patients how their disease was progressing. Thomas and Wilson link these differences in semantic profiles with assessments of patient satisfaction with the treatment they were receiving. The more interactive doctor, who talked about the treatment rather than the disease, was perceived as more supportive than the other one.

Thomas and Wilson's research again illustrates a synergy between methods. It is possible to criticise the semantic categories as lacking in finesse. Does *unnecessary* in *with unnecessary fierceness* belong to the 'Causality/Chance' class in the same way as it does in *There's too much litigation . . . most of it unnecessary*, for example? On the other hand, the automatic annotation plays an important role in dealing with large quantities of data that would be unreasonably time-consuming and difficult to annotate consistently by hand (Thomas and Wilson 1996: 106). Qualitative analysis is then used to interpret the findings and to account for the quantitative differences.

'How a meaning is made'

The final kind of annotation to be mentioned here is a variation on semantic annotation, described by Biber and Finegan (1989) and Conrad and Biber (2000). This is a partial annotation, in that only certain categories are selected, for example expressions of 'stance'. Candidates for belonging to this category, such as adverbs (e.g. *probably*), clauses (e.g. *I think*) and prepositional phrases (e.g. *on the whole*) are selected by the computer from a tagged and parsed corpus and the human researcher can accept or modify the categorisation. Calculations can then be made in terms of how frequently a meaning is made in a number of registers, and how the meaning is most frequently made in each register. Conrad and Biber (2000), for example, note that adverbs are the most frequently used way of expressing stance grammatically in all three registers investigated (conversation, news reporting and academic prose), and that they are most predominant in conversation. Clauses such as *I think* and *I guess* are also frequent in conversation. Academic prose and news reporting, in addition to adverbs, use prepositional phrases extensively. In academic prose they limit the range of what the writer is saying, as in *on the whole* and *in most cases*.

Corpus annotation of this kind provides a basis for approaching a corpus from the point of view of meaning first and can be linked with a notional approach to language teaching. Put simply, a corpus annotated in this way allows this question to be answered: If a learner has something to say in a particular context, what are the most useful words and phrases for that situation?

One development of this idea is the concept of a 'local grammar' (Gross 1993; Barnbrook and Sinclair 1995; Hunston and Sinclair 2000). A local grammar attempts to describe the resources for only one set of meanings in a language, rather than for the language as a whole. For example, Hunston (1999b) describes several ways of talking about sameness and difference. The words that are used to indicate this meaning are identified, together with the patterns in which they are used, such as 'verb + plural noun group' (*equate two things*), 'verb + *between* + plural noun group' (*differentiate between two things*), and 'verb + *from* + noun group' (*one thing differs from another*). Because meaning and pattern are linked, in each case there are several verbs used with the same pattern. Elements in the local grammar are also identified, in this case 'comparer', 'comparison', 'item 1' and 'item 2'. The elements in the local grammar can then be mapped on to the elements in the pattern, as in the following examples.

There are people who equate those two terrible video tapes.
        comparer   comparison   item 1, 2
                   Verb   **plural noun group**
Also: *compare, conflate, connect, contrast, distinguish, juxtapose, match, mismatch, muddle, reconcile, relate, separate, mix up, muddle up.*

It's difficult to differentiate between chemical weapons and chemicals for peaceful use.
          comparison   item 1   item 2
          Verb   *between* **plural noun group**
Also: *discriminate, distinguish.*

Make your advertisement stand out from all the others by having it printed in bold type.
         item 1   comparison   item 2
                 Verb   *from* **noun**
Also: *differ, diverge, grow apart, grow away, stand out, stick out.*

How <u>does</u> your job <u>measure up to your ideal?</u>
       item 1   comparison   item 2
              Verb   *to* **noun**

Also: *answer, approximate, conform, correlate, correspond, equate, relate, hark back, match up, measure up, stack up.*

The Cuban musicians themselves often <u>liken their music to the works of Bob Dylan</u> . . .
       comparer   comparison item 1   item 2
                                         Verb   **noun** *to* **noun**

Also: *compare, connect, correlate, link, match, relate, match up.*

This type of study is in its infancy at present, but it can easily be seen that if pattern recognition can be automated, the frequency of different ways of making similar meanings can easily be calculated.

Issues in annotation

The accounts of various annotation projects given above indicate something of the range of applications of corpus annotation. Many research projects depend on particular kinds of annotation, and it may seem churlish to suggest that annotation could be anything other than wholly advantageous. There are, however, several interlinked issues connected with annotation which are worth consideration.

There are three basic methods of annotating a corpus – manual, computer-assisted and automatic (see Biber et al 1999: 35–37, how the corpus used for the Longman Grammar of Spoken and Written English was annotated using these methods) – but only the second two are suitable for use on anything but the smallest corpora. In automatic annotation, the computer works alone, following whatever rules and algorithms the programmer has determined. Once the program has been written, a corpus of any size can be annotated relatively quickly. On the other hand, an automatic annotation program is unlikely to produce results that are 100% in accordance with what a human researcher would produce; in other words, there are likely to be errors, as discussed above in the section on tagging. A computer-assisted annotation program allows the human researcher to edit the computer-generated output (as with most Parsers) or provides an interactive interface between human being and machine so that what is essentially a manual annotation can be performed with the minimum of effort (as with the anaphora annotation mentioned above). Computer-assisted annotation is slower than automatic, allowing for less corpus material to be annotated, but it is likely to be more accurate.

The difficulty in automating most annotation procedures has implications for corpus design and research. Access to large, tagged corpora is easily available, but the amount of parsed corpus data publicly available is more limited. The more specialised kind of annotation is available only within specific research projects. A heavily annotated corpus, even an edited parsed corpus, is a valuable commodity and cannot lightly be discarded. The work involved in annotation acts as a constraint against updating or enlarging a corpus. For example, the 1961, 1 million word LOB Corpus is still used as a source of data, small and outdated though it is, precisely because it is parsed. To a certain extent, then, the benefits to be found in corpus data – the availability of large amounts of current material – tend to be undermined by annotation.

The discussion about annotation, and category-based methods of corpus research, will be continued in the section below.

Competing methods

This survey of methods of investigating a corpus has dealt with concordance lines, collocational statistics and corpus annotation, moving from the least to the most complex. It began with methods that are based on word-forms alone, noting the patterning of particular words and phrases, and the co-occurrence of sets of words, and moved on to methods that put words into categories, whether syntactic or semantic. The preference for prioritising words alone tends to go along with a preference for a plain text corpus, that is, one with a minimum of annotation (for example, a corpus which is tagged but not parsed). The preference for prioritising categories often goes along with a preference for an annotated corpus, although some work, such as that by Halliday and by Stubbs mentioned above, is category-based but works with plain text (and see Stubbs and Gerbig 1993: 78–79 for an argument in support of using plain text to investigate categories).

It is important to recognise that no method of working is neutral with regard to theory. To regard simple word-forms as more important than categories, or to regard a set of categories as 'given' and unproblematic, are both theoretical positions which will influence the way a corpus is investigated. Although it may be considered an ideal to 'have the data speak for itself', in practice what the data says will depend to a large extent on how it is able to be accessed.

Basically, category-based methods and word-based methods each answer different sets of questions. For example, a question such as, 'What kind of anaphora is most frequently used in academic prose?'

needs an annotated corpus. A question such as, 'How is the word *way* used?' is best answered with a plain text corpus. A question such as, 'Is *START* most frequently used transitively or intransitively, and is it more frequently followed by a to-clause or an '-ing' clause?' can be answered by either concordance lines or with an annotated corpus (though the annotated corpus would calculate the number of in-transitive uses more accurately). The follow-up question, 'What function does the word and its phraseology perform in this register?' is best answered with plain text.

A plain text corpus has obvious disadvantages in that certain categories cannot easily be counted, so certain questions are difficult to answer. For example, Rissanen (1991) traces the history of 'object clauses' beginning with *that* (e.g. *I had always thought that deserts were hot and dry*), and those beginning with 'zero' (e.g. *I thought she was sleeping*) in unparsed corpora, and comments:

collecting the object clause subordinators from among the other conjunctive and pronominal uses of *that* means toil and trouble. Furthermore . . . there is no direct way of picking out the instances with the zero link. The problem of tracing zeros must, in this case, be solved in an indirect way, by checking all occurrences of all verbs which take an object clause with *that*, in order to find the possible instances of zero. (Rissanen 1991: 275)

The search was only possible at all because a relatively small corpus was being used.

As was mentioned above, the 'added value' that annotations give a corpus can be a double-edged sword. The corpus is more useful, but it is also less readily updated, expanded or discarded. In addition, the categories used to annotate a corpus are typically determined before any corpus analysis is carried out, which in turn tends to limit, not the kind of question that can be asked, but the kind of question that usually is asked. Most of the work that is done using annotated corpora uses categories that have been developed in pre-corpus days, such as nominal clauses, anaphoric reference or direct and indirect speech (Short et al 1996). Phenomena such as frames (Renouf and Sinclair 1991) or semantic prosody (Louw 1993; 1997), and the pervasive influence of phraseology (Sinclair 1991) tend to have been identified from plain text corpora and word-based studies. Theory and practice form a circle here: a reluctance, on theoretical grounds, to use categories that already exist in linguistics has led to a word-based practice of corpus investigation, which in turn has led to a revised theory of what language is like (see chapter 6 for more details of this argument, and also Tognini-Bonelli 2001).

Paradoxically, the most interesting and useful annotations seem to be those which are either added *ad hoc* to a corpus to enable the researcher to answer a particular question or those which are able to be added to a corpus quickly and automatically. An example of a quick, automatic annotation program is a tagger. An example of *ad hoc* annotation is Sealey's (2000: 10–28) work on a corpus of newspaper texts, which she annotated to identify all references to children, whatever the lexical item used (*child, kid, young person* etc). This then allowed her to gather together all these instances and to observe similarities in patterning which might not have been so obvious if the words had been seen individually.

What we can perhaps hope for is a synergy between word-based and category-based methods of corpus analysis, in which the one can inform the other, much as qualitative and quantitative methods of research complement each other. Much of the work by Biber and his colleagues, for example, moves between categories and words as necessary. Thomas and Wilson's work on semantic annotation moves between calculations of frequency to interpretation in terms of phraseology.

Conrad (2000) has suggested that in the future researchers must go 'beyond the concordance line' in exploiting corpora. This is a useful reminder that corpus studies need to progress beyond making *ad hoc* observations about individual words. It is worth remembering, however, that the interpretation of information found by looking beyond the concordance line frequently involves returning to those same concordance lines. (The investigation of *BEGIN*, above, was a case in point.) There needs to be a constant movement between the more sophisticated search techniques and looking at the raw data.

As corpora are exploited more and more for purposes other than simply 'looking at language' (see chapter 5), it seems obvious that a mixture of plain text and annotation will always be needed. From the above discussion, the following points have emerged with regard to corpus annotation:

• However much annotation is added to a text, it is important for the researcher to be able to see the plain text, uncluttered by annotational labels. The basic patterning of the words alone must be observable at all times.
• It is important to be able to use unconventional, *ad hoc* annotations as necessary. Annotation should serve the needs of the corpus user, not determine the direction the investigation must take.
• Unless a very small-scale study is being carried out, it is important to make the process of annotation as automatic as possible, so that

the annotated corpus does not become 'over-valued', and so that annotation is consistent (Leech and Eyes 1997: 40). Conversely, the corpus needs to be large enough to minimise the importance of inaccuracies in annotation. (See Sinclair 1992: 396 for a similar emphasis on speed and automaticity.)

And finally:

- Corpus linguists can be very partisan as regards the methods they prefer (and readers of this book will no doubt be aware that I am no exception to this). It is important when reading about corpus work to be critically aware of the methods being used, and of the theories that lie behind them.

5 Applications of corpora in applied linguistics

The application of corpora expected to have most relevance to readers of this book – language teaching – is dealt with in chapters of its own (chapters 6–8). In this chapter, other applications are described. These are:

- The production of dictionaries and grammars, that is, reference books for language learners and translators.
- The use of corpora in critical linguistics, illuminating items of importance to the study of ideologies.
- The use of corpora in translation.
- The contribution of corpora to literary studies and stylistics.
- The use of corpora in forensic linguistics.
- The use of corpora in designing writer support packages.

Dictionaries and grammars

Introduction

Corpora have so revolutionised the writing of dictionaries and grammar books for language learners (or rather, for learners of English) that it is by now virtually unheard-of for a large publishing company to produce a learner's dictionary or grammar reference book that does not claim to be based on a corpus. As a result, this is probably the application of corpora that is most far-reaching and influential, in that even people who have never heard of a corpus are using the product of corpus investigation. Accounts of using corpora to write dictionaries are found in Sinclair (ed.) 1987; Summers 1996; Baugh et al 1996; Clear et al 1996.

This section will concentrate on those areas in which the use of corpora has changed dictionaries and other reference books. These can be summarised as a series of new emphases:

- an emphasis on frequency;
- an emphasis on collocation and phraseology;
- an emphasis on variation;
- an emphasis on lexis in grammar;
- an emphasis on authenticity.

Each of these will now be dealt with in turn.

Emphasis on frequency

One area in which speaker intuition is acknowledged to be of very little use is in the assessment of relative frequency between words, meanings and usages. A very important impact of corpora upon dictionaries, therefore, is the inclusion of information about relative frequencies. Such information may be given explicitly to the dictionary user, or it may be used by the dictionary writer in deciding, for example, which sense of a word to show first.

Because a corpus can show the diversity of use, and the importance, of very frequent words, current learner's dictionaries tend to include more detailed information than the old ones did about these words. A rough indication of this can be given by comparing the number of senses given for certain frequent words in different dictionaries.[1] Here are some comparisons between the *Longman Dictionary of Contemporary English* 2nd edition (1987), which was written without a corpus, and two dictionaries written with the aid of a corpus: the *Longman Dictionary of Contemporary English* 3rd edition (1995) and the *Collins* COBUILD *English Dictionary* (1995).

KNOW

Longman 1987 gives 20 senses of *KNOW*. Longman 1995 gives over 40 and COBUILD 1995 gives over 30.

MATTER

Longman 1987 gives 10 senses of the noun and verb *MATTER*, including phrases such as *as a matter of fact*. Longman 1995 gives over 30 senses. COBUILD 1995 gives over 20.

MAY

Longman 1987 gives 7 senses of the modal *may*. Longman 1995 gives 8 senses. COBUILD 1995 gives 15 senses.

PLACE

Longman 1987 gives 20 senses of the noun *PLACE*. Longman 1995 and COBUILD 1995 each give over 30 senses.

---

[1] A comparison between number of senses can only be a very rough guide to comprehensiveness because dictionaries do not divide information between senses in consistent ways. One dictionary may include a lot of information in a single sense, where another dictionary may choose to divide the information between two or more senses.

Many of the increases in number of senses is explained by more information being given about the very frequent uses, involving the division of one sense into two or more. For example, Longman 1987 gives as one sense of *matter* the meaning 'something wrong', as in *What's the matter?* Longman 1995 expands this to four senses: the question asking about illness or a state of being broken; the question asking about feelings; the statement *there's something the matter with*; and the negative statement *there's nothing the matter with*.

There are also 'new' senses, that is, meanings or uses that seemed unimportant before a corpus showed how frequent they were. One example is the phrase *I know*, which was included in Longman 1987 only as a phrase uttered when someone gets a sudden idea (as in *What can we get her for her birthday? Oh I know, we'll get her some flowers*). In Longman 1995, two additional uses are given: agreement (as in *'I'm so worn out.' 'Yeah, I know'*) and forestalling disagreement (as in *It sounds silly I know, but try it anyway*). COBUILD 1995 gives three uses of *I know*: agreement; prefacing a disagreement (as in *'There are trains straight from Cambridge.' 'I know, but it's no quicker'*); and showing sympathy and understanding (as in *I know what you're going through*). Another example is *may*. One meaning of *may* in Longman 1987 is the 'degree of certainty' meaning. Longman 1995 divides this into a 'future' meaning (something may or may not happen) and a 'present' meaning (something may or may not be true). COBUILD 1995 adds another sense which indicates a degree of usuality rather than a degree of certainty, that is, something is certain but is only sometimes true (as in *Up to five inches of snow may cover the mountains*). Finally, *place* with a possessive (*my place, your place*) is noted by Longman 1995 and COBUILD 1995 to indicate 'the house or flat where someone lives'. In addition, COBUILD 1995 notes that *the place* is used anaphorically, referring to somewhere that has already been mentioned in the discourse. Neither of these uses of *PLACE* were given in Longman 1987.

Another innovation in dictionaries that has been made possible by the use of a corpus is the inclusion of explicit frequency information. COBUILD 1995, for example, places all the words in the dictionary in one of 6 frequency bands. Longman 1995 notes words that are particularly frequent in spoken and written English and compares the frequency of some words in the two modes. The verbs *BET, MEAN* and *THINK*, for example, are shown to be much more frequent in spoken than in written English, because of the colloquial use of phrases such as *I bet, I mean* and *I think*. *NEED* is shown as more frequent than *REQUIRE* in both written and spoken English, but the difference is greater in spoken English, indicating that *REQUIRE* is more frequently used in written English than in spoken.

Using tagged corpora, it is possible to compare the frequency of the same word, for example, as a noun and as a verb. The dictionary definitions can then be presented in a sensible order, with the most frequent use first (Summers 1996: 262). For example, *GORGE* as a noun (meaning 'a valley with steep sides') is approximately four times as frequent as the verb *GORGE* (meaning 'eat greedily'), so it is sensible to put the noun sense before the verb sense in a dictionary. What would help lexicographers even more would be automatic sense recognition (Clear 1994; Summers 1996), which would enable senses to be identified in terms of frequency also. Given that the different senses of words have different collocations and patterning, automatic sense differentiation is in theory possible, but has not yet been achieved.

Frequency and grammar reference books

There are two ways of dealing with information about frequency in grammar books. One approach is simply to focus on usages that are relatively frequent. Sinclair et al (1990), for example, take this approach. More recently, some writers of grammar books give precise statistical information based on frequency counts in specially designed and annotated corpora (Biber et al 1999; Mindt 2000). Much of this information is to do with variation, and examples are given in the section below on 'Emphasis on variation'. One very interesting type of frequency that is given is the distribution of meanings across a given form. Mindt (2000: 224), for example, identifies four meanings of the present perfect (the indefinite past, past continuing into present, the recent past, and a use indicating that an action is completed, though at an unspecified time).[2] Of these, the first (indefinite past) accounts for almost 80% of all occurrences of the present perfect, with the second (past continuing into present) accounting for all but 5% of the others. The 'recent past' and 'completed action' meanings are comparatively rare. This is in conflict with many course books, which teach uses such as *I have lived here for 12 years* (past-into-present) or *they have recently had their third child* (recent past) as prototypical, when in fact they are less common than the indefinite past use. Most of the other tense

[2] Mindt (2000) in fact divides the indefinite past use into two: resultative and non-resultative. Of these, the resultative use, where the present situation is a result of a past action, is more frequent.

forms presented by Mindt have similarly asymmetrical patterns of use.

This kind of work is probably most useful when frequency can be linked to discourse. For example, Biber et al (1999) point out that the most frequent use of *the* in academic prose is at the beginning of complex noun phrases (such as *the disorientating effect of zero gravity*). Also, the most frequent use of *this* and *these* in the same register is to refer back to ideas previously mentioned. Knowledge of this raises awareness of the use of *the* and *this/these* in academic writing such as the following:

During the past year, three Danish engineers working at the Technical University of Denmark . . . have been studying a detailed model of *the* side-to-side motion of train wheels. Like all models of train wheels, theirs has a single left/right symmetry − reflectional symmetry about a line perpendicular to *the* axle that connects the wheels. *The* equations of motion that describe *this* system have reflectional symmetry too. But *the* solutions to *these* equations may or may not be symmetric − that is, the wheels need not stay 'centred' on the rails. (*New Scientist*)

For the most part, though, frequency information of this kind is more useful to the syllabus designer or coursebook writer than to the class teacher. For example, according to Biber et al (1999: 388−389), the verb *TELL* is most frequently found in the pattern 'verb + indirect object + complement clause' (e.g. *You can't tell her to get off*) whereas *PROMISE* is most frequently found in the pattern 'verb + complement clause' (e.g. *They promised to write*). *PROMISE* occurs fairly frequently as an intransitive verb (e.g. *I promise*), whereas *TELL* very rarely does (e.g. *time will tell*). If a language course consists of fairly large quantities of authentic language, it is likely that this proportion of frequencies will be mirrored in that language. If only small quantities are used, or if invented language is presented to the learner, frequency information such as this can be used to ensure that the more frequent patterns are presented earlier and more frequently than the infrequent ones.

The limitation of frequency information of this kind is that it can suggest that very infrequent uses can legitimately be ignored. For example, Mindt (2000: 182) reports that 98% of verbs in the past tense refer to past time, which is hardly surprising. References to a hypothetical future, for example, are very rare indeed. It seems safe to assume, therefore, that hypothetical meanings are unimportant from the point of view of the past tense, and learners can safely not be taught this meaning. However, it is important for learners to learn to express the hypothetical, and for this the past tense is significant;

in some contexts (such as following *what if*) the past tense is the most frequent. In other words, a student learning the past tense can safely ignore hypothetical meaning, but for a student learning to express hypotheticality the past tense cannot be ignored.

In addition, lexical variation needs to be taken into account when considering frequency (as in the example of *TELL* and *PROMISE* above). For example, Mindt (2000: 185) reports that 'quasi-subjects' such as *it* and *there* are very infrequent with lexical verbs, compared with other subject types. This observation masks a considerable amount of lexical variation. There are a fairly large number of verbs (see Francis et al 1996: 518–542 for lists) for which the sequence '*it* + verb + clause' is very important. The point is that a teacher should not be misled into thinking that the sequence is unimportant just because it occurs frequently only with some lexical items.

Emphasis on collocation and phraseology

The attention paid to phrases such as *I know, your place* and *there's something the matter with* in dictionaries written using corpora reflects the tendency of a corpus to highlight collocation and phraseology (Hanks 1987; Sinclair 1987a; 1987b; Summers 1996). For example, in Longman 1987, one sense of *brink* was given as 'as far as one can go without being in a condition or situation'. In Longman 1995, the word by itself is not defined but the phrase *be on the brink of* is defined as 'to be almost in a new and very different situation', with the example *Karl is on the brink of a brilliant acting career*. COBUILD 1995 includes the phraseology in the definition: 'If you are on the brink of something, usually something important, terrible, or exciting, you are just about to do it or experience it.' This definition includes reference to the emotive nature of the situation you might be on the brink of. The examples given reflect the 'central and typical' use of *on the brink of* by indicating a bad situation rather than a good one: *Their economy is teetering on the brink of collapse . . . Failure to communicate had brought the two nations to the brink of war*. The examples illustrate frequent collocates of *the brink of*: the preposition *on* and the verb *TEETER*, and the preposition *to* with the verb *BRING*. (See Sinclair 2000 for a more complete study of *brink*.)

This example illustrates several characteristics of the 'new' dictionaries:

- the tendency, where possible, to define a phrase rather than a word: *be on the brink of* rather than *brink*;

- the use by some dictionaries of the definition sentence to illustrate phraseology;
- the possibility of introducing further collocational information into the definition: 'usually something important, terrible, or exciting';
- the use of examples to introduce more information about collocation.

It also illustrates a dilemma of the dictionary writer: how to be selective from a wealth of information. The word *brink* is used in a variety of phrases, of which *on the brink of* is the most frequent. The most frequent verb before this phrase is *BE*, but *TEETER*, *STAND* and *be poised* are also common, as is *HOVER*. The second most frequent phrase is *to the brink of*, preceded by verbs such as *BRING*, *TAKE*, *DRIVE* and *PUSH*. All these phrases are typically, but by no means invariably, followed by nouns indicating something bad. Examples such as *Roy Evans is guiding them to the brink of a glorious new era* or *was on the brink of promotion* are unusual but not 'wrong'. The problem is that there is too much information here to be dealt with in a brief dictionary entry. Longman 1995 and COBUILD 1995 both choose the most frequent phrase for their definitions. COBUILD 1995 tries to deal with the other phrases in examples, hoping that the learner will extrapolate what is essential (the phrases *on the brink of* and *to the brink of*) and what is useful (the verbs *teetering* and *has brought*).

Phraseology is particularly important in the case of very frequent words, the majority of whose uses may be in fairly fixed phrases (Sinclair 1987b; 1999; Summers 1996). Summers, for example, notes that *day* most frequently occurs in phrases such as *one day, the other day* and *some day* (1996: 262–263). Sinclair (1999) argues that dictionaries sometimes do not go far enough in identifying such phraseology, particularly in relation to grammatical, as opposed to lexical, words. He points out, for example, that many instances of the word *a* are accounted for by phrases such as *come to a head*, rather than occurring as an alternative to *the* or another determiner, but that dictionaries (and grammar books) rarely record such usage.

Emphasis on variation

In a keynote lecture at the 2nd North American Symposium on Corpora and Language Teaching (2000), Susan Conrad argued that reference books must cease to be 'monolithic', that is, must cease to treat English as a single entity. Instead, Conrad advocated the approach adopted in the *Longman Grammar of Spoken and Written English* (Biber et al 1999), in which grammatical features are presented in terms of a comparison of frequency between four broadly defined 'registers': fiction, academic prose, 'news' (newspaper reportage), and conversation. Each section of Biber et al (1999) includes corpus evidence of comparative frequency, together with an interpretation which relates the figures to contexts of use. For example, instead of simply describing the formation and use of present and past tense in English, Biber et al (1999) note that present tense occurs more frequently than past tense in conversation and in academic prose whereas past tense occurs more frequently than present tense in fiction. News uses both tenses about equally (1999: 456). These figures are interpreted in terms of the typical meanings made in each register. Conversation frequently uses present tense, for example, because of 'speakers' general focus on the immediate context' (1999: 457). For academic writing, the reason for the preponderance of present tense is different: there is a concern with 'general truth', in which specific time is not relevant (1999: 458). Past tense is typical of narrative, which makes up most of fiction.

A similar approach is taken by Mindt (2000), though he uses only three registers: conversation, fiction and expository prose. As an example of his results, he notes that passives with *BE* are most frequent in expository prose and least frequent in conversation (2000: 269). For passives with *GET*, however, the reverse is true: these forms are most frequent in conversation and least frequent in expository prose (2000: 282). Passives with *BECOME* are most frequent in fiction and least frequent in conversation (2000: 282).

Work of this kind raises the question as to whether the registers selected for comparison are sufficiently homogeneous, or whether they themselves are open to the charge of being monolithic. The news texts used by Biber et al, for example, come from a variety of newspaper types (tabloid and broadsheet, for example) and from different parts of the newspapers (international news, arts reviews, business reports and so on). It is not possible to tell whether certain grammatical features are more prevalent in some of these newspapers or parts of newspapers than others. Similarly, their academic corpus is made up of both academic articles and books, from a range of different disciplines (Biber et al 1999: 31–33). Research reported in chapter 8 of this book, which relates grammatical features to the specific concerns of individual disciplines, suggests that the notion of 'academic prose' as a single register might be an overly blunt instrument. Other questions arise regarding the usefulness of this comparative quantitative information to the teacher; these will be discussed in chapter 7.

Emphasis on lexis in grammar

Another striking feature of the *Longman Grammar of Spoken and Written English* is the degree to which lexical information forms an integral part of the grammatical description. For example, part of the study of present and past tenses in English includes lists of verbs which are overwhelmingly found in present tense (such as *BET, DOUBT, KNOW, MATTER, MEAN, MIND, RECKON, SUPPOSE* and *THANK*) and those which are more frequent in past tense (e.g. *EXCLAIM, EYE, GLANCE, GRIN, NOD, PAUSE, REMARK, REPLY, SHRUG, SIGH, SMILE* and *WHISPER*) (Biber et al 1999: 459). In this concern for lexis the writers concur with Sinclair, who, in fact, rejects the distinction between lexis and grammar (see chapter 6). The *Collins* COBUILD *English Grammar* (Sinclair et al 1990) was a pioneer in this respect. Describing the imperative, for example, it notes the use of this verb-form in sentences such as *Consider, for example, the contrast between the way schools today treat space and time* which focus the reader's attention on a particular aspect or example of the topic being explained (p204). A list of verbs used in this way is included: *compare, consider, contrast, imagine, look at, picture, suppose* and *take*. (Note that Sinclair et al take a rather different view of the importance of frequency than do Biber et al. Whereas Biber et al tend to give the most frequent verbs to be found with a certain form in a given register, Sinclair et al list the verbs which are most important to a given meaning made in a particular way.)

Sinclair et al (1990) in fact contains many lists, including lists of verbs with particular complementation patterns (p139–193), lists of nouns followed by prepositions (p131) and a list of adjectives used after a noun (p75). What emerges from many of these lists is the fact that words with similar behaviours tend to have similar meanings. For example, nouns followed by *for* mostly indicate a reaction or feeling towards someone or something: *admiration, disdain, dislike, love, regard, respect* or *sympathy*. The feeling is often one of intense wanting: *appetite, craving, desire, hunger, need*, and *thirst*. Another meaning is 'looking or asking for': *bid, demand, quest* and *search*.

The association between pattern and meaning provides the basis for a larger COBUILD project: the Grammar Patterns series (Francis et al 1996; 1997; 1998, see also Hunston et al 1997; Hunston and Francis 1998; 1999). These books are based on the grammar codings used in the *Collins* COBUILD *English Dictionary* (CCED) (1995), in which a sequence of codes illustrates the sequence of elements in a pattern. Here are some examples of the verb *DECIDE*, together with their pattern coding (taken from the CCED):

- *She decided to do a secretarial course.* The verb is followed by a to-infinitive clause. The coding is **V to-inf.**
- *He has decided that he doesn't want to embarrass the movement* . . . The verb is followed by a that-clause. The coding is **V that.**
- *The house needed totally rebuilding, so we decided against buying it.* The verb is followed by a prepositional phrase beginning with *against.* The coding is **V *against* n.**
- *Its outcome will decide whether Russia's economy can be reformed at all.* The verb is followed by a clause beginning with a wh-word. The coding is **V wh.**
- *Think about it very carefully before you decide.* The verb is intransitive; it is not followed by anything. The coding is **V.**

A pattern is identified from a corpus, rather than from a single example. To qualify as a pattern, a phrase or clause or word must frequently occur with the node word and must be dependent on it, as was discussed in chapter 3 with relation to the noun *SUGGESTION*.

When the words that share a pattern are listed, most of them can be seen to share an aspect of meaning. For example, many verbs with the pattern **V n *to* n** (as in *conceded victory to the ruling party*) have something to do with 'giving', e.g. *accord, administer, allocate, allot, arrogate, assign, award, bequeath, bring, cede, commit, concede, contribute, dedicate, delegate, deliver, devolve, dispense, distribute* and so on. Other groups with the same pattern include:

- verbs to do with communication: *address, admit, announce, bid (farewell), break (news), commend, communicate, confess, confide, describe, dictate, disclose, divulge* and so on;
- verbs to do with ascribing a quality to someone or something: *ascribe, assign, attach, attribute, credit, impute, put down;*
- verbs to do with change: *abbreviate, change, commute, convert, decrease, demote, drop, increase, lower, promote, raise, reduce, shorten, swell, turn, cut down, narrow down, whittle down;*
- verbs to do with devoting yourself to something: *abandon, address, apply, commit, confine, dedicate, devote, enslave, limit, pledge, restrict, rivet, tie, give (oneself) over;*
- verbs to do with adding something to something: *add, affix, annex, append, attach, bind, bolt, chain, clamp, clip, connect, couple* and so on;

- verbs to do with attracting someone: *attract, commend, draw, endear, recommend*;
- verbs to do with moving someone from one job or position to another: *accredit, appoint, apprentice, demote, nominate, ordain, promote, recall, recruit, relegate, transfer, upgrade*;
- verbs to do with betrayal: *betray, denounce, report, shop, grass up, turn in*;
- verbs to do with changing awareness or attitude: *acclimatise, accommodate, accustom, adapt, adjust, alert, awaken, blind, desensitise, inure, reconcile, resign, sensitise*;
- verbs to do with directing attention: *direct, divert, draw, give (thought), pay, switch, turn.*

(For complete listings, see Francis et al 1996: 417–433. Comparable corpus-based studies of pattern and lexis are Rudanko 1996; Levin et al 1997.)

Reference books of this kind emphasise the connection between meaning and pattern and provide a resource for vocabulary building in which the word is treated as part of a phrase rather than in isolation. They also provide evidence for a challenge to the traditional distinction between lexis and grammar (see chapter 6), and indeed challenge our view of what a grammatical description is. To illustrate this, consider how grammar is used to account for a particular instance of language. Here is an example from a letter to a newspaper:

I consider myself to be a so-called 'new man' because I gave up a profession to bring up our son. My wife went back to work a year ago, and since then I have been astonished to discover how many women consider bringing up a baby is a woman's job. I meet a lot of women who find it incomprehensible that I run the household. It's time that more women changed their attitudes – or they can never hope to change those of their menfolk!

Possible grammatical approaches to this text might include examining the tense usage, or the balance between material and mental processes, or the level of modality. A lexical approach to grammar, however, would see it in terms of the patterns belonging to each of the various lexical items, as shown in Table 5.1.

Emphasis on authenticity

When reference books are written with the aid of a corpus, examples can be chosen that illustrate the most typical use of a word or phrase and, if examples are taken from the corpus itself, authenticity is guaranteed, in the sense that each example has been used in genuine

Table 5.1. Grammar patterns in a short text

Text	Pattern
<u>consider</u> myself to be	V n to-inf
<u>be</u> a so-called 'new man'	V n
<u>gave up</u> a profession	V P n
<u>bring up</u> our son	V P n
<u>went</u> back to work	V adv prep
have been <u>astonished</u> to discover	v-link ADJ to-inf
<u>discover</u> how many women consider	V wh
<u>consider</u> bringing up a baby is a woman's job	V that
<u>bringing up</u> a baby	V P n
<u>is</u> a woman's job	V n
<u>meet</u> a lot of women	V n
<u>find</u> it <u>incomprehensible</u> that	V *it* ADJ that
<u>run</u> the household	V n
It's <u>time</u> that	*it* v-link N that
<u>changed</u> their attitudes	V n
<u>hope</u> to change	V to-inf
<u>change</u> those of their menfolk	V n

communication. It is important to recognise that authenticity and typicality are not the same thing. Any corpus contains numerous examples of a given word that are authentic – they are part of actual texts – but are the product of innovation, word-play, or simple odd circumstances, and are therefore not typical. Conversely, some dictionary writers invent sentences that reflect typical usage but which have not been used in authentic situations.

Although all dictionary writers agree that typicality is important, they do not all agree that absolute authenticity is desirable. Baugh et al (1996: 43) argue that:

Most citations are unsuitable for a learner dictionary because they are too complex grammatically, contain unnecessary difficult words or idioms, or make culture-dependent allusions or references to specific contexts.

The introduction to Longman 1995 (xvi) says:

All the examples in this dictionary are based on what we find in the spoken and written corpus material in the Longman Corpus Network. Some examples are taken direct from the corpus; some have been changed slightly from the corpus to remove difficult words; and some have been written specially for the entry.

The *Cambridge Learner's Dictionary* (2001: 5) stresses naturalness and typicality rather than authenticity:

The corpus . . . helps us find natural and typical examples to show how words and phrases are used.

COBUILD 1995 (xxii) makes the strongest claim to authenticity itself:

The majority of the examples in the dictionary are taken word for word from one of the texts in the Bank of English. Occasionally, we have made very minor changes to them, so that they are more successful as dictionary examples.

Fox (1987) argues the case for authentic examples, pointing out that invented examples often do not reflect nuances of usage. The phrase *take aback*, for example, is typically used in the passive (*I was taken aback by . . .*) rather than in the active, whereas an invented example may be of the type *His reaction took me aback* (though not, of course, if the writer has observed the data accurately). Invented examples, which do not make reference to specific contexts, are often over-explicit. Fox illustrates this with the example *'We'll try to salvage your leg,' said the doctor to the trapped man*, which sounds stilted because in a narrative of which this sentence was a part it would be unlikely that both the doctor and the man would need to be identified at this point. (On the other hand, it might be argued that a less stilted version – *'We'll try to salvage your leg,' he told him* – is less informative and so less helpful.) Fox also indicates the pitfalls of shortening sentences for inclusion in a dictionary. She cites the example *His anguish was terrible*, which comes from an actual sentence reading *His anguish was terrible for her to behold*. Fox comments:

What seems to be wrong with the short version is that it is too bald and also comes too close to stating the obvious – we naturally assume that anguish is terrible. Perhaps more importantly, in the short version the word 'terrible' describes 'his anguish', whereas in the original it is more plausibly interpreted as referring to her reactions to his grief. (Fox 1987: 148)

Summary of reference books discussion

Reference books for learners of English, then, have been transformed by the use of corpora in their compilation and have become, on the whole, even less like similar books for native speakers. They are greatly influenced by the ease with which information on frequency and typicality is obtained from a corpus, or from contrasting corpora, and tend to emphasise phraseology and the interaction between lexis and grammar. Whilst there is disagreement on the extent to which examples should be authentic in the sense of 'have been said or written', there is a concern for idiomaticity and realism in examples.

Studying ideology and culture

Ideology in a specialised corpus

A growing concern in Applied Linguistics is the relation between language and ideology, in particular, the role of language in forming and transmitting assumptions about what the world is and should be like, and the role of language in maintaining (or challenging) existing power relations. The dominant school of research into language and ideology is critical linguistics (Fowler 1987) or critical discourse analysis (Fairclough 1995). Critical linguistics looks at language, not as a system on its own but as something that 'intervenes' in the social world, largely by perpetuating the assumptions and values of that world (Fowler 1987: 482–3). Fowler mentions three aspects of what critical linguists do that are important when considering their use of corpora.

1. Critical linguists study texts in the context of the social circumstances in which they have been produced.
2. Critical linguists aim to reveal 'the ideology coded implicitly behind the overt propositions'.
3. Critical linguistics 'challenges common sense by pointing out that something could have been represented some other way, with a very different significance'.

It is clear that the techniques of corpus investigation have much to offer the second and third of these objectives. Patterns of association – how lexical items tend to co-occur – are built up over large amounts of text and are often unavailable to intuition or conscious awareness. They can therefore convey messages implicitly and even be at odds with an overt statement. The different options open to speakers can be illustrated by the various ways that individual words are used. For example, a process indicated by the word *change* can be expressed as a noun, as in *One change that has begun to emerge within the republic over the last ten to twenty years has been a revival of Islam*, or as a verb, as in *people who were trying to change society*. In the noun example, the process of change has no agent, that is, no-one is made responsible for the change. But this is not an inevitable way of expressing what has happened. In the verb example, *people* are shown as responsible for social change (see Fairclough 2000: 32–34 on metaphors associated with *change* as a noun).

With respect to the first objective – to study texts in their social context – the role of a corpus is less clear. If a corpus is composed of a number of texts, corpus search and processing techniques, such as word-lists, concordance lines and lists of collocations, will tend to obscure the character of each text as a text. Each individual example is taken out of context – that, in a sense, is the point. Furthermore, the corpus treats texts as autonomous entities: the role of the text producer and the society of which they are a part tends to be obscured. Perhaps for this reason, some critical linguists have avoided using corpora, though Krishnamurthy (1996), Stubbs (1997), Caldas-Coulthard and Moon (1999), Piper (2000a) and Mautner (2000) are among those who argue for the value of corpora in such studies.

In this section we look at the role of corpora in critical linguistics in the light of a number of studies. These are:

- Teubert's (2000) study of the language of Euroscepticism in Britain, based on a corpus of texts downloaded from web-sites taking an antagonistic stance regarding the European Union.
- Flowerdew's (1997) discussion of speeches by the last British governor of Hong Kong, Chris Patten. Flowerdew argues that Patten created through these speeches a mythical picture of Britain as a benevolent colonial power.
- Fairclough's (2000) investigation of the language of New Labour, the re-modelled version of the Labour Party that became the party of government in Britain in 1997 after many years in opposition.
- Piper's (2000a, b) analysis of a key concept in the New Labour programme – that of *lifelong learning* – based on a corpus of texts downloaded from British government and EU web-sites.
- Morrison and Love's (1996) study of letters to Zimbabwean magazines ten years after independence.
- Stubbs and Gerbig's (1993) comparison of textbooks in Geography and Ecology, particularly with relation to their use of ergative verbs.
- Wickens' (1998) account of computer-aided teaching materials in Law, which he compares with seminars and textbooks in the same subject.

Most of these writers acknowledge the influence of Stubbs (1996), whose work is discussed further in the next section.

Teubert's (2000) study is one of those that focuses on 'keywords' in the sense used by Williams (1976, cited in Stubbs 1996), that is, words that have a particular significance in a given discourse (though not identified statistically as described in chapter 4). In Teubert's case some of the words are identified intuitively as conceptually significant in some texts, while others occur as the collocates of those words. They include what Teubert, following Hermanns (1994), calls 'stigma keywords', which indicate an adversary, such as *bureaucrat, corruption*, and, in the context of Europe, *federal*, and 'banner keywords', which indicate a positive value, such as *independence, peace* and *prosperity*. Teubert notes a considerable amount of repetition between the texts forming his corpus, with phrases such as *bureaucratic dictatorship* and *signing away . . . rights* appearing in several different texts. He relates this repetition to the minority stance of the writers: 'It is this tight net of intertextual references that is indicative of groups basing their identity on an ideological foundation not shared by their environment' (2000: 53). Teubert also points out the density of co-occurrence of the stigma and banner keywords in his texts. Out of 17 examples of the sentences containing the stigma words *unelected* and *faceless*, for example, ten include other stigma words, such as *bureaucrats, unaccountable* and *dictators*. A similar pattern is repeated across the other keywords discussed.

The contrast between stigma and banner keywords allows Teubert to draw attention to the inconsistencies in the Eurosceptics' position. For example, *unaccountable bankers* are evidence of the perfidy of Europe, whereas an *independent central bank* is held up as an ideal, yet both *unaccountable* and *independent* indicate institutions which do not answer to a political power (2000: 55). Some words are identified as the site of conflict. *Anglo-Saxon*, for example, is quoted in the corpus as a term of abuse (*nasty Anglo-Saxon capitalist excesses . . . detested Anglo-Saxon model . . . dreadful Anglo-Saxon inequality*), but this use is ascribed to others, and the writers in the corpus themselves use the term positively (*the ideals of Anglo-Saxon democracy . . . Anglo-Saxon economies with their greater flexibility*). The term becomes a rallying point, delimiting quite effectively those for whom it is a stigma term and those for whom it is a banner word (2000: 66).

Teubert uses the identification of recurrent items, phrases and collocations to unpack the assumptions behind the Eurosceptic discourse and to make explicit what is implied but left unsaid: that, according to the Eurosceptics, only Britain out of the whole of Europe is a true democracy with a truly accountable government (2000: 76–77). In doing so he reveals the 'subliminal message' conveyed by the repetition of lexical items and the formation of pattern of association.

Flowerdew (1997; see also Flowerdew 1998) reveals an analogous hidden message in Patten's speeches, arguing that 'lexical reiteration and patterning' is important in suggesting (or 'creating the myth') that Western ideas about the market economy, freedom of the individual, the rule of law, and democratic participation had a benign influence on Hong Kong during its period as a British colony. Evidence for this argument again comes from collocational information. For example, in Patten's speeches the words *economy* and *economic* are usually found in positive environments. Typical collocates are *choice, freedom, fairness, cheerfulness, growth, good health, virtues, benefits, positive change, success, talent* and *initiative*. These words not only create a prosody of 'goodness', but also link *economy* to other Western values such as *choice* and *freedom*. Similar points are made about the words *wealth, individual* and *rule of law*. Here are Flowerdew's selected examples illustrating Patten's use of the words *individual, individuals* and *individuality*:

> the individual against the state
> the individual against the collective
> the rights of the individual
> decency and fairness, individuality and enterprise
> respect for the individual's rights
> the individual's rights to privacy
> individuals and families free to run their own lives
> opportunities for individuals to shape their own lives
> the privacy of individuals
> individuals and their right to seek the protection of the courts
> the freedom of individuals to manage their affairs without fear of arbitrary inte

The words that co-occur with *individual* here are positive ones: *rights, respect, free, opportunities. Individuality* co-occurs with *decency* and *fairness*, and the concept as a whole is set against *the state* and *the collective. Individuality*, then, like *economic freedom*, is presented as entirely positive; moreover the worth of *individuality* is assumed rather than stated: there is an assumption that the people of Britain and Hong Kong share the same values. Through this and other methods, Flowerdew argues, Patten builds up the myth of the 'good colonial'.

A similar example from Fairclough (2000) is the use of the word *business* in a corpus of British Prime Minister Blair's speeches and other texts concerned with New Labour.[3] In the New Labour corpus, *business* clearly has a positive prosody, collocating with words

---

[3] The Labour Party was the main socialist party in British politics. In the 1990s it revised its policies and discarded much of its socialist agenda. Party leaders now refer to it as 'New Labour'.

indicating co-operation, such as *partnership, involvement, collabora-tion, dialogue* and *relationships,* as well as with words indicating support, such as *help, promote, boost, empower, enhance, encourage* and so on (2000: 30–31). The implicit message is that New Labour is breaking with the traditions of the past, which set the Labour Party in opposition to the values of the business world.

Fairclough makes more explicit comparison between two corpora – the New Labour corpus and a corpus of earlier Labour Party documents – with respect to a number of words and phrases. This comparison allows him to show changes in the ideology of the party through its language or, to take a critical linguistics view, to trace the intervention of language in those changes. He also uses a general corpus for comparison. Fairclough identifies words which are dis-proportionately frequent in the New Labour corpus (i.e. 'keywords' in Scott's 1996 sense), such as *new, MODERNISE, partnership, business* and *together.* These keywords serve to identify what the proponents of New Labour see as the significant differences between their party and its predecessor. New Labour is forward-looking (not old-fashioned, as Old Labour was perceived to be); it is interested in co-operation between different segments of society (not concerned with conflict, as Old Labour was perceived to be); and it is concerned with the interests of business (not anti-capitalist, as Old Labour was perceived to be). The reiteration of these keywords represents an establishment of difference between Old and New Labour.

Collocations, too, indicate the gap between Old and New Labour. The word *rights* collocates with *responsibilities* and *duties* in the New Labour corpus; conversely, *responsibilities* and *duties* collocate strongly with *rights* (Fairclough 2000: 40–41). Both rights and responsibilities are expressed as belonging to individuals. In the earlier Labour corpus, *responsibilities* is found mainly in the context of mention of public authorities and other corporate bodies. Com-menting on this corpus, Fairclough observes that '. . . the close relationship between 'rights' and 'responsibilities' in New Labour language is absent, and we have rather the divorcing of rights from responsibilities . . .' (2000: 41). Another example of changing use is the word *values,* which is found much more frequently in the New Labour corpus than in the earlier one (2000: 47). In the earlier corpus, *values* (except in its economic sense) collocates most strongly with *socialist, socialism* or *Labour,* and occurs in almost half the instances in the context of 'conflict between Labour and its political opponents'. In the New Labour corpus, *values* does not co-occur with *socialist* or with indications of conflict; instead, *values* occurs most frequently in the context of indications of change and modernity, as in *we have applied these values to the modern world*, and in the context of shared perceptions of decency, as in *common values, essential values* and *traditional values*.

Piper's work (2000a, b) examines some key items such as *lifelong learning* in a corpus of government and EU documents. Her study is wide-ranging and important for its integration of corpus observation and social theory. Here I shall concentrate on her methods of interpretation of corpus data, not because her methods are different from those of other researchers, but because she explicates them so clearly. For example, in considering the collocates that the words she is studying have, she classifies those collocates into types and then draws a connection between the collocational behaviour of the word and its social significance. For example, she notes that *learning* in a general corpus precedes words indicating problems (*disabilities, difficulties*) and 'experiential aspects of learning' (*curve, methods, process, experiences*). In the specialised 'Lifelong Learning' corpus, the same word has some of the same uses, being followed by *difficulties* and by *activities, methods, materials* and *programmes*, but it also 'modifies more institutionalised concepts', such as *society, age* and *culture* (Piper 2000a: 12). She comments that in these phrases 'the human subject is subsumed within superordinate and all-embracing social, cultural and temporal entities'. The term 'lifelong learning' is often preceded by *of*, and this in turn often follows words reflecting newness, such as *adoption, challenge, champion, implementation*, as well as words which indicate thought, such as *awareness, concept, definition, form, idea, issue* and *vision* (2000a: 16). Thus Piper's interpretation of *lifelong learning* as a new concept which still has to be defended with argument arises from a classification and interpretation of collocates.

As well as lexis, Piper uses grammatical concepts in her arguments. For example, she notes that the frequent phrase *for lifelong learning* most commonly follows nouns indicating provision, enablement and control (such as *foundation, framework, planning, policy, resources* and *support*) (2000a: 17). This, she notes, suggests that lifelong learning is the responsibility of institutions, who must organise it, rather than of the individual who will, hopefully, do the learning. Using Halliday's terminology, 'the people who do the learning are not agents but patients, the goals and beneficiaries of processes which are as likely to be controlled by someone else as by themselves' (2000a: 17). A related study of the term *individuals* is reported in Piper (2000b). Thus, the word, its collocates and its grammatical patterning are linked to its semantic roles and to the ideology of the texts comprising the corpus.

A somewhat similar approach is taken by Morrison and Love (1996) in their analysis of letters to the editor from issues of two Zimbabwean magazines. They use word-frequency lists to identify high-frequency content words, such as *people, party, president* and *Zimbabwe*. They then note the semantic roles that each item most often takes. For example, *President* is often the subject of verbal or mental process verbs (e.g. *the President again promised . . . as the President said himself*). Morrison and Love comment that 'the writers position the President as the articulator of government policy' (1996: 62).

The word *people*, on the other hand, is used in a number of different ways which none the less combine to form a consistent picture of oppression and suffering. *People* in Morrison and Love's corpus is the subject of clauses indicating difficulty (*. . . are facing starvation, . . . travel at least 15 kms*), or of verbs indicating a negative reaction (*. . . are grumbling, . . . are disgruntled*), or of passive verbs indicating powerlessness (*. . . are still being exploited, . . . are prevented from*). It is the object of verbs indicating 'violence and abuse' (1996: 65) (*. . . suppress the people, . . . beat up people*), and of verbs indicating manipulation of the way people think (*. . . misinforming people, . . . confusing the people*). Morrison and Love see in such patterns of use evidence of the 'discourse of disillusionment' referred to in their title.

Stubbs and Gerbig (Gerbig 1993; Stubbs 1996; Stubbs and Gerbig 1993) also focus on grammar, and on the importance of grammatical choice. Ergative verbs, such as *CLOSE*, for example, can be used to reveal or hide responsibility for a given event, as in these contrasting versions:

Several firms have closed their factories
Factories have been closed
Factories have closed

A writer who consistently chooses the intransitive option in examples such as these presents economic events as if they were natural events, outside human control. A writer who consistently chooses the transitive, active option tends to stress the responsibility borne by people who take decisions to do things like close factories. The ideology of the text produced cannot be interpreted from a single instance of use: it is the cumulative effect of many choices that is important.

It is important also to recognise that a single grammatical choice does not have a single meaning. For example, in the discussion above, it was stated that the intransitive choice with an ergative verb 'means' that the writer or speaker fails to ascribe cause or responsibility. The implication was that the writer or speaker would be on the side of major institutions such as government, industry etc who would be the prime movers behind events such as factory closures and who may prefer to leave this unsaid. However, this is only one interpretation, Gerbig (1993, in Stubbs 1996: 145–146) argues that in texts produced by environmental agencies the intransitive in clauses such as *the crisis deepens . . . the size of the Antarctic ozone hole has increased* implies a situation that is out of control, rather than an absence of blame. Caution needs to be exercised in the interpretation of corpus data with respect to the ideology of the text-producer. This point will be returned to below.

Another example of grammatical features being used to interpret ideology is Wickens' analysis of on-line teaching materials designed for use in British university Law departments (Wickens 1998). Wickens analyses projected clauses, i.e. that-clauses following verbs such as *SAY, THINK, ARGUE, CLAIM* and adjectives such as *likely, possible, doubtful* and so on (cf Hunston 1993d; Stubbs 1996). He concentrates particularly on instances where an assertion is attributed to a source, either the speaker themselves (as in *I think the Law doesn't make it their policy to . . .*) or someone else (as in *Economists recognise that . . .*) and undertakes a careful classification of the possible sources. Wickens (1998) notes that in textbooks attributions are used to make statements about generalised circumstances and to quote other academic and legal texts. He suggests that:

. . . the textbook is concerned to fit its knowledge claims into the linguistic structure of the academic discourse community and explicitly draws on intertextual resources to place itself within the framework of the cumulative knowledge of the field.

In seminars and lectures, on the other hand, attribution is mainly to the self, as the tutor spends some time giving his or her own opinion based on experience of the law. Quoting examples such as *Now I'm sure that the parties didn't mean that when they drafted . . ., And I think that that's a borderline case*, and *I was relieved to see that the House of Lords overturned this*, Wickens comments:

[The tutor] presents the Law not as a clear cut set of rules or principles but as a fallible process which one should not take at face value.

The on-line practice materials are like the seminars in that students are presented with actual cases and are asked to discuss them in the light of legal theory and precedent. Unlike seminars, however, the on-line materials contain few statements attributed to personal opinion, of the type quoted above.

Wickens' interpretation of this is that the on-line materials are impoverished in comparison with both the textbooks and the lectures and seminars, in that students receive a less critical interpretation of what 'Law' is about. In the textbooks, Law is presented as a multi-layered, intertextual construct that is in a continual process of renegotiation. In the seminars, Law is presented as a site of personal interpretation and argument. In the on-line materials neither process – construction or interpretation – is revealed in the practices of attribution. This conclusion has implications, not just for one set of on-line materials, but for the movement towards computer-assisted learning support materials in many academic areas.

Ideology in a general corpus

In the work described above, the discourse of a particular community, in a particular context, is examined to reveal ideological implications. Writers such as Piper often use comparison with a general corpus to highlight these. Piper (2000a) notes that *learning* in her specialised corpus has collocates not found in a general corpus. On the other hand, in Piper (2000b) she notes that *individuals* has a wider range of usage in a general corpus than in the specialised one. She argues (Piper 2000b: 24) that the difference suggests that 'policy-making discourse' does not simply arise from socio-cultural norms, but quite specifically contributes to them.

Another step is to use a general corpus, not as 'background' to a specific study, but as the focus of a study itself. To do so implies regarding the general corpus as a repository of cultural information about a society as a whole (Hunston 1995b). Like the specific studies, work of this kind uses comparative frequency, collocation and phraseology, and evidence for semantic prosody as its data. Lexical items are selected for study that have a cultural saliency and which can be said to embody key ideas in a given society.

Much of the discussion below will focus on Stubbs' (1996) examples of 'cultural keywords', that is, words which capture important social and political facts about a community. Stubbs summarises his work thus:

The main concept is that words occur in characteristic collocations, which show the associations and connotations they have, and therefore the assumptions which they embody. (Stubbs 1996: 172)

Stubbs gives numerous examples, most notably words connected with education (*falling standards, back to basics* and so on), work (*worker, job, career, employment* and so on), nationality, and a network of interconnected words: *service, care, family* and so on. Some of the most important points he makes are these:

- Frequency information can be used to deduce what aspect of a situation the society considers to be most salient. Using simple comparative frequency, for example, Stubbs notes that in the BBC corpus from the Bank of English, the abstract word *unemployment* is much more frequent that the more personal word *unemployed*. According to Stubbs, *unemployment* 'applies to areas and populations, rather than to the people who are unemployed. It collocates not with references to individual people, but with references to groups and categories of people and to areas, and with quantitative expressions' (1996: 180). An interpretation of this is that public discourse in Britain focuses on the abstract demographic phenomenon of unemployment more frequently than on the personal experience of people who are unemployed and, by extension, that it is concerned with society as an abstract, quantifiable notion more than as a collection of individuals.

- Newly emerging collocations can be used to indicate the growth of new concepts, and changes in the meaning of words. For example, Stubbs notes that collocations such as *single parent families* and *unmarried mothers* 'signal important changes in social structures' (1996: 184). In these cases, a new phrase indicates the increasing prevalence of a particular family structure.[4] Another novel collocation, *working mother*, which means 'a mother in paid employment outside the home', is evidence for a change in the meaning of the word *work*, from a general 'doing something' to 'paid employment'.

- The range of collocates that a word has can reveal the range of associations that it has. Taking Stubbs' work on *family* a stage further, for example, it is interesting to examine the compounds consisting of *family* followed by a noun in the Bank of English. From this evidence, views of the family appear to include: the family as a cohesive group of people acting as a single entity (*family home, family friend, family holiday, family business, family reunion, family income, family gatherings, family outings,*

---

[4] In the Bank of English corpus, the phrase *one parent family/ies* occurs 319 times, *single parent family/ies* 280 times, *two parent family/ies* 111 times, and *lone parent family/ies* 29 times. The relative frequency of *one/single/lone parent family/ies* suggests the social salience of such families, whereas the significant presence of *two parent family/ies* suggests that family 'norms' are a site of conflict.

family bereavement); as a historical entity comprising continuity between generations (*family history, family tree, family tradition, family heirloom*); as the site of conflict and breakdown (*family therapy, family support, family breakdown, family problems, family feuds, family squabbles, family counsellor*); as a unit within the political and bureaucratic life of the state (*family law, family doctor, family health service, family policy, family unit, family structure, family allowance*); and as the site of particular social virtues (*family values, family entertainment*).

- Strong collocations become fixed phrases that represent a packaging of information, such that the assertion behind the phrase is less open to question than it would be in a less fixed expression. For example, Stubbs suggests that, in the context of discourse about education, the collocation *falling standards* has become a fixed phrase. It is therefore less easy to challenge the assertion that 'standards are less high now than they were previously'. He says '. . . if collocations and fixed phrases are repeatedly used as unanalysed units in media discussion and elsewhere, then it is very plausible that people will come to think about things in such terms' (1996: 195). Another example might be the phrase *illegal immigrant*. The collocation between *illegal* and *immigrant* (which has both a high t-score and a high MI-score) suggests that this is a fixed, 'unanalysed' phrase. The existence of such a fixed phrase might be said to lead people to accept without question that the movement from one country to another under some circumstances is reprehensible, and, further, that all immigration is illegitimate. (At the time of writing, the term *bogus asylum seeker* seems to be, depressingly, well on the way to becoming another such fixed phrase.) See also Dodd (2000) for examples of 'information packages' in compound nouns used in East and West German newspapers.

- Because of semantic prosody, a word or phrase can carry a covert message. For example, Stubbs (1996: 188) notes that the word *intellectual* co-occurs with words which many people would regard as negative, including *contempt, hippie, leftist* and *students*. He goes on to suggest that this negativity carries over to other collocations, such as *Jewish intellectual* and *Marxist intellectual*. He argues that, although a speaker might argue that a phrase such as *Jewish intellectual* is a purely objective description, a negative judgement is being implied, because of semantic prosody. This is perhaps controversial where a word has more than one meaning – does the prosody of one meaning carry over to the other? For example, words such as *blind* and *deaf* have 'literal' meanings ('cannot see/hear' and 'without the full range of sight/hearing') and 'metaphoric' ones. The metaphoric meanings occur in phrases such as *turn a blind eye to* and *turn a deaf ear to*. These phrases mean 'do not pay attention to', and construe the blindness and deafness in question as a deliberate avoidance strategy. It could be argued (e.g. Hunston 1999a) that the meaning of *blind* and *deaf* in these phrases constitutes a prosody that influences attitudes to literal blindness and deafness; however, there is no evidence for this influence, and a counter-argument would be that the different meanings exist independently, having no influence upon each other.

There are, it seems, two important questions in the application of corpus techniques to the study of ideology and to the practice of critical linguistics. These are: What is to be observed? and How are interpretations to be made? Stubbs, and the researchers who have been influenced by him, appear to utilise the following steps. In terms of method, frequency of occurrence, regularities of co-occurrence and of usage are observed, comparatively where appropriate. This information is used to draw conclusions about collocation, semantic prosody, and typical grammatical and semantic roles. That information in turn is used in the identification of salient concepts, of inconsistencies and sites of conflict, of difference and of change. A further level of interpretation is needed to relate these aspects to covert attitudes, implicit messages, and the discontinuity between discourse and experience.

Corpus evidence for disadvantage

One of the key concerns of critical linguistics is the perpetuation of inequality and disadvantage by a community's public discourse. There are many studies showing how groups identified by ethnicity, gender, or class, are construed in ways that constitute oppression, either in the media as a whole (e.g. van Dijk 1991, van Leeuwen 1996) or in texts of a particular type (e.g. Caldas-Coulthard 1996). More recently there have been attempts to show how information from a corpus can contribute to studies of this kind. Krishnamurthy (1996) considers the typical contexts of the words *tribe/tribal*, *ethnic/ethnicity* and *race/racial* and suggests that these words are used to construct 'otherness', in that they mark a clear difference between the groups referred to and the target readership of the texts they are used in. The use, particularly of *tribal*, is often pejorative, and Krishnamurthy argues that the use of any of these words may be evidence of racism. Similarly, Stubbs' (1996) discussion of the prosody of *intellectual* (see above) suggests that the term *Jewish intellectual* is covertly anti-semitic.

Similarly, Caldas-Coulthard and Moon (1999) investigate a corpus of the *Sun* and *News of the World* newspapers to discover the adjectives collocating with words such as *man* and *woman*. The two lists of adjectives are significantly different, with only *woman* being modified significantly often by adjectives indicating physical appearance, such as *beautiful, pretty* and *lovely*, and only *man* being modified significantly by adjectives indicating importance, such as *key, big, great* and *main*. Further investigation confirms this asymmetry. For example, the adjective *right* is used to modify both *woman* and *man*, but *right woman* most often means 'the right woman for this man' whereas *right man* most often means 'the right man for the job' (Hunston 1999a). These findings suggest that women and men are construed differently by the discourse of popular newspapers, affirming inequality between the genders in society.

Corpus work of this kind seems to me to raise two important questions. The first is the nature of the outcome of the corpus research. One interpretation of Caldas-Coulthard and Moon's findings would run along these lines: 'We know that our society is sexist, and we know that this sexism is reflected and perpetuated by the discourse of popular journalism. The study of adjectives reveals one of the ways that these newspapers represent women and men differently and unequally.' In other words, sexism is assumed; how it is manifested is discovered. A second interpretation would be: 'Our study reveals a sexism in popular newspapers, and therefore in society, which we suspected but did not know before.' In other words, sexism is discovered; nothing is assumed. The second of these interpretations is attractive because it seems more 'objective', but it is a more difficult one to sustain. For example, I have assumed that the predominance of the personal relationship meaning of *the right woman* in a corpus of newspapers meant that women in those newspapers were construed as belonging to the domestic sphere more than to the sphere of work. The work-related meaning of *the right man* indicated that the opposite was true for men; taken together this was an argument for the perception of women as less significant in the world of paid work than men. This assumption has been challenged, however, and an alternative interpretation offered: that men are being construed as less emotionally competent because they more frequently need 'the right woman' to make their lives complete.[5] The point here is that if it is assumed, because of other evidence, that women are in

[5] This was suggested by Chris Tribble (personal communication).

general disadvantaged with respect to men, my original interpretation can be allowed to stand as the more likely of the two: newspapers reflect and perpetuate the disadvantage. But if the aim is to determine whether or not women are disadvantaged, the second interpretation must be given due weight, and the verdict must be 'unproven': the newspapers may be interpreted as perpetuating a negative view of women or men (or indeed both).

The second question relates to the effectiveness of statistical information in a situation of heteroglossia. What is the relation between a dominant pattern of usage and a less-dominant one? Piper (2000b: 11), for example, points out that her corpus includes one text whose use of the word *individuals* is different from the use in the rest of the corpus, avoiding 'the institutionalised networking model of the individual' which is the dominant use in the corpus as a whole. The more heterogeneous a corpus, the more it will include a multitude of voices, which statistical approaches tend to mask. For example, turning again to the word *deaf*, the Bank of English shows a variety of uses (Hunston 1999a). These include the *fall on deaf ears* use mentioned above as oppressive, other insulting uses such as the taboo *deaf-mute* and *deaf and dumb*, and a range of other uses such as the following:

- Deaf people are a minority language group with rights:

  one hysterical older teacher, are deaf. Not since Children of a Lesser
  to staff to improve its service to deaf customers. After consultations
  was valued. Diana spreads word to deaf; Princess of Wales PRINCESS
  that this was because they were deaf British Sign Language users. Would
  Lyndsay and Alexandra. Sarah, who is deaf, read a prayer in sign language as

- Deafness is a handicap that can be overcome through technology:

  sighted people. Even the blind and deaf can receive their daily paper usin
  equencies too high for the human ear, deaf people are able to understand
  of the police raids. PHONES FOR DEAF A scheme to assist the deaf to

- Deafness is linked to disability, and deaf people are to be pitied:

  usband Abdullah was 60 and blind and deaf, but the Serbs had taken him anywa
  more so since I realised I was going deaf, because my visual perception of
  wnership to a new commitment to help deaf and partially sighted people.
  them is Andrew Readman, 19, who is deaf and dyslexic and works as a butche
  kidneys. Wife Yvonne, 46, who is deaf, had already suffered a failed
  soldiers claiming they were made deaf by firing rifles. Defence Minister
  that involves phlegm sends me deaf these days. My hearing is generall
  our greatest fear? Going permanently deaf. With which historical figure do
  whose daughter was born profoundly deaf as a result, according to her
  ne-to-one situations, being slightly deaf. But he loves company. Purr has
  but I'm extremely impatient with the deaf. The deaf don't have the same

- Deafness is a simple description:

pound; 30-a-week she earns escorting deaf children to school is all going on
are deaf and dumb. I get a lot of deaf people coming to my concerts. They

From the above it would appear that the 'disability' use is the most frequent, and it is possible to argue that the word *deaf* has this prosody in British society. Such an argument, while having some validity, masks the divergence of discourses that exist, and whose competing existence is arguably more important than the overall comparative frequencies.

Summary of ideology discussion

Many of the arguments that critical linguists use depend upon assumptions about the influence upon people and on society of repetitions of ways of saying things, and about the power of language whose meaning is covert. It seems apparent, then, that corpora are a very useful tool for the critical linguist, because they identify repetitions, and can be used to identify implicit meaning. Because data in corpora are de-contextualised, the researcher is encouraged to spell out the steps that lie between what is observed and the interpretation placed on those observations.

Translation

Translation is an increasingly important application of corpora, partly because of the needs of institutions such as the European Union, for whom translation is crucial, to improve and automate translation processes. Research into corpora and translation tends to focus on two areas: practical and theoretical. In practical terms, the question is: What software can be developed that will enable a translator to exploit corpora as an aid in the day-to-day business of translation? In theoretical terms, the question is: What does a corpus consisting of translated texts indicate about the process of translation itself? We will take each of these areas in turn.

Because corpora can be used to raise awareness about language in general, they are extremely useful in training translators and in pointing up potential problems for translation. Kenny (2000), for example, discusses examples where German writers have exploited unusual collocations (in German), and where this poses a problem for translators rendering the texts into English. In some cases the translators have found a translation that captures the creativity and the sense of strangeness of the original. For example, corpora show that the German suffix *freundlich* typically collocates with non-concrete nouns, as does the English suffix *friendly*. So the English *high-heel-friendly* sounds as odd as the word for which it is a translation: *stöckelschuhfreundlich* (Kenny 2000: 146). On the other hand, *super-friendly*, offered as a translation for *stinkfreundliches*, is less successful, because whereas *stink* in German can be shown to collocate with negative words, *super* in English has a fairly positive prosody (Kenny 2000: 151).

It is obvious that corpora in different languages are of use to translators. It is often even more useful if these corpora match each other. For example, many documents from the European Union are produced in several languages simultaneously. It is possible to align these documents so that sentences can be extracted that include a word or phrase in one language and its equivalent in one or more other languages every time it has been used. A translator using corpora and software such as this can see at a glance what possible translations are available for a given word or phrase. Corpora used in this way often comprise original texts and their translations. For example, corpora of English and French might consist of books which were written in English and translated into French, and books which were written in French and translated into English. The English corpus, then, would include both texts originally written in English and those that have been translated from French. Another alternative, useful for literary translators or those researching the translation process, is to build a corpus consisting of several different translations of the same book. The corpus user can then see how a particular expression has been translated in each translation. The challenge for the software is to match the texts up automatically, so that equivalent sentences can be placed alongside each other without the need for human intervention (see, e.g., Johansson et al 1996; King and Woolls 1996; Somers 1998). It is important to remember that when a translator uses a corpus of this kind, they are not looking at the 'correct' translation of a given word, but are being shown how previous translators have dealt with a particular problem.

One example of a multilingual concordancing program is MULTI-CONC (King and Woolls 1996; Johns 1997a).[6] This program has been developed as part of an EU-funded project which has also collected a multilingual parallel corpus (King 1997). King describes some of the results. In the English translation of the French novel *Le Petit Prince* ('The Little Prince'), for example, the French word *on* is

---

6 See also the program *Paraconc* developed by Michael Barlow (http://www.ruf.rice.edu/~barlow.parac.html).

variously translated by the English *one*, *you*, the passive, *it*, *anyone*, *he*, *I*, *we*, *nobody*, subject ellipsis, *people* and so on. Perhaps most interesting are those instances where the translator has used a totally different phrase. The French *on se console toujours* (literally: 'one always comforts oneself') is translated as *time soothes all sorrows* (King 1997: 398). Translations in English of German car manuals show a similar diversity in dealing with the German word *Hinweise* (for which dictionaries normally give equivalents such as *information* or *hint*). The English words used are *information, points, hints* and *procedure*. King again notes that sometimes the translator chooses to omit the word altogether. *Wichtige Hinweise* [*Important Information*], used as a heading, is translated simply as *Important*. King (1997: 399) observes that dictionaries typically do not give 'translation by zero' as an option. He comments:

This is not surprising since dictionaries have a bias in favour of finding lexical equivalents or paraphrases – but the more successfully they do this, the less they faithfully reproduce actual translator behaviour.

As another example of this use of parallel corpora, below are some examples of the word *still* from the English part of the multilingual parallel corpus described by King (1997), along with the equivalent sentences from the French corpus. Some of these examples are from texts originally written in English and translated into French; others are from French texts translated into English. In each case, the original language is shown by italics. In each example, the word *still* is underlined, as is the French equivalent, if there is one.

1 *Before her was another long passage, and the White Rabbit was <u>still</u> in sight, hurrying down it . . .*
Devant elle s'étendait un autre couloir où elle vit le Lapin Blanc en train de courir a toute vitesse . . .

2 The building which it <u>still</u> owned in the twentieth century preserves its austere appearance of a barracks and a warehouse.
Le bâtiment qui lui était propre conserve <u>encore</u> au XXe siecle l'aspect austère d'une caserne et d'un entrepôt.

3 Those heirs, at the end of the twentieth century, <u>still</u> have difficulty conceiving of a balanced cooperation, which requires a transformation of mindsets as well as sacrifices.
Ceux-ci, au terme du XXe siècle, conçoivent avec peine une coopération équilibrée exigeant une transformation des esprits et des sacrifices.

4 . . . they must early on breathe the air of sea, play a little with the marine element while they are <u>still</u> in the cradle . . .

. . . il faut respirer de bonne heure l'air de la mer, badiner en quelque sort avec l'élément marin dès le berceau . . .

5 All the same, a distinction seems to impose itself and <u>still</u> be valid up to the present time.
Toutefois une distinction paraît s'imposer et valoir jusqu'au temps présent.

6 Enchanted, the emperor planted a commemorative sequoia which <u>still</u> stands in the park.
Charmé, l'empereur planta dans le parc un séquoia commémoratif que l'on peut <u>toujours</u> admirer.

7 *All this was lost on Alice, who was <u>still</u> looking intently along the road, shading her eyes with one hand.*
Tout ceci était perdu pour Alice qui, une main en abat-jour au-dessus de ses yeux, <u>continuait</u> à regarder attentivement sur la route.

8 Are you <u>still</u> there?
Tu es <u>toujours</u> là?

9 Nevertheless, he <u>still</u> had some more questions.
Cependant il posa <u>encore</u> des questions.

10 *In our society it is <u>still</u> customary for parents and teachers to answer most of these questions with a shrug . . .*
Dans notre société parents et professeurs répondent <u>couramment</u> à de telles questions en haussant les épaules . . .

11 <u>Still</u> unsatisfied, he then wrote an anonymous review of the report in the Royal Society's own periodical.
Pas <u>encore</u> satisfait, il écrivit alors un article anonyme consacré à ce rapport dans le journal périodique de la Royal Society.

12 *They <u>still</u>, however, do not agree on the distance the light has traveled . . .*
Ils ne sont cependant pas d'accord sur la distance parcourue . . .

The adverbs *toujours* and *encore* are among the translation equivalents of *still*, while *continuer* and *couramment* convey the same information. In examples 1 and 12, the translator from English into French has chosen to omit *still*, whereas in examples 3 and 5 the translator from French into English has added *still* although the French had no equivalent word. From the evidence of these lines some hypotheses about French might be made: that *encore* is preferred for a repeated activity (9) and *toujours* for a continuous one (6, 8); that *encore* is used with a negative (11); and that whereas *still* is sometimes used to indicate a contrast to expectation (3, 5, 12), French only needs a time adverbial, such as *jusqu'au temps present*, to convey the same information.

Corpora can be used to identify what terms are used in a

particular discipline in a given language (Pearson 1998; Thomas 1992) and can therefore improve the dictionaries available to translators. They might also help in developing machine translation. The problem for automatic machine translation is that a single word may be translated differently depending on the context. A corpus approach that identifies phrases rather than individual words can help to make machine translation more accurate. Baker (1995: 233), for example, cites the example of the Swedish word *låna*, which is translated into English differently depending on its phraseology:

låna followed by *ut* is translated as *LEND*
låna followed by *in* is translated as *HIRE*
låna followed by LOCALITY is translated as *USE*
låna in all other contexts is translated as *BORROW*

All these examples show how corpora can be used to create reference tools for translators. Now we turn our attention to the theoretical study of the translation process.

One area of interest to those who study the process of translation is the difference between texts that are written in a language and those which are translated into the same language. Corpora are needed if these differences are to be quantified (Baker 1993; 1995; Laviosa 1997). Laviosa, for example, has built a corpus of texts in English which have been translated from non-English sources, and another corpus of texts of similar types and on similar topics which were originally written in English. Comparisons can be made between the two, such as the ratio of types to tokens, or the frequency of particular words. These indicate the difference between 'real English' and 'translators' English'. Her findings suggest that translated texts tend to make greater use of frequent words and correspondingly less use of less frequent words (Laviosa 1997: 315). This points to a measure of simplification in the translated texts: these texts make greater use of a relatively small number of frequent words.

Baker (1993: 243–245; 1995: 236; 1999) suggests that certain features which have been noticed in translated texts might be observed more systematically using corpora. She notes, for example, that translations are often more explicit than their source texts, in that they include background information that the source text omits. If this tendency is a general one, then grammatical features which show relations explicitly (such as that-clauses with *that* rather than without) would be expected to occur more frequently in a corpus of translated texts than in a corpus of original texts. Another example is that translated texts often reduce ambiguity, for example by replacing pronouns by more explicit references to individuals. A corpus of translated texts might, then, be expected to contain fewer pronouns than a corpus of original texts.

Corpora, then, have more to offer translators than might at first sight be apparent. Not only can they provide evidence for how words are used and what translations for a given word or phrase are possible, they also provide an insight into the process and nature of translation itself.

Stylistics

The place of corpora with respect to literary studies is ambiguous. On the one hand, there is a whole discipline – stylometrics – devoted to the statistical study of literary texts (for overviews see Burrows 1992 and Holmes 1998). These studies 'measure' style and have been used to establish authorship of dubious texts and to trace developments in literary style over centuries. On the other hand, there is resistance in the 'literary critical' world to the use of corpora as an aid to interpretation of individual literary texts (Louw 1997: 241).

Barnbrook (1996: 46) and Louw (1997: 244) both suggest using a large, general corpus as a means of establishing a norm for comparison when discussing features of literary style. Louw comments that 'there is general agreement that the difference between the norm and features of the text is responsible for many of the 'devices' which give the reader so much pleasure'. He also suggests that 'hidden meaning' in a literary work might be revealed by comparison with a large corpus. He quotes an example from a poem by Yeats which contains the lines 'One had a lovely face, / And two or three had charm, / But charm and face were in vain . . .'. Louw reports one of his students who felt intuitively that Yeats was demonstrating 'sexism and conceitedness' in these lines but was unable to provide evidence from the poem itself to back up her intuition (1997: 246). Concordance lines from the Bank of English, however, showed that the phrase *in vain* typically follows the word *efforts* or a reference to an intentional, motivated activity, such as *complaints, sacrifices, insults* and *protests*. Examples include:

Even if [the scheme] had succeeded, I suspect that the government's <u>efforts</u> would have been <u>in vain</u> because education has such a multiplicity of goals, many of which cannot be easily measured.

There is a widespread feeling that the <u>sacrifices</u> of World War II were <u>in vain</u> . . .

In other words, *in vain* is used to indicate that someone has made a deliberate attempt to achieve something, through effort or sacrifice perhaps, but that that attempt has been unsuccessful. The line 'charm and face were in vain', therefore, can reasonably be taken to imply that the (female) possessors of the charm and the lovely face were deliberately attempting to use these assets, unsuccessfully. Armed with these observations about the typical use of *in vain*, Louw's student was able to mount a well-corroborated attack upon Yeats' 'male arrogance'. (See also Jackson 1997 on students of literature using corpora in project work.)

Burgess (2000) and Lawson (2000) use corpora consisting of a single work and, like Barnbrook (1996), show how corpus investigation techniques such as word frequency lists, concordance lines and collocations can be used to illuminate aspects of a writer's style. A more concerted attempt to quantify aspects of style is to be found in Short et al (1996) and Leech et al (1997). The writers describe a project to annotate a corpus of narrative texts (fiction, newspaper reports and biography) in terms of the representation of speech and thought (cf Leech and Short 1981). This topic is important to the study of narrative and literature because how a writer represents the words and thoughts of his/her characters is one of the ways in which the point of view or focalisation of the writer is construed (Simpson 1993). As Thompson (1994) points out, newspaper reports can offer different versions of the same events depending on whom they report and how, while fiction writers often create complex effects by merging the thoughts of a character with the narrator's own voice. The categories of 'Free Indirect Speech' and 'Free Indirect Thought' are crucial to these effects, and are a key topic in stylistic analysis (Leech and Short 1981; Simpson 1993: 21–30; Toolan 1988: 119–137). Researchers in stylistics frequently contrast different writers by quoting samples of their work, but can offer no figures to support claims that, say, direct speech is typical of Hemingway, but Free Indirect Thought is typical of Woolf. Given that Free Indirect Speech indicates a high level of intervention by the narrator into the character's world, it might be expected that this mode of representation would be used more in fiction than in biography or newspaper reporting, but without an annotated corpus it is impossible to test this hypothesis.

Short et al (1996: 128–129) report some of the findings from this project, though without data on the biography part of the corpus. They find that the representation of speech comprises a larger proportion of the text in newspaper reports than in fiction, while figures for the representation of thought are the other way round. In other words, speech is more important to news reporting than it is to fiction, but thought is of little importance in news reporting. This is not surprising, in that journalists report what people tell them, and do not have other options of representing character open to them, but it is also important ideologically because the relatively high proportion of speech reporting represents one of the ways in which journalists give an impression of 'objectivity'. Another distinction between fiction and journalism is that fiction uses more Direct Speech and Free Direct Speech than the other categories. Broadsheet newspapers prefer Direct Speech and Indirect Speech and tabloids use mainly Direct Speech. Free Indirect Speech occurs marginally more frequently in broadsheet newspapers than in 'high literature', but very rarely in either. Free Indirect Thought, on the other hand, is the most frequent way of representing thought in fiction (both 'high' and 'popular'), confirming its importance to this mode. Another frequent category in fiction is 'Narrative Report of Internal State' (Leech et al's terminology).

Unfortunately, the researchers in this area have not yet found a way to automate their annotation process (which is carried out entirely by hand), largely because some categories are ambiguous or difficult to identify. Leech et al note, for example, that 'the important and interesting category of free indirect speech (FIS) is more or less defined by the absence of formal features to identify it' (1997: 100).[7]

In addition to stylistic studies of the kind mentioned above, literary texts often form a large part of historical corpora, simply because they are likely to have been preserved, and therefore often form part of studies of how a language has changed over time (e.g. Rissanen 1991; Knowles 1997; Nordlinger and Traugott 1997; Biber et al 1998: 203–229; Hundt and Mair 1999; Fitzmaurice forthcoming). The availability of even very ancient manuscripts in electronic form allows corpus techniques to be applied to them (Prescott 1997; Pidd et al 1997).

Forensic linguistics

Forensic linguistics is the application of linguistics to matters involving the law, that is, criminal or civil court cases. There are many branches. A forensic linguist may be asked to identify a voice in a tape recording, or establish whether a suspect was able to understand questions put to them at the time of arrest, or say whether two

---

[7] Geoff Thompson (personal communication) has suggested that FIS might be recognised by the mismatch of features typical of writing and of speech, and that identification of these features might offer a basis for automatic annotation, but this possibility remains in the future.

documents were written by the same person, or whether a document has been written by one or two people, or judge how accurate a written record of what someone has said is likely to be. A general review of the work of forensic linguists is to be found in Levi (1994); a review of the use of corpora for forensic linguistics is in Coulthard (1994).

Corpus techniques are used particularly in comparing documents with each other, or parts of a document with other parts (in order to establish who wrote or said what), and in offering evidence about the naturalness of the language in a document (in order to establish whether it is genuine or not). The documents under investigation may themselves comprise a corpus, or the documents may be compared with another, larger or more general corpus. One problem that forensic linguists often have is working with documents, such as letters, that are very short, making statistical analysis difficult. They also often run into problems in explaining linguistic concepts to judges and juries and having their opinions as experts taken seriously (Coulthard 1997; Storey-White 1997).

In this section I shall consider only two aspects of corpus-based forensic linguistics. The first is: how a single text, such as a confession, can be compared with a large, general corpus in order to find evidence for it being genuine or otherwise. The second is: how texts can be compared with each other in order to find evidence for or against plagiarism.

Coulthard (1994; Woolls and Coulthard 1998) compares some aspects of the confession made by Derek Bentley, who was hanged for murder in 1953,[8] with the spoken corpus in the Bank of English. For example, he examines the use in Bentley's statement of the word *then*. All the occurrences of this word are presented here as concordances:

```
                           I then ran after them
        We all talked together and then Norman Parsley and Fank Fazey left.
                Chris Craig and I then caught a bus to Croydon
       ot off at West Croydon and then walked down the road where the toilets are
                          Chris then jumped over and I followed
                          Chris then climbed up the drainpipe to the roof
                        Up to then Chris had not said anything.
          the flat roof at the top. Then someone in a garden on the opposite side shone
              The policeman and I then went round a corner by a door
```

---

[8] In this notorious miscarriage of justice, Bentley's companion (Chris Craig) shot and killed a police officer, but was too young to be hanged for murder. Bentley, who was older, was reported to have encouraged his friend to fire, and was hanged. He was acquitted posthumously in 1999 – forensic linguistic evidence by Professor Coulthard forming part of the appeals procedure.

> Chris fired again then and the policeman fell down
> <u>The policeman then</u> pushed me down the stairs

Coulthard notes, firstly, that Bentley uses *then* more than is typical. There are 11 occurrences in a short statement of 582 words, giving a frequency of one in every 58 words. In the Bank of English spoken corpus, *then* occurs on average once every 500 words. On the other hand, Coulthard collected a small corpus consisting of police officers' statements, in which *then* was used once every 78 words. A comparable corpus of witnesses' statements, totalling 930 words, has only one instance of *then*. In other words, Bentley's statement is unlike 'ordinary' speech as evidenced in the Bank of English corpus. The difference cannot be explained by saying that statements are not ordinary language, because the other witness statements corresponded well with the Bank of English data. Only the police statements use *then* as frequently as Bentley is supposed to have done.

Secondly, Coulthard points out that in most of the occurrences of *then*, it is placed after the subject and before the verb (these examples are underlined in the concordance lines above). This is itself unusual. The sequence *then I* is ten times as frequent in the Bank of English spoken corpus as the sequence *I then* is. (Figures from the current Bank of English show an even wider discrepancy.) On the other hand, Subject + *then* is a feature typical of police officers giving evidence. Thus a comparison of Bentley's statement with a larger corpus of spoken English suggests that, at least in its use of and placement of *then*, the statement is unlikely to be an accurate account of what Bentley said. Evidence of this kind (and obviously evidence about more words than this is needed in a court case) can be used to throw doubt on the validity of written confessions.

Our second topic in this section is the study of plagiarism. Plagiarism is sometimes the subject of criminal or civil legal action, but it is also an increasingly contentious and important issue in education. On the one hand, the availability of information, and even sample essays, over the Internet make plagiarism easy to do and difficult to detect. On the other hand, many teachers of writing consider the term 'plagiarism' to be too widely used, in particular against writers who are struggling with the problem of how to integrate read material into their own writing and for whom the injunction 'don't plagiarise' is unhelpful and indeed meaningless (Ivanic 1998). In addition, there is a growing emphasis on co-operation in education, with students often advised to discuss their work with each other, even being required to co-produce texts of various kinds. Under these circumstances, the dividing line between 'sharing ideas' and 'copying' can be a fine one. The blunt instrument of a computer program may seem inadequate to deal with these circumstances.

Accounts of software designed to identify essays which have been copied from each other are to be found in Johnson (1997) and Woolls and Coulthard (1998). This software is part of a package called 'CopyCatch', developed by David Woolls. Information here is also taken from Finlay (2000).

The 'CopyCatch' package essentially compares 'suspect' texts, whose writers are suspected of copying, and 'control' texts, whose writers are not suspected. All the texts, both suspect and control, are written on the same topic, following the same preparation in terms of classes attended. If the similarity between texts is due to the writers dealing with the same material, then all the texts should show a similar degree of sameness. Finlay (2000) identifies a number of features which are important in distinguishing suspect texts from control ones.

The first feature is the amount of lexical vocabulary (that is, lexical words, not grammar words) that the essays have in common. All essays on the same topic will share some vocabulary (Finlay suggests up to 35%), but texts that share over 50% give rise to suspicion. In Johnson's study, 49% of the tokens in the suspect texts are shared between those texts, whereas the equivalent percentage for the control texts is 17%.

Of the shared vocabulary, words which occur only once in a text (hapaxes) but which are common to more than one text are particularly significant, as 'these are the words that are not so predictable in a text and are a result of the writer's personal choice' (Finlay 2000). Woolls and Coulthard (1998) looked at the shared once-only vocabulary in the same texts that Johnson used. Their results show that in the suspect texts 27 once-only words are common to all three texts, and that the two texts which overlap the most share no fewer than 59 additional once-only words. In the control texts only one word occurs once in all three texts, and the two most overlapping texts share 10 additional once-only words.

The other side of the shared-lexis coin is uniqueness. Johnson (1997) found that in each of the suspect texts, the percentages of tokens that are unique to that text are 16%, 15% and 39%. In the control texts the comparable percentages are 61%, 54% and 54%. In other words, in each of the control texts, more than half the words (tokens) are used only by that writer. In each of the suspect texts, fewer than half the words are used only by that writer. In two of the suspect texts the number of unique words is very small indeed.

Another diagnostic used by 'CopyCatch' is the frequency of the most frequent lexical words in the essays. In the texts studied by Finlay, each of two 'suspect' writers uses the same words about the same number of times. The most frequent lexical items in these essays are *children*, *school*, *language* and *system*. *Children* is used 8 times and 5 times by each writer respectively; *school* is used 7 times and 6 times; *language* is used 6 times and 5 times; and *system* is used 4 times by both writers. In the control essays the most frequent items are *languages*, *school*, *language* and *children*. (The use of the same items by both suspect and control writers is to be expected because they were answering the same essay question.) These writers use *language* an equal number of times (6), but for the other words the differences are greater than in the case of the suspect essays: *languages* is used 5 and 9 times; *school* is used 12 and 1 times; *children* is used 6 and 3 times. The greater similarity in the suspect essays is quite marked.

Finally, the 'CopyCatch' software identifies same and similar strings of words. The control texts studied by Finlay have no strings in common, whereas two of the suspect texts share 25 strings and other pairings share 8 and 7 strings.

These calculations suggest that the suspect texts have more in common than the control texts do, even though the topics are the same and the circumstances of writing the essays should have been the same. A possible interpretation is that plagiarism in the sense of direct copying might have taken place. Another possibility, though, is that the suspect texts were written by less able students who relied more heavily on their discussions, and on the source texts used, and who were less flexible in their use of language than the writers of the control texts. If that were the case, the 'suspect' writers would be in need of remedial assistance in writing but would not be guilty of copying. It would be interesting to test the feasibility of this hypothesis by setting up an experiment involving students of different standards who would be given the same source materials and asked to write essays on the same topic under conditions where collaboration was impossible. I would expect that the essays of the weaker students would show more similarities, for the reasons given above. Whether the similarities would be as marked as in the suspect essays studied by the writers mentioned in this section remains to be seen.

Help for writers

Dictionaries, grammars, and translation aids may all be of help to writers, and many of these are now available, either on-line or as CD-ROMs. Recent innovations include the on-line *Longman Web Dictionary* and the *Collins* COBUILD *English Collocations on CD-ROM*. There is, however, enormous potential for growth in this area, as observations regarding the phraseology and use of individual words could be made available to writers in the form of lexically sensitive grammar-checkers, on-line thesauruses and the like.

Current work in providing help for writers seems to focus on writers in specific areas, who have fairly narrow identifiable needs. Haller (2000), for example, reports a suite of aids available to writers who are producing multilingual technical documents, and who therefore need to be consistent in their use of terminology and accurate in finding accepted translation equivalents. On-line tools check each document for consistency of spelling and match technical terms against an electronic style guide to alert the writer to possible incorrect usages. In addition, parallel corpora are used to suggest to the writer possible translations of given terms. This approach focuses on the difficulties of translating technical terms and achieving consistency within and between languages.

For many writers who are expert in their own field, however, it is not the technical terminology but what might be called the terminology of rhetoric that causes problems. This is a problem facing, for example, experts in academic disciplines attempting to write papers in a language not their own. For them, signals of organisation and purpose may be more difficult to use than the technical terminology. Corpus analysis of particular kinds of paper may be used to identify the words and phrases linked with specific moves and functions, the aim being to provide on-line assistance which will supply the writer with the most appropriate phraseology at each point of the article (Noguchi 2001). The disadvantage of this approach is that a large amount of research is needed to provide a resource for a relatively small group of people.

Turning from on-line assistance to a more general use of corpus research, Campanelli and Channell (1994) use information from a general corpus to advise writers of government documents intended for the ordinary reader on the most appropriate use of language. Corpus evidence is used to identify typical and atypical phraseologies, and to suggest what words such as *training* are typically used to mean. This evidence in turn can indicate what an ordinary reader might find unusual and difficult to process, or how questions might most usefully be phrased.

Conclusion

The work described in this chapter suggests that, increasingly, corpus techniques are being used to solve real-world problems. This in turn locates those problems in the field of language and of discourse. The methods used are those described in chapters 3 and 4 and may be summarised as:

- observing frequency of occurrence;
- observing regularities of co-occurrence;
- observing regularities of use.

From these observations of regularity come the identification of collocation, of semantic prosody and of typical grammatical and semantic roles. Where appropriate, the regularities are compared between corpora.

6 Corpora and language teaching: Issues of language description

The development of corpora has the potential for two major effects upon the professional life of the language teacher. Firstly, corpora lead to new descriptions of a language, so that the content of what the language teacher is teaching is perceived to change in radical ways (Sinclair 1991: 100; Stubbs 1996: 231–232). The question 'What is language like?' will be answered in this chapter. Secondly, corpora themselves can be exploited to produce language teaching materials, and can form the basis for new approaches to syllabus design and to methodology. These topics will be explored in the next chapter.

Language as phraseology

Introduction

In chapters 1 and 3 of this book, attention was drawn to the tendency of words to occur, not randomly, or even in accordance with grammatical rules only, but in preferred sequences. Some examples of this are:

- Collocation: for example, *utterly* frequently occurs before *different* but not before *similar,* and before *ridiculous* but not before *sensible.*
- Phrases and variation: for example, one of the uses of the noun *smoke* is in the phrases *where there's smoke there's fire* and *no smoke without fire.* These phrases are open to considerable creativity and exploitation, with examples such as *many Americans came to believe that where there was smoke there must be fire* or *Sometimes there is smoke without fire.* There is regularity here but not fixedness.
- The tendency of certain verbs to occur in the passive rather than the active, or in the negative rather than the positive, or in the present or the past tense: for example, *Manchester is hemmed in by industrial areas* is more likely than *industrial areas hem Manchester in;* and *it never entered my head to be scared* is more likely than *it entered my head to be scared.*

- The occurrence of complementation patterns: *suggestion that, decision as to whether, obligation to do* are examples.

These and the other consequences of sequence preference together might be called 'phraseology'.

It is by now well-documented that phrases (sometimes called 'lexical phrases', 'lexical bundles', 'formulae', 'routine formulae', 'prefabricated routines', 'sentence stems', 'formulae' and 'formulaic language') are frequently used in English and are therefore important to the teaching and learning of English (see, for example, Nattinger and DeCarrico 1989; 1992; Cowie 1988; Pawley and Syder 1983; Peters 1983; Weinert 1995). Unfortunately, phrases tend to be seen as tangential to the main descriptive systems of English, which consist of grammar and lexis, and learners are sometimes described as learning phrases as a short-cut to fluency before going on to a more analysed and accurate command of the language. Phraseology, however, is more than just a collection of phrases: it encompasses all aspects of preferred sequencing as well as the occurrence of so-called 'fixed' phrases. Sinclair (1991) puts phraseology at the heart of language description, arguing that the tendency of words to occur in preferred sequences has three important consequences which offer a challenge to current views about language:[1]

- there is no distinction between pattern and meaning;
- language has two principles of organisation: the idiom principle and the open-choice principle;
- there is no distinction between lexis and grammar.

Following a discussion of each of these points, we will ask how far this approach to language can be taken. Can phraseology indeed be taken to be the basis of what a learner needs to know, or is phraseology simply an important adjunct to grammar?

Pattern and meaning

A key observation that always emerges from investigation of a corpus

---

[1] Sinclair's phrase 'more or less fixed' is important. A 'more fixed' phrase might be *on the whole*, which admits of little, if any, variation. A 'less fixed' phrase might be *teetering on the brink*, where *teetering on the edge, teetering on the verge, hanging on the brink, hovering on the brink, tottering on the brink* and *trembling on the brink* are also found, as well as *hovering on the edge, hovering on the verge, teetering at the edge* and so on. Sinclair (1991) argues that so-called 'fixed phrases' allow more variation than might be expected, and that apparently unmotivated sequences of words turn out to be unexpectedly patterned. It is therefore unhelpful to propose a category of 'phrase' that is different from all 'non-phrases': the difference is one of degree only.

is the association between pattern and meaning. This was noted in various examples in chapter 3, and the phenomenon has several important aspects. Firstly, if a word has several senses, each sense will tend to be associated most frequently with a different set of patterns (Sinclair 1991). For example, when the adjective *mobile* is used of things, meaning 'can be moved', it usually precedes the noun (*mobile unit, mobile library*) but when it is used of people, meaning 'not prevented from moving by disability or lack of resources', it usually comes after a link verb (*I'm still very mobile*). Another example is the verb *MAINTAIN*. This has three main meanings, each associated with one or more patterns:

- the 'do not allow to weaken' meaning, as in *They have maintained their relationships over 50 years*. The pattern is usually 'verb followed by noun';
- the 'say something strongly' meaning, as in *I have always maintained that Jorge's death was a political assassination* or *One railway engineer maintains: 'Nothing short of a machine-gun nest will stop people stealing the fencing'*. The most usual patterns are 'verb followed by that-clause' and 'verb used with quote';
- the 'keep at a particular level' meaning, as in *The manufacturers are trying to maintain prices at too high a level*. The pattern is 'verb followed by noun followed by *at* followed by noun'.

This relation between meaning and pattern is not one-to-one. For example, other meanings of *MAINTAIN* besides 'do not allow to weaken' share the 'verb followed by noun' pattern. These meanings include 'maintain a road or building' and 'maintain a person'. The phrase 'maintain one's innocence', which belongs to the 'say strongly' meaning, also has this pattern, but only with a few collocations. In the main, however, the connection between pattern and meaning holds. It would be reasonable, therefore, not to treat *MAINTAIN* as a single word with three meanings (as a traditional dictionary must do), but to propose three phraseologies – 'maintain something', 'maintain that something is true', and 'maintain something at a level' – each of which has its own meaning. These phraseologies replace the word as the unit of vocabulary teaching. The learner's task is in one sense more difficult, as there are three 'lexical items' to be learned instead of one. On the other hand the learner's task is simplified, as each 'lexical item' contains more information about its use.

The second aspect of the pattern/meaning association is that words with the same pattern tend to share aspects of meaning, as shown in the section on 'Emphasis on lexis in grammar', in chapter 5. A further example of this phenomenon is the pattern 'verb followed by noun followed by *as* followed by noun', as in *he described it as legalised theft*. Verbs with this pattern on the whole share a meaning of 'making someone or something be or seem to be something', by:

- thinking or talking about it in a particular way, as in *She seems to view marriage as an unpleasant duty*);
- classifying something or someone, as in *People tend to characterise him as a 'preppy' director*; *He revealed himself as a man of deep culture*;
- giving someone a job, as in *I would like to appoint you as Managing Director.*

There are other groups of meanings (notably, e.g., *began her career as an accountant*; *ended his life as an outcast*), but this is the main one. The association of pattern and meaning is such that the meaning may be said to belong to the whole phrase, rather than to the individual words in it.

The association between pattern and meaning is so strong that using the pattern with any verb implies a meaning of 'think of someone in a particular way', whether or not the verb normally has that meaning, as in these examples:

The Lord commanded the young man to sell everything he had, give the money to the poor, and follow Him as Lord.

She was living with a man who was never able to welcome her as a full human being with separate needs of her own into his life.

Another example is the verb *MISTAKE*, normally used in a pattern with *for*, as in *they mistook a taxi for a police car*. However, *MISTAKE* has the meaning 'think of someone in a particular way', and it is occasionally (7 times in the Bank of English) used with *as*, presumably by analogy with other verbs with the same meaning, such as those mentioned above. One example from an Australian newspaper is:

A common mistake made in identifying frilled neck lizards was in mistaking it as a bearded dragon.

Finally, the following unusual use of the word *sleaze* is taken from a magazine dedicated to pop music:

It's just plain old Billy Ray, Cyrus The Virus, trying to sleaze his way into our hearts again with his treat-your-woman-right, patronising, slimy puke.

This pattern of 'VERB one's way (in)to' is often used with verbs such as *bribe, bully, cheat, fiddle, hustle, insinuate, trick* and *wangle*, which indicate that someone achieves something by illegal or immoral means. Although *sleaze* is rare in this pattern, indeed is rare as a verb at all, it fits comfortably into this meaning.

It seems plausible that one of the ways that language can change is through a word being used with a new pattern, by analogy with another word. Hunston and Francis (1999) give some examples of verbs which are not typically followed by an '-ing' clause, but which are occasionally found in this pattern. One example is CONFESS, which is usually followed by a that-clause or a to-infinitive, but which does sometimes occur in examples such as . . . *any officer who confesses being corrupt*, apparently by analogy with ADMIT (Hunston and Francis 1999: 98).

Without a large diachronic corpus of modern English, it is not possible to track the development of such innovations, but it seems highly possible that these analogous pattern usages are one of the ways in which English changes over time.

In examples such as these, meaning cannot be said to belong to a single word, but to the phraseology as a whole. The term **semantic prosody** is used to describe phenomena such as this. It usually refers to a word that is typically used in a particular environment, such that the word takes on connotations from that environment (Sinclair 1991; Louw 1993; 1997; Stubbs 1996; Hunston 1995a; Channell 2000). The phrasal verb *SIT through* shown in chapter 3 is an example of a lexical item with semantic prosody. Because it is often used with items that indicate something lengthy and boring, connotations of boredom tend to attach to the phrasal verb itself. Another example, given in chapter 5, was the poem including the line *But charm and face were in vain* (Louw 1997). As Louw's student observed, *in vain* is usually used in the context of something involving effort and intention, and this in turn suggests that *charm* and *face* are to be interpreted as deliberate strategies rather than matters of chance. This illustrates one of the characteristics of semantic prosody: it can be used to hint at a 'hidden meaning' or it can reveal a speaker's hidden attitudes (Louw 1993). Other commonly cited examples of semantic prosody are the phrasal verb *SET in* (Sinclair 1991), which usually co-occurs with subjects indicating something bad such as *bad weather, gloom, decline* or *rot*, and the verb *CAUSE* which also usually co-occurs with nouns indicating a negative evaluation, such as *illness* or *disaster* (Stubbs 1996). Channell (2000) gives several examples, including the negative *in the sticks* and its positive equivalent *off the beaten track*. Hunston (1995a) extends the notion to the implications of some verbs of attribution.

The features of semantic prosody can be summarised thus:

- The semantic prosody of a lexical item is a consequence of the more general observation that meaning can be said to belong to whole phrases rather than to single words.
- Semantic prosody can be observed only by looking at a large number of instances of a word or phrase, because it relies on the *typical* use of a word or phrase.
- It accounts for 'connotation': the sense that a word carries a meaning in addition to its 'real' meaning. The connotation is usually one of evaluation, that is, the semantic prosody is usually negative or, less frequently, positive.
- It can be exploited, in that a speaker can use a word in an atypical way to convey an ironic or otherwise hidden meaning.
- The semantic prosody of a word is often not accessible from a speaker's conscious knowledge. Few people, for example, would define *SET in* as meaning 'something bad starts to happen', but when the negative connotation is pointed out in many cases it accords with intuition (*A spell of fine weather set in* sounds very odd, for example).

Because semantic prosody is not always part of a speaker's conscious knowledge of a language, it may be something that learners are not taught. Because of the kind of meanings that it can convey, however, it is an important aspect of language. Vocabulary teaching needs to take account of semantic prosody, and can do so only if the approach is phraseological rather than word-based.

There is some evidence that phrases and clauses as well as individual lexical items might have a semantic prosody. For example, Hunston (2001) points out that the phrase *may not be* is frequently used as part of a concession–counter-assertion pair, as in *Circle of Friends may not be a world beater, but it has a charm that mostly avoids being cloying*. Furthermore, the two items being compared (*world beater* and *a charm that mostly avoids being cloying*) often follow the pattern of 'ideal thing' + 'not ideal but satisfactory thing'. Some example pairs are shown in Table 6.1.

There are also examples of sentences which convey a covertly evaluative message by this phraseology. For example, the sentence:

There may not be a woman in the pulpit yet in [place name], but there is a preacher of sorts.

suggests that the speaker (on America's National Public Radio) regards *a woman in the pulpit* as the ideal, even though he does not actually say so. Similarly, because of the prosody, the sentence:

Carey may not be a scientist but he is a doyen of the literary world . . .

Table 6.1. Examples of *may not be . . . but*

... may not be	a genius	but ...	he will never have to worry about the mortgage
	a good thing		it is the one card that has not been played
	a jewel of incomparable price		it has its fine moments
	a world beater		it has a charm that mostly avoids being cloying
	a major discovery		it is a fascinating baroque oddity
	a just peace		it is more than just a continuation of war

hints that for this writer *a scientist* is the ideal, with *the literary world* coming in second place. This sets the theme for the rest of the text from which this example comes.

Moreover, because the meaning of a concession is that it is given information, preceding the new information of the counter-assertion, the prosody of 'may not be . . . but' constructs consensus around the first item of the pair. The reader as well as the writer is expected to hold the opinion that women in the pulpit and scientists are to be evaluated positively.

The idiom principle

If we look at English from the point of view of the words that make it up, then, each word can be described in terms of its preferred phraseologies. Mostly, though, users of a language encounter that language as a piece of speaking or writing, not as a set of concordance lines. Sinclair (1991) argues that much of what appears in spoken or written texts follows what he calls the 'idiom principle', that is, each word in the text is used in a common phraseology, meaning is attached to the whole phrase rather than to the individual parts of it, and the hearer or reader understands the phrase as a phrase rather than as a grammatical template with lexical items in it. When a stretch of text cannot be interpreted in the light of the idiom principle, the language user falls back on the 'open-choice principle', following which principle words are much less predictable.

It is not possible to prove or disprove the existence of the idiom principle, but it is possible to argue that some sequences of words

Table 6.2. Demonstrating the Idiom Principle

Phraseology	Evidence
after a few moments of	Key word: *moments*. Most significant word immediately to the right: *of* Key words: *moments of* Most significant word immediately to the left: *few* Key words: *few moments of* Most significant word immediately to the left: *a* Key words: *a few moments of* Most significant word immediately to the left: *after*
furious scribbling	Key word: *scribbling* Adjectives immediately preceding: *frantic, furious, hurried, manic, quick, tireless, uncontrolled*. None of these is by itself significantly frequent, but note that they all have similar meanings.
shifted her position	Key word: *shifted* Most significant words two places to the right: *the, from, focus, **position**, weight, balance, attention*. 'shifted . . . position' has two meanings: the physical (as here) and the metaphoric. In news reports (newspapers and broadcasts) the latter is almost the only meaning. In fiction the former is almost the only meaning.
much as . . . would	Key words: *much as* (not preceded by *as* or *so*) Most significant words two places to the right: *had, **would**, did, might*.

constitute preferred phraseologies, using a large corpus as evidence. It is then not an unreasonable assumption that such phraseologies are encoded and decoded as single entities rather than as strings of individual words. To demonstrate the principle, here is a sentence from a book describing psychotherapy sessions:

After a few moments of furious scribbling, she shifted her position, grasping the pen in her fist with the point down, much as a young child would do.

Some of this sentence is made up of preferred phraseologies, evidence for which can be found in the Bank of English corpus. These are shown in Table 6.2.[2]

---

[2] In the table, the phrase 'most significant word' means 'the collocate with the highest t-

It is reasonable to suppose, then, that these parts of the sentence are interpreted in line with the idiom principle, in that they represent significantly re-occurring phrases. What of the rest of the sentence?

- *grasping the pen in her fist*. Neither the whole Bank of English corpus, nor the British and US books sub-corpora show *pen* as a collocate of the verb *GRASP*. (Collocates include parts of the body, such as *arm, shoulder* and abstract nouns such as *opportunity, significance*.) On the other hand, the phrase *in . . . fist* usually follows a verb indicating 'holding', as in *a sudden handkerchief clutched in her fist* or *trying to hold water in a fist*; *grasping* would belong to this category. Possessives occur significantly frequently before *fist*, and *in* occurs significantly frequently before *her fist*.
- *with the point down*. The phraseology of *point* has been discussed in chapter 3. When *the point* follows *with*, the meaning is usually (though not always) a physical point, such as a sword or finger, rather than a metaphoric one. However, the most frequent phraseology is *with the point of*.

The idiom principle seems to operate not at all in some of these instances (e.g. *grasping the pen*) and only weakly in others (*in her fist*). The open-choice principle is more important here, with word-choice constrained only by the general grammatical rules of English (such as: *GRASP* is followed by an object; determiners such as *the* and *her* come before a noun). In the example sentence, then, some phrases can be interpreted according to the idiom principle, others according to the open-choice principle.

Sinclair suggests that any group or sequence of words is con-structed and understood in the light of one or other of the principles, but not both. In other words, meaning is made either by the phrase as a whole, operating in accordance with the conventional phraseology, or (less often) it is made by the individual words, operating in accordance with grammatical rules. The choice between the idiom or open-choice principles makes ambiguity theoretically possible; the fact that either one or other is employed by a language user at any one time explains why ambiguity is rarely a problem for speakers and hearers. For example, *grasp the point* is in theory ambiguous. Interpreted according to the idiom principle, it means 'understand the main idea of something'; interpreted according to the open-choice principle, with *GRASP* combining with anything indicating a solid object, it means 'take hold of the sharp end of something'. In

score in that position'. Where more than one word is given, the one with the highest t-score is first.

practice, however, only one interpretation is activated, and few readers will be undecided as to which meaning is intended in a sentence such as: *Perhaps, finally, this terrible accident will help the islanders grasp the point.* (The Bank of English, incidentally, contains no examples of *GRASP the point* interpretable according to the open-choice principle, though it is possible – just – to invent one: *When performing a hilt-and-point circle, each dancer holds out her sword by the hilt and her neighbour grasps the point.*)

There is evidence that much of the language met in everyday life does not consist of one phrase tacked on to the end of another, but that one phrase overlaps with the next. In this way, the typicality of each phrase and the originality of their co-occurrence combine. This has been called 'pattern flow' (Hunston and Francis 1999) and 'collocation cascade' (Gledhill 1995). To illustrate the phenomenon, here is a short extract from an article written for English language teachers (*English Teaching Professional* January 2000: 17):

Conventional accounts of recent changes in English language teaching rightly identify the advent of Communicative Language Teaching (CLT) in the late 70s/early 80s as a significant turning point. The paradigm shift from an approach based largely on form and structure to a plurality of approaches informed by a concern for meaning introduced a new 'reality principle' to syllabus design and classroom delivery. One unintended side effect, however, has been the marginalising, or even the exclusion, of the cultural dimension of language learning.

Words in this extract which are used in a way that represents a typical patterning for them include:

accounts	*account of* noun (**N** *of* n)
changes	*change in* noun (**N** *in* n)
identify	*identify* noun *as* noun (**V** n *as* n)
advent	*the advent of* noun (*the* **N** *of* n)
shift	*shift from* noun *to* noun (**N** *from* n *to* n)
based	*based on* noun (**V-ed** *on* n)
plurality	*plurality of* plural noun (**N** *of* pl-n)
informed	*informed by* noun (**V-ed** *by* n)
concern	*concern for* noun (**N** *for* n)
introduced	*introduce* noun *to* noun (**V** n *to* n)
has been	*be* noun (**V** n)
exclusion	*the exclusion of* noun (*the* **N** *of* n)
dimension	adjective *dimension of* noun (**adj N** *of* n)

Overlap between patterns occurs when a word that is part of one pattern has a pattern of its own. For example, *changes* is the second noun in the **N** *of* **n** pattern belonging to *accounts*, and it also begins a pattern (**N** *in* **n**) of its own. Therefore, the noun *changes* represents a point of overlap between two patterns. If all the patterns identified above are mapped on to the extract, the degree of overlap between one pattern and the next is shown (and see Hunston and Francis 1999 for more examples). This is shown in Table 6.3; the extract has been slightly shortened to make the layout easier to follow.

Practical application of Sinclair's theory is not without problems. As might be expected, the idiom principle is easier to demonstrate than the open-choice one. Application of the open-choice principle can be established only by a negative: by the *absence* of phraseology. Yet presence and absence are difficult to quantify. In the 'furious scribbling' example above, the phrase *After a few moments of* is a candidate 'phrase' in English. The Bank of English has 642 instances of *after a moment*, 99 instances of *after a few moments* and 12 instances of *after a few moments of*. How many examples of a three-, four- or five-word sequence are necessary for it to be considered a phrase? As this is not an answerable question, in Table 6.2 a different methodology was used, with the collocates of the least frequent word, *moments*, being considered first, then the collocates of *moments of*, and so on. What is being built up here is not a 'phrase' but evidence of idiomatic phraseology. On the other hand, *grasping the pen in her fist with the point down* was said to be produced by the open-choice principle, in spite of the collocation between *grasping* and *fist* and between *pen* and *point*, and in spite of the relatively frequent *in her fist* and the association of *with* with the literal sense of *point*. What was said to be 'open choice' was the co-occurrence of *grasping* and *pen*, of *fist* and *point*, and of *point* and *down*. In all these cases, the meaning apparently belongs to the word rather than to the phrase.

The problem with establishing the influence of the open-choice principle, then, lies in setting the boundaries of phraseology. Whilst this problem remains, the boundaries between parts of a text that are influenced by each principle will remain open to debate. On the other hand, there is considerable evidence, as illustrated briefly above, for the usefulness of the idiom principle in explaining how discourse in English is composed. It appears to be a considerably more powerful theory than previous approaches to the phraseology of English, as it accounts not only for fixed phrases but for the much less tangible preferences of phrasing that appear to exist. The idiom principle and the open-choice principle together provide a theoretical account for two observations: that phraseology is extremely pervasive in English, and that phraseology alone cannot account for how sentences or

Table 6.3. Demonstrating 'Pattern Flow'

Conventional accounts of recent changes in ELT rightly identify the advent of CLT as a turning point.
N ...... of .... n   V .... n .... as .... n
    N .... in .. n   N ...... of .. n

The shift from an approach based on form to a plurality of approaches informed by a concern for meaning
N .. from .... n .... to .. n
    V-ed on .. n   N .... of .. pl-n   V-ed ...... by .. n
                                    N ...... for ... n

introduced a new 'reality principle' to syllabus design and classroom delivery.
V .... n .... to .... n

One side effect has been the exclusion of the cultural dimension of language learning.
V .... n
    the N .... of .... n
        adj ...... N .... of .... n

utterances are made up. The principles also account for the fact that ambiguity causes much less of a problem in everyday communication than might be expected from the many words that have more than one meaning. As an explanation for how sentences are interpreted, the theory is extremely persuasive.[3]

Lexis and grammar

If, then, language as word list may be described in terms of phraseology, and language as text may be accounted for in terms of the idiom principle, the question arises as to how this view of language relates to the traditional distinction between lexis and grammar. As was noted above, there is a tradition (among lexico-graphers, for instance) of treating phrases as an aspect of lexis. The wider notion of phraseology is not so restricted. Sinclair (1991) argues that a view of language as phraseology – a view informed by looking at a lot of language word by word – necessitates the rejection of lexis and grammar as separate entities. Sinclair's thesis is based on two arguments: that there is no essential difference between 'lexical words' (or 'content words') and 'grammatical words' (or 'empty words'); and that the observed patternings of lexical items are observations about both lexis and grammar.

The more traditional assumptions about language are that lexical words and grammatical words are readily distinguished (calculations of lexical density such as those by Halliday 1985 and Ure 1971 rely on this, as do more recent applications such as the CopyCatch program described in chapter 5), and that lexical facts such as collocation are separable from grammatical facts such as transitivity. The distinction between lexical and grammatical words is in turn based on at least three notions about the words: first, that grammatical words are more frequent than lexical words; second, that grammatical words are most readily accounted for in terms of paradigm, lexical words in terms of syntagm; third, that grammatical words have no meaning of their own, but lexical words do.[4] Each of

---

[3] The two principles also explain how some jokes work (Hunston and Francis 1999). In this dialogue: 'It's unpleasantly like being drunk. . . .What's so unpleasant about being drunk? . . . You ask a glass of water.' (Adams 1979: 49), the phrase *being drunk* is interpreted by the reader first according to the idiom principle, meaning 'intoxicated through the effects of alcohol' (where *drunk* is an adjective), then according to the open-choice principle, meaning 'being ingested' (where *drunk* is a past participle). The humour depends on both meanings <u>not</u> being available at the same time.

[4] Some grammatical words have formal means of identification as well. Modal verbs, for example, do not inflect, though auxiliary verbs do. Grammatical words belong to closed sets, though the argument about the failure of the paradigm lessens the importance of

these common sense notions about words is challenged by corpus evidence. Although it is roughly the case that grammatical words do occur at the top of any word list, with lexical words occurring less frequently, it is not the case that all the grammatical words come before all the lexical words. In the frequency list from the 1998 Bank of English, for example (Sinclair 1999), the most frequent words are *the, of, to, and, a, in, that, is* and *it*, as might be expected. The lexical word *said*, however, comes before *one, there, will* and *their*, the word *new* comes before *do, two* and *than*, and *time* and *people* come before *them, into* and *some*. The least frequent grammatical words, including *each, must* and *might*, are less frequent than many lexical words, including *life, man, woman* and *week*. Sinclair (1999) also points out that very frequent, grammatical words such as *a* participate in the idiom principle just as lexical words do. Phrases such as *COME to a head* account for a sizeable proportion of the occurrences of *a*, but in these phrases the word *a* does not occur in contrast with another article such as *the*. In other words, the paradigmatic behaviour of the word is nullified, and *a* is behaving in this respect in a way that is similar to the lexical word *head* in the same phrase. Hunston (2000) makes similar points with respect to modal auxiliary verbs such as *may* and *must*. She also points out that phraseology can distinguish between the meanings of modal verbs, just as it does between the meanings of lexical words. The third traditional distinction, that grammatical words have no meaning but lexical words do, can easily be countered. The lexical word *point*, in phrases such as *from your point of view, the point is that* and *from that point on* has very little isolatable meaning. On the other hand, Willis (1990) has argued that a grammatical word such as *would* is best taught to language learners as having a meaning of its own, rather than as part of a grammatical abstraction termed the 'conditional'.

The point about lexical and grammatical facts being separable has been countered by the notion of 'pattern grammar' (Francis et al 1996; 1998; Hunston and Francis 1998; 1999). As explained in chapter 5, this approach to grammar prioritises the behaviour of each individual lexical item, and patterns can be given for both lexical words such as *demonstration* and grammatical words such as *each* and *of*. Patterns include those traditionally associated with transitivity (transitive verbs have the pattern **V n**, intransitive verbs have the pattern **V**, and ditransitive verbs have the pattern **V n n**) as well as

---

this factor. Usually, grammatical words are the only ones that are shorter than three letters long in written English, though American spelling of words such as *ax* breaks this rule.

those involving the collocation between a lexical word and a grammatical word such as a preposition, sometimes called colligation. They thus blur the distinction between grammatical and lexical facts.

So far, then, there seems to be some evidence that the distinction between grammatical and lexical words is insufficient to support on its own a distinction between lexis and grammar. There is also evidence that some facts traditionally accounted for under the heading of 'grammar' might better be dealt with as 'lexis', and vice versa. All of this lends credence to Sinclair's assertion that there is no distinction between the two categories of observation. It might be argued, however, that 'grammar' encompasses many more facts than these. Tense choice in English, for example, is said to be part of the grammar of orientation (Willis 1994). The choice between present and past tense is a genuine paradigmatic choice, dependent on the meaning of the verb phrase in relation to the discourse as a whole. In the extract from *English Teaching Professional* quoted above (Table 6.3), for example, the tense difference between *identify* the advent of *Communicative Language Teaching* and *introduced* a new 'reality principle' can be explained in terms of the level of generality. It seems perverse to suggest that the tense choice might be affected by the choice of the verbs *IDENTIFY* and *INTRODUCE*. As Sinclair has noted (1991: 53–66), however, different word-forms of a single lemma do not exhibit equivalent phraseologies. This observation affects tense choice as well as meaning. Although, overall, present and past tenses occur in English in approximately equal amounts (Halliday 1993), many verbs have very different frequencies of tenses. According to Sinclair (1991: 45), for example, the verb-form *declined* is much more frequent than the verb-form *decline*. Thus, *DECLINE* is much more likely to be met in the past tense than in the present tense. Biber et al (1999: 459) give lists of verbs that occur more than 70% or 80% of the time in one of the two primary tenses. Of the two verbs considered above, *IDENTIFY* . . . *as* appears to be used slightly more in the base form (*identify*) than in the past tense (*identified*), and the past tense *introduced* is half as frequent again as the base form *introduce* (based on data from the Bank of English). These proportions are not large enough to indicate that lexis and tense are inextricably linked, but they are perhaps enough to suggest that a holistic choice is being made: that is, just as verb and pattern are chosen together, so tense and verb are chosen together, with neither one determining the other.

How far can you go?

To summarise the argument so far: there is considerable observational evidence that words do not occur randomly in language. Not only is there the kind of non-randomness to be expected from a rule-governed system of categories (*child* often follows *the* but does not follow *she*, for example; *might* is followed by *go* but not by *going*), but there is apparently further non-randomness in the choice between members of a paradigm. Two questions seem to arise from this. For the teacher, the question is: To what extent can phraseology be used as a description of what happens in English, in lieu of, say, a grammatical rule or explanation? Will phraseology as a descriptive technique lead to a 'phrase-book' approach to English, where learners can produce many phrases fluently but cannot analyse them to attain a more creative mastery of the language? For the language theorist the question is: Can phraseology be used as an explanation for why speakers speak as they do, or is it simply an observation, for which further explanation must be found? What is the status of the idiom principle as a tool of language description?

As an illustration of the teacher's question, consider the use in English of the definite article and the possessive before nouns indicating parts of the body.[5] English is unusual, among European languages at least, in allowing the possessive (*her head*) as well as the definite article (*the head*) in this context. Explanations as to when one is preferred over the other range from the stylistic (*the* is said to be less personal and is used when the part of the body is seen as an object) to the logical (*the* is used when the possessor of the body part has already been established so that further information would be superfluous).

An alternative to finding such an explanation is to examine the phraseologies of the words concerned. For example, *his leg*, where the noun is preceded by a possessive, is typically found in the following phrases:

BREAK/LOSE/HURT *his leg*
wound/pain in his leg
ligament/muscle/blood vessel in his leg
have an operation/treatment on his leg

The phrase *the leg* is typically found in the following:

[5] I am indebted to Nobutaka Hayashi for raising this issue, for educating me on the language typology background to the debate, and for valuable discussion on the corpus evidence.

SHOOT/STAB/HIT someone in the leg
HIT/BITE/CLUB someone on the leg

Similarly, *her face* occurs mainly in expressions such as:

look/smile/expression/frown on her face
put her hands over her face
a smile/look spread/came over her face
TURN her face
BURY her face

whereas *the face* occurs in expressions such as:

in the face of death/evil
a slap in the face
on the face of it
SLAP someone across the face.

These phraseologies are consistent enough to allow learners to be taught them as typical patterns, which they can then build on by analogy, rather than being taught a rule about the use of *the* or the possessive. Some phrases, such as *a slap in the face* and *on the face of it* are essentially single vocabulary items.

In theoretical terms, the question is essentially about the relationship between phraseology (the syntagm) and the paradigm. The essence of the notion of paradigm is that two words are alternatives to one another. For example, *the* and *his* are paradigmatic alternatives before a noun, and *is* and *are* are paradigmatic alternative forms of the verb *BE*. The choice between items in a paradigm is usually said to be determined by the wider discourse context and by the precise meaning that the speaker or writer wishes to express. For example, the choice between present and past tense will be determined by the speaker's wish to indicate general/present or specific/past time-reference. The examples shown above, as well as Sinclair's (1999) discussion of words such as *a* mentioned above, and Gledhill's work, to be discussed in chapter 8, however, suggest that the selection of an item in a paradigm is more holistic than might have been thought. The examples of *the/his leg* or *the/her face* are examples of general phraseology constraining the choice of an item in a paradigm. Sinclair's work offers further examples of this. Gledhill's examples are more ambiguous. Gledhill notes that in the abstracts he investigated, *is* was found in expressions such as *there is no evidence* and *it is apparent that* whereas *was* is found in passives such as *was observed, was found, was reacted* and so on. Here we might be more cautious about suggesting that the phraseology constrains the paradigm choice, if 'constrain' here implies 'cause'. We might be unhappy to argue that, in writing *it was observed*, the writer rejects an alternative *it is observed* because of phraseology instead of because of the time-reference of the phrase. On the other hand, the observations about the different distributions of *is* and *was* suggest that paradigms can be viewed instantially rather than absolutely. That is, within a particular register, or within a particular language function, a paradigm may come into or out of existence in a way that is not true for the language as a whole.

Local grammar

The notion of 'local grammar', which was introduced in chapter 4, utilises the connection between pattern and meaning. Because meanings are mapped on to patterns in predictable ways, elements of meaning can be identified via the elements of pattern that realise them. It is easier to identify automatically elements of patterns than elements of meaning, because the patterns are surface configurations.

A local grammar is described as 'local' because it accounts for only one type of meaning rather than for all sentences of English, for example. Gross (1993) uses the term to describe ways of accounting for time expressions, such as *at the beginning of the twenties, in the early 70s* and *late in the nineties*, which show a limited amount of variation. Barnbrook and Sinclair (1995) apply a similar notion to a restricted set of items – the definitions in the *Collins* COBUILD *Students Dictionary*. Because the definitions use a restricted set of sentence patterns (such as *An* x *is a* y *which* z, or *If you* x *something, you* y *it in a* z *manner*), they can be parsed automatically in such a way as to show the function of each part of the definition. For example, the sentence –

*An **abstract** of an article or speech is a short piece of writing that summarizes the main points of it.*

– might be parsed by a general grammar as in Table 6.4a. This shows the relations of the parts of the clause to each other, using the terms that are applicable no matter what the meaning of the clause: subject, verb, complement.

A local grammar of definitions, however, analyses the same sentence using terms which are specific to this function, as in Table 6.4b (a simplified version of the analysis in Barnbrook and Sinclair 1995).

Local grammars can be written for language functions that occur

Table 6.4a. Parsing with a general grammar

Subject	Verb	Complement
An abstract of an article or speech	is	a short piece of writing that summarizes the main points of it.

Table 6.4b. Parsing with a local grammar

Left-hand side: the thing defined	Link-word	Right-hand side: the definition		
headword	hinge	**discriminator**	**super-ordinate**	**discriminator**
An abstract of an article or speech is	a	short	piece of writing	that summarizes the main points of it.

(adapted from Barnbrook and Sinclair 1995: 31–32)

in any texts, not just in the specialised context of a dictionary definition. Hunston and Sinclair (2000) propose a local grammar of evaluation, which would apply to sentences or parts of sentences which function to evaluate some entity. To illustrate this, below are three sets of concordance lines, each demonstrating a pattern used with evaluative nouns, such as *difficulty, problem* or *nuisance.* The concordance lines illustrate the variety of evaluative nouns found in each pattern. Table 6.5 shows how the examples belonging to each pattern set might be analysed in terms of a local grammar of evaluation. The elements of the local grammar are:

- Evaluative category, such as *problem* or *blessing;*
- Evaluated entity, that is, the thing that is being evaluated;
- Affected entity, that is, the thing that is affected by the *problem* or the *blessing.*

Set 1: *the* Noun *of* -ing

 would remain, as would the **absurdity** of letting Rottweilers and the rest roam
 levels, job-sharing has the **advantage** of ensuring that there is always a
  and going through all the **agony** of developing and becoming aware of my
 e ought to be rising to the **challenge** of helping one another, but instead we
  never she was left with the **chore** of looking after him. Mind you take care
 offers convenience and the **comfort** of sorting out your finances from your
 em seemingly committing the **crime** of speaking with an English accent. In

t the country now faces the **danger** of returning to dictatorship. Mr
does not acknowledge the **difficulty** of reaching any sort of agreement. It is
anfani, but they had the **disadvantage** of living in the historic centre of Rome
Keegan's honesty over the **disgrace** of being sent off stood him in good
and he has avoided the **embarrassment** of having possessions seized from his
never quite get over the **excitement** of driving through the early light of
illustrates once more the **folly** of leaving the provision of transport
f us have experienced the **frustration** of looking through our electronic
so guests are spared the **hassle** of parking and we generally strive to
is still getting over the **horror** of finding out about her daughter's
but you don't want the **inconvenience** of paying by cash or cheque, our
although he did suffer the **indignity** of being clouted back over his head for
notes that parenting brings 'the **joy** of watching a person become a person,
last few years, I've had the **luxury** of picking and choosing what jobs I
Not really. I made the **mistake** of overestimating you. I didn't think
wondered which bishop had the **ordeal** of keeping him in order. The service
ever do it. Because you know the **pain** of being on the other side of the
16 September). I had the **privilege** of working in the NHS for 40 years, from
20 years, has solved the **problem** of selling live, but dormant, insects I
If not, you'll have the **satisfaction** of knowing for sure." He was
then we'd have to live with the **shame** of selling out and being commercial
Mediterranean, cutting out the **slog** of going all the way round Spain. First
ong journey wash over her, the **strain** of trying to keep a smile fixed on her
have also had to cope with the **stress** of telling anguished parents there is no
workers break off from the **tedium** of making things and chat endlessly
ut this week suggests that the **threat** of losing no-claims discounts is
as you do in a vehicle. The **thrill** of being on your own two feet in the

Set 2: noun link-verb Noun *for* noun

The break was probably a **blessing** for Blackburn, who needed to
he drought has been a mixed **blessing** for those with sheep as the cost
The Eastbourne result remains a **blow** for Neil Kinnock, with Labour
d: 'This is another devastating **blow** for the car industry and is
The win was nonetheless a **boost** for Downing Street, which promoted
Victory would be a tremendous **boost** for the development of rugby league
isbane. This is some **consolation** for the other losses. The
ow in. However, it is no **consolation** for the unemployed, especially
thing. The attack is a new **headache** for college bosses. They are in a
s. B&Q has become a growing **headache** for the group. It is expected to
The scheme will also be a **lifeline** for scientists who have run out o
shared activities can be a **lifeline** for the sufferer. After being
omen. Would you think it's a **problem** for men too? Erm
I mean this was an enormous **problem** for Orwell. He he
The figures are a major **setback** for the Prime Minister, who hopes
h. The incident is a further **setback** for the Tories who have been

Set 3: *it* link-verb Noun *that*

so degenerately? Well, it was a **blessing** that she hadn't responded. He
their drinking water, it was a **blessing** that local supermarkets keep large
e following that. It is a **disappointment** that they don't pull it off
s of Tory rule). It was a **disappointment** that Robinson began by bearing
it has confronted. It is a **disaster** that a once-thriving industry has

ay or even more. He says it is a **fallacy** that the body cannot absorb more
es. Despite the numbers, it is a **fallacy** that mass tourism has scarred
ocking was so gymnastic it was a **miracle** that no bones were broken. It was
beaten so severely that it was a **miracle** that I survived he recalls with years
to bullets. Also, it is a **misconception** that White Middle Class males
upting his rhythm. It is a **misconception** that you have to hit harder
advance and I feel it is a **pity** that some of the well-known shows do
people riding my horses. It is a **pity** that so many people still think that
Hazel Slater. In a way it is a **relief** that they died together. That is
as scary. But in a sense it was a **relief** that it was over. For 14 years my
start up again. I think it is a **shame** that girls have to carry a lot of
for all Australians. It is a **shame** that many of these issues have
t the Royal Family, said: 'It is a **shame** that Buckingham Palace should take
normal 20-year-old woman. It is a **shame** that many young athletes miss out
ea. Eventually I said: 'It was a **tragedy** that those inherent weaknesses
and religious dissent. It is a **tragedy** that Sydney did not take this

The disadvantage of a local grammar is that the target sentence has to be found before it can be analysed: the nouns illustrated above have to be identified as evaluative, for example. The advantage is that once the necessary patterns have been identified, the elements of the local grammar are more useful than elements of a general grammar are. That is, for most purposes it is more useful to know that a clause is an 'Evaluated Entity' than that it is an object etc.

The aim of devising local grammars is to enable computer programs to identify the elements in them automatically. This can be done if the local grammar elements are mapped on to the pattern elements (as in Tables 6.5a, b and c), and if programs can be written to identify patterns correctly. At the moment, local grammars remain one of the ways that an emphasis on phraseology will contribute to different descriptions of English in the future.

Language variation

Introduction

Another major aspect of language study that has been assisted by the development of corpora is the study of variation between language produced in different situations. There is, of course, a long tradition in the investigation of register variation (e.g. Halliday et al 1964; Halliday 1985; Halliday and Martin 1993; Ghadessy ed. 1988; 1993) and the study of genre (e.g. Swales 1990; Bhatia 1993), but corpora have added a new dimension to the kind of research that can be undertaken.

The use of corpus investigation techniques to discover variation in

Table 6.5a. *the* noun *of* -ing

Elements in the local grammar		Evaluative category		Evaluated entity
Elements in the pattern	*the*	noun	*of*	-ing
Example	*the*	*ordeal*	*of*	*keeping him in order*

Table 6.5b. link-verb *a* noun *for* n

Elements in the local grammar	Evaluated entity		Evaluative category	Affected entity
Elements in the pattern	noun	link-verb	noun	*for* noun
Example	*The attack*	*is*	*a new headache*	*for college bosses.*

Table 6.5c. *it* link-verb Noun *that*

Elements in the local grammar			Evaluative category	Evaluated entity
Elements in the pattern	*it*	link-verb	noun	that-clause
Example	*It*	*was*	*a blessing*	*that she hadn't responded.*

patterns of language use is largely associated with the team who produced the *Longman Grammar of Spoken and Written English* (Biber, Johansson, Leech, Conrad and Finegan 1999) and with the CANCODE project (e.g. Carter and McCarthy 1995), although variation has also been studied in research projects as diverse as Granger's studies of learner language (Granger ed. 1998), Hyland's studies of academic disciplines (e.g. Hyland 1998), and Gledhill's comparison between parts of a research article (Gledhill 1995; 1996). In this section I shall refer mainly, though not exclusively, to the work of Biber and his colleagues (e.g. Biber 1988; 1992; 1996; Biber and Finegan 1988; 1989; Biber et al 1998; 1999; Conrad and Biber 2000).

Sites of variation

The study of variation is essentially the study of comparisons between discourses produced at different times, or for different purposes, or by different groups of people, or under different conditions. Some of the sites of comparison are listed here.

Regions, gender and social groups. Comparisons are made between speakers from different regions, socio-economic groups, and genders following in an established sociolinguistic tradition of variation studies. For example, Rayson et al (1997), using the spoken component of the British National Corpus, find that men and women, older and younger speakers, and speakers from different social classes, are differentiated in terms of the words used most frequently. Men use the components of noun phrases, such as *the* and *of*, more frequently than women do, whilst women use more pronouns and proper nouns. Women in particular use the pro-forms *she/her/hers* and *I/me/my/mine* more than men do. Certain vocabulary items are favoured more by younger speakers than older ones, noticeably interjections such as *okay, hi, hey* and *wow* and adjectives such as *weird, massive, horrible, sick* and *funny*. Speakers from the economically more advantaged social groups use *actually* and *really* more than the other speakers, while those from the less advantaged groups use *SAY*, numbers and taboo words more frequently than the others.

Biber et al (1999) offer many differences between British and American English. As well as predictable findings, such as the American preference for *DO not have the* over the British *HAVE not got the*, there are more surprising discoveries. With negative *HAVE*, for example, the preferred American form is *HAVE no*, while *DO not have any* is more frequent in British than American English (p161). Ellipsis is more frequent overall in British English than in American English. British speakers frequently omit the beginnings and ends of clauses, as in *Depends* instead of *It depends* and *She's not* (as a response) instead of *She's not coming*. (Carter and McCarthy 1995, using their British corpus of spoken English, comment on the high frequency of initial ellipsis.) American speakers use this type of ellipsis less frequently. American speakers, however, omit parts of verb groups, such as *What she say* instead of *What did she say*, more frequently than British speakers do (p1108). Also comparing regional varieties, Farr and O'Keeffe (forthcoming) note that speakers in Ireland use hedges such as *would* more extensively and in different contexts than speakers in Britain do. They cite examples such as *my hair <u>would be</u> brownish now*, where a British speaker would be more likely to say *my hair is brownish now*.

Regional variation of a different kind is studied by Granger and others (Granger ed. 1998; and see chapter 8) who investigate corpora of writing by learners of English from different language backgrounds. For example, Ringbom (1998: 43) notes that whereas most learners use *BE* and *HAVE* more than native speakers of English, Swedish learners use those words much less frequently.

Time periods. Comparisons are made between the English used at different dates. Changes in grammatical features have been noted, such as the development of zero object clauses (i.e. without *that*) between the fourteenth and seventeenth centuries (Rissanen 1991). Registers can also be compared over time. Geisler (forthcoming), for example, uses dimension analysis (see below) to suggest that during the nineteenth century writing in history became less narratorial and more abstract in nature. Studies such as these can add more material to the studies of discipline development such as those carried out by Bazerman (1988), for example.

There are two major difficulties in the study of language over time, using corpora. First, texts from previous centuries are not as readily available as those from today are, and it may be difficult to compile comparable corpora. It is not possible, for example, to collect samples of 18th century spoken English! Second, searches in old texts in a language such as English are complicated by the large amount of spelling variation. Barnbrook notes, for example, that in the Helsinki corpus the word now spelt *blood* appears as *blod, blode, blood, bloode, bloud, bloude, blot, blota, blud* and *blude* (1996: 105), and that such variation is far from exceptional. This complicates calculations of frequency and collocation immensely.

Register. Currently the most important site of variation studies lies in the difference between different registers. 'Register' is of course a technical term in Systemic Linguistics, with a meaning in terms of theory that is sometimes contrasted with 'genre' (e.g. Martin 1982). Frequently, however, it is used in a less theoretically precise way to mean simply discourse occurring in a particular context. Comparisons between registers may take broad groupings, such as texts found in newspapers, or texts found in academic contexts, or they may compare much more narrowly defined discourses, such as research papers in contrasting academic disciplines, or the different parts of research papers in a single discipline.

As described in chapter 5, Biber et al (1998; 1999) use the broad definition of register, identifying large groupings of texts, such as newspaper reporting ('news'), fiction, conversation and academic prose. Mindt (2000) similarly identifies conversation, fiction and expository prose. The types of difference found will be dealt with in some detail below. Here I shall simply make the point that whereas clear and significant differences are very usefully identified between these broad registers, it is also possible to find clear and significant differences within them. Within academic prose, for example, Biber et al (1998) themselves identify important differences between disciplines, as do Charles (in preparation), Rizomilioti (in preparation) and Poos and Simpson (forthcoming), for example, while Gledhill (1995; 1996) identifies significant differences between the sections of research articles in a single discipline. (These topics will be dealt with further in chapter 8.) Carter (2000) has stressed that what might be called 'conversation' is in fact composed of a large number of discrete registers, each of which has different characteristics. For example, the use of the progressive in report verbs (e.g. *she was telling me that* . . .), noted by Carter and McCarthy (1995), is typical of spontaneous oral narratives but not of other conversational registers. It seems that variation is found wherever it is sought, and that there is no end to the fine distinctions that can be made. This raises the question of the validity of the broader registers used by Biber et al and by Mindt. If general grammars are to be criticised for being 'monolithic' (Conrad 2000), might not the categories of 'news', 'conversation' and so on be criticised on the same grounds? One answer is purely practical: a grammar of the scope of Biber et al (1999) that tried to make distinctions between 'smaller' registers would quickly become unmanageable. The broad categories provide a pragmatic basis that establish a kind of baseline for studies of this kind.

Parameters of variation

Biber and others focus on a number of different parameters of variation between registers.

Word frequency. As was illustrated in chapter 1, and as might be expected, many words are not distributed evenly across registers, but occur more frequently in one register than another. Biber et al (1999: 373) report that the twelve overall most frequent lexical verbs, such as *SAY, GET, GO, KNOW* and *THINK*, are much more frequent in conversation than in other registers. Together they make up over 40% of all lexical verbs in conversation, whereas in academic prose they make up less than 20% of total lexical verbs. The most frequent lexical verb in fiction and in news is *SAY*, but *GET* is more frequent in conversation (1999: 375). Word-classes, as well as individual words, also differ. Nouns (excluding pronouns) are more frequent in news and in academic prose than in other registers, and least frequent in conversation (Biber et al 1999: 65). This reflects the density of information in the various registers, particularly the complexity of noun phrases in academic prose (Halliday and Martin 1993). On the other hand, conversation has a greater frequency of pronouns than other registers, reflecting its immediacy of context (Biber et al 1999: 92).

The words used in individual patterns also vary across registers. Looking at verbs followed by a that-clause, for example, Biber (1996) notes that *THINK that*, *SAY that* and *KNOW that* predominate in conversation, but *SAY that*, *SEE that*, *SHOW that* and *SUGGEST that* are significant for academic prose.

Word meaning and use. Different frequencies of words in different registers is sometimes associated with different meanings and uses, as was also illustrated in chapter 1. For example, the word *platform* and the phrase *SHIFT position* tend to be used in journalism with abstract meanings associated with political debate (*a platform of reforms*; *shifted his position on reform*) whereas in fiction they usually have a physical meaning (*they made their way towards the platform*; *she shifted her position slightly*). The adjective *massive* is used in science writing with a technical sense of 'large in mass' and modifies nouns such as *star*, *black hole* and *planet*. In journalism, it is used with a more general sense of 'very big' and modifies nouns such as *blow*, *boost*, *gamble* and *profits* (Lee 1999: 24). Biber et al (1998: 34–39) compare the word *DEAL* as a noun and as a verb. In a combined corpus of fiction and academic prose, the frequencies are approximately equal, but in fiction the noun is more frequent than the verb, whilst in academic prose the reverse is the case. The relative high frequency of the noun in fiction is explained by the wider range of meanings used. The 'amount' meaning (*a great deal of*, *a good deal more*) is frequent in both registers, but fiction also uses the 'agreement' meaning (*make a deal with*, *cut a deal*).

Frequency can also be associated with the different ways that a meaning can be made. Conrad and Biber (2000) and Biber et al (1999: 982) discuss the ways that writer/speaker stance is indicated by adverbials in different registers. Stance adverbials are most frequent in conversation and least frequent in news, suggesting the 'subjectivity' and 'objectivity' of these registers. Single adverbs (such as *possibly*) are the most frequent indicator of stance overall, but prepositional phrases (such as *in fact*) are very frequent in academic prose, while clauses (such as *I think*, *I believe*) are particularly frequent in conversation. *I think* is overwhelmingly most frequent in

Table 6.6. Non-finite verb forms in three registers

	To-infinitives	Present participles	Bare infinitives
Conversation	low	low	high
Expository prose	high	low	low
Fiction	high	high	high

(adapted from Mindt 2000)

British English, whilst American English uses *I think* and *I guess* with almost equal frequency.

Feature frequency. Grammatical features, as well as words, are distributed unevenly across registers. Negative forms, for example, are much more frequent in conversation than in writing (Tottie 1991: 17) and more specifically than in academic prose (Biber et al 1999: 159). This is due in part to other features of conversation, such as the relatively high frequency of verbs, the high degree of repetition, the frequency of features such as tag questions (which may be negative), and the frequency in conversation of verbs which are often negative, such as *FORGET, KNOW* and *MIND*. Biber et al offer other aspects of explanation too, focusing on the immediate interactiveness of conversation. Speakers frequently express (dis)agreement with each other, and negatives are used for this function. Negatives are used for interactivity in academic prose too, as they position the reader to hold certain assumptions, but this function is less frequent overall than the conversational function.

Certain verb forms, too, are unequally distributed across registers (Mindt 2000). As well as differences in tenses, with past tenses more frequent in fiction, present tenses more frequent in conversation, Mindt finds that to-infinitive patterns are more frequent in expository prose and fiction than in conversation (2000: 473), present participles are more frequent in fiction than in expository prose and conversation (2000: 524), and bare infinitives are more frequent in fiction and spoken conversation than in expository prose (2000: 502). These differences are summarised in Table 6.6, with similarities between registers highlighted. As the table shows, there is no consistency of similarity between the registers in terms of these features.

As with lexis, the meaning of grammatical items can vary across registers. Noun groups with a definite article in conversation most frequently refer to something in the immediate context, as in *there's someone at the door* (Biber et al 1999: 264–66). In fiction, such noun groups usually refer to something in the preceding text. In academic prose, the definite article usually refers to something later in the text, often in the same noun group (e.g. <u>the</u> *patterns of industrial development in the United States*). The immediacy of context in conversation, and the need for written registers to establish their own contexts, account for these differences.

Biber (1992) studies types of referring expressions in a range of registers. He finds, for example, that the number of referring expressions is higher in news reporting than in conversation, and that the number of different expressions is also higher. The average 'chain length', comprising the number of expressions that refer to the same entity, is long in conversation and short in news reporting. Biber interprets this as resulting from the tendency in news reporting to mention people and places as additional detail to a story. In conversation, on the other hand, there are fewer topics and each is dealt with at greater length (1992: 229). Using another measure, Biber notes that news reporting uses more repeated lexical items than pronouns, whereas for conversation the reverse is true. He links this finding to the concept of 'informativity': news stories, like academic prose, are more heavily informative than conversation is.

Co-occurrence of variation

The features which distinguish registers do not occur independently, but co-occur in clusters. Biber (1996: 173) refers to these as 'association patterns': 'the systematic ways in which linguistic features are used in association with other linguistic and non-linguistic features'. Under this heading can be included collocation (the association of one lexical item with another) and the co-occurrence of grammatical features, as well as the tendency of words and features to associate with given genres, and indeed the term 'association pattern' has been used throughout this book.

The tendency of given features to co-occur leads Biber to propose what he calls **factors**: clusters of language features which can be shown statistically to co-occur significantly or to fail to co-occur, that is, to attract or repel each other. For example, Biber (1988: 102; Biber et al 1998: 148) finds that the following features co-occur (the order has been changed here to group similar features together; in doing so the comparative strength of co-occurrence noted by Biber has been lost):

private verbs (e.g. *THINK, FEEL*)
present tense verbs
do used as a pro-form

BE as a main verb
second-person pronouns
demonstrative pronouns
first-person pronouns
pronoun *it*
indefinite pronouns (e.g. *someone*)
analytic negation (using *not* rather than *no* or *neither*)
general emphatics and amplifiers (e.g. *definitely, really*)
discourse particles (e.g. *well*)
general hedges
possibility modals
sentence relatives (e.g. . . . *which I think is ridiculous*)
deletion of *that* at the beginning of that-clauses
wh-questions
wh-clauses
causative subordination (e.g. *because*)
non-phrasal coordination (*and* used at the beginning of sentences)
prepositions at the end of clauses
adverbs
contractions

Where these features predominate, the following features tend not to be found in large numbers:

nouns
long words
prepositions
a large number of types relative to the number of tokens
attributive adjectives
place adverbials
agentless passives
reduced relative clauses beginning with past participles

An example of a small sample of English with some of the co-occurring features is:

No that's not the one anyway so I don't know I mean there's no tickets in the in the box for that one so er I don't know what the other one was.

As this short extract illustrates, the co-occurring features are not a random collection but are all associated with a particular kind of meaning. In this case, Biber argues, they indicate a personal involvement between speaker and hearer. Texts with large numbers of the co-occurring features, and low numbers of the 'repelled' features, exemplify a concern with personal involvement. Texts with low numbers of the co-occurring features exemplify a concern with efficient information-giving, at the expense of personal involvement. Biber calls the interpretation of the factor a **dimension**. Texts may be measured along the dimension 'Involved versus informational production' by counting the instances of the relevant features they have. Analysis of several genres indicates that telephone conversations and face-to-face conversations score particularly highly on this dimension, personal letters and public conversations score fairly highly and prepared speeches just gain a positive score. Fiction has a score that is just negative (that is, it is more informational than involved), press editorials have a more negative score and academic prose and official documents have a very negative score (Biber et al 1998: 152).

Biber (1988) identifies six dimensions in all. These are:

1 Involved versus informational production.
2 Narrative versus non-narrative concerns.
3 Explicit versus situation-dependent reference.
4 Overt expression of persuasion.
5 Abstract versus non-abstract information.
6 On-line informational elaboration.

The dimensions vary independently of each other. In other words, two genres which are close together on one dimension may be far apart on another. For example, professional letters and official documents are very similar along Dimension 2, but they are very different along Dimension 5. Both letters and documents are non-narrative, but the documents are much more abstract than the letters. Thus, Biber demonstrates that differences between genres are by no means simply described: they are truly multi-dimensional. Even less simple is the relation between speech and writing. Spoken and written genres do not necessarily cluster together on any of the dimensions. Along dimension 3, for instance, spontaneous speeches have a slightly positive score, but telephone conversations and broadcasts have negative scores. Few people nowadays would argue that speech and writing are different simply because one uses the airwaves as a channel and the other uses paper (Halliday 1987, for instance, uses the terms 'speech' and 'writing' to indicate a style rather than a channel). Biber's work confirms this trend.

The place of variation in language description

In this concluding section we consider the work of Carter and McCarthy and of Halliday and Stubbs in relation to variation. We raise briefly the question of whether different registers of English require descriptions that are different in terms of the categories used, that is, descriptions that differ in design as well as in outcome. We also return to Conrad's (2000) comment that the days of the 'monolithic' grammar are over, and ask whether variation studies leave any space for general studies of frequency.

In the examples given in the previous section, exponents of the same grammatical feature are counted in different registers. The work of Carter and McCarthy (1995), however, suggests that spontaneous spoken English may need to be described in terms that are different from those used to describe the grammar of written English. Most notably, they suggest that in casual conversation, speakers have available to them elements of clause structure which they call 'topic slot' and 'tail slot'. The topic slot occurs before the subject and is filled by a noun phrase that is co-referential with a noun or other reference item elsewhere in the clause. The tail slot occurs at the end of the clause and is filled by, for example, a question tag, or by a noun phrase which amplifies a noun or pronoun occurring elsewhere in the clause (see Carter and McCarthy 1995: 148; 150). Examples of topic slot offered by Carter and McCarthy include:

The one chap in Covent Garden who I bought the fountain pen off he was was saying that . . .
This friend of mine her son was in hospital . . .

An example of a tail slot is:

It's very nice that road up through Skipton to the Dales.

Examples such as these are not just more frequent in spoken English than in written, but would often be described as incorrect in written English, and learners may be strongly discouraged from using such structures. The presence of 'topics' and 'tails' suggests that analyses of speech and writing might be not just quantitatively different, in that the same grammatical categories occur with different relative frequencies, but also qualitatively different, in that a different set of categories are needed to account for clause structure in the two modes. Biber et al (1999: 1072–1082), for example, following Carter and McCarthy, suggest that basic clause structure in spoken English consists of 'preface + body + tag' – a structure which is not proposed for written English.

We now turn to the question of whether it is worth trying to make descriptive statements about English that do not explicitly take register into account. Halliday (1992) addresses this point. He interrogates a general corpus to determine the 'global probabilities' relating to particular choices in English. The ratio of past to non-past tenses, he finds, is about 50:50, whereas the ratio of positive to negative clauses is about 9:1 (Halliday 1993; Halliday and James 1993). He hypothesises, on the basis of information theory, that all binary choices in English will be weighted in one of these two ways: either equally or in the proportion 9:1. But what is the point of carrying out such an exercise, if what matters is not how something is done in 'the language' but how something is done in a register of that language? Halliday (1992: 68) comments:

There has been some misunderstanding on this topic, with the argument being put forward that since every text is in some register or other only register-based frequencies have any meaning, and it is meaningless to talk of global probabilities in grammar. This is rather like saying that since it is always spring, summer, autumn or winter a mean annual precipitation is a meaningless concept.

The upshot of Halliday's argument here is that it is useful to establish a norm with which observations about specific registers can be compared. Stubbs' (1996) work on ideology, described in chapter 5, gives an illustration of how this works. He finds that in his Geography text, most ergative verbs are intransitive, whereas in the Ecology text most of them are transitive and active. In other words, the Geography book prefers instances such as *The old coalfield-based steelworks closed* while the Ecology book prefers instances such as *When BSC closed the iron and steelmaking part of the plant* . . . As pointed out in chapter 5, it may be presumed that different ideologies are at work here: is factory closure a natural occurrence, for which no-one is responsible (the intransitive choice), or should responsibility for the action be attributed (the transitive choice)? It might be supposed that the ideological basis of the Ecology text might be more easily observed in the text, because the writer's intention as an Ecologist is to present a principled view of humankind's relationship with the natural world, whereas the Geography text might be more 'neutral' and impersonal, because the discipline of Geography has no such overt ideological basis. Stubbs' next step is to compare both books with the LOB corpus, which as a general corpus provides a background reading on ergativity in English. In the LOB corpus, ergative verbs are most frequently used transitively. In other words, the Ecology text is more in keeping with general English use, and in that sense is more neutral, whereas the Geography text shows a greater difference from the norm.

Conclusion

In this chapter, two kinds of argument have been made that are applicable to professionals applying linguistics to a particular task. It has been indicated that a great deal of useful descriptive work can be undertaken using corpus investigation techniques, and that a number of reference works now exist that include such descriptions of English. These works are enormously detailed and raise the question of how they will inform applications such as the design of teaching materials. This question will be considered in chapters 7 and 8.

It has also been indicated that descriptions of English using corpora may involve different principles of description than have been used in traditional grammar books. The concern with variation is one such principle, another is the need to consider qualitatively different categories of description, such as Carter and McCarthy's 'topic slot' and 'tail slot'. Sinclair's work is even more radical, involving totally new concepts such as the competing principles of idiom and open-choice.

It is possible to see old and new concepts as existing in counterpoint with each other. For example, traditional clauses, with their clear boundaries, co-occur with fuzzy-edged 'units of meaning'. Hierarchical units such as clauses and groups co-exist with the more fluid 'pattern flow'. One description does not necessarily supersede or replace another, but reminds us that language has many more dimensions than a single model of description can comfortably encompass.

7 Corpora and language teaching: General applications

In this chapter, applications of corpora to the practice of language teaching (mainly English language teaching) will be considered. There are sections devoted to data-driven learning and reciprocal learning, and to issues relating to methodology and syllabus design. The final section is a discussion of recent challenges to the use of corpora in language teaching.

Data-driven learning

Introduction

As Leech (1997c: 3) comments, the use of corpora in language teaching situations owes much to the work of Tim Johns, who developed data-driven learning (DDL) for use with international students at the University of Birmingham. An often-quoted comment by Johns is that 'Research is too important to be left to the researchers' (1991: 2). The theory behind DDL is that students act as 'language detectives' (Johns 1997a: 101), discovering facts about the language they are learning for themselves, from authentic examples. This supports learning, partly because students are motivated to remember what they have worked to find out. In addition, because corpus data can reveal previously unnoticed patterns, a student may well notice something that a teacher has overlooked, or that no textbook covers. As well as being beneficial in teaching specific items, DDL is hypothesised to improve general skills of using context to deduce meaning.[1] DDL involves setting up situations in which students can answer questions about language themselves by studying corpus data in the form of concordance lines or sentences. The questions may arise out of something the student is writing, and may be formulated as 'Is it better to say x or y?' or 'What is the difference between saying x and saying y?' In this case, the questions are the student's own. Alternatively, self-access materials may be written that

---

[1] The hypotheses about the benefits of DDL have not yet been adequately tested, but see Stevens (1991), Cobb (1997) and Cobb and Horst (2001) for small-scale studies.

allow students to explore general issues such as 'that-clauses', using information from a corpus. In this case, the teacher aims to teach items which are known to be problematic or useful for the groups of students concerned. The first kind of study will use a 'raw corpus', in the sense that the student and tutor will look at the corpus together, without either of them necessarily knowing what they will find. For the second kind of study, the tutor has to carefully select and possibly edit the concordance lines in order to demonstrate the target language feature.

The first kind of study has the advantage of maximum student motivation: the student asks a question for which an answer is urgently required (for the student to complete a piece of written work, for example), and is therefore highly motivated to discover information in the corpus data consulted. A possible disadvantage for the teacher is that they have very little control over what happens. If the corpus is consulted and no answer is apparent to student or teacher, or if further difficult questions are raised, the teacher may feel that a loss of expertise has occurred. A more basic problem is that not every teaching situation allows the luxury of one-to-one consultations, or sufficient computer access for students to undertake investigations on their own. In the second kind of study, the teacher, having selected the information, has more control. Materials can be printed on to paper to be used with a whole class. The disadvantage is that, as the teacher has selected the topic for study, the students are potentially less motivated to search for or remember the target information. In these circumstances, DDL may appear to the students to be a tangential activity to the main business of the class.

More recent developments in data-driven learning (e.g. Bernadini 2000) stress the benefits of encouraging students to design their own corpus investigations and to take advantage of the 'serendipity' effect of searching a corpus when the agenda is not too firmly fixed and a student can follow up any interesting observations that they happen across. This Discovery Learning, as it is sometimes called, is most suitable for very advanced learners who are filling in gaps in their knowledge rather than laying down the foundations. At the other end of the scale, Cobb and Horst (2001) describe an experiment to teach large amounts of vocabulary to EAP students, using concordances from a corpus of texts from the students' language course. In this very controlled environment, students learned lists of vocabulary items more successfully when they had access to the concordance lines than using other methods.

DDL with a 'raw' corpus

Advanced learners can safely be encouraged to use a raw (unedited) corpus to make observations about the language. Dodd (1997), for example, describes advanced learners of German using a corpus of German newspapers. Among other activities, the students test out statements made in standard reference books, about grammar, such as rules for the use of particular conjunctions, and lexis, such as differentiation between near-synonyms. The newspaper corpus can also be used to test hypotheses about the use of various key terms in East and West Germany. Many teachers nowadays use the worldwide web to allow students access to a range of corpora, both monolingual and parallel (Foucou and Kübler 2000) or to encourage students to build their own corpora (Pearson 2000).

The challenge for the teacher who wishes to encourage students to do work of this kind is to formulate a task in such a way that the student will obtain maximum benefit from it. If teacher and student are in a one-to-one consultation, the teacher can 'play it by ear'. In other circumstances, however, the teacher will have to do some planning of the activity to be undertaken. Here are two examples of activities which a student may undertake, using an unedited version of the Bank of English corpus.

Example 1: prevent

A student writes the following phrase in an essay: . . . *in their efforts to prevent such incidents to ever happen again.* The teacher disagrees with this use of *prevent*, and sends the student to a corpus to investigate the conventional usage of this verb. There are two alternative ways of doing this. One is to focus on the verb *PREVENT* and its patterns. The student can be asked to obtain 30 random lines from the corpus for the verb. This will yield useful information, but it does not reflect how the student probably built up the problem sentence, in which the focus could have been on *incidents* and the notion of 'happening again' as much as on *prevent*. If the corpus used is large enough, the student can be instructed to search for *PREVENT* and *INCIDENT* together. Here are 23 concordance lines from the Bank of English for each of these searches:

PREVENT
of the whole human family, has to prevent the horrific toll of 40,000
48, who was stabbed as he tried to prevent a gang attacking William Njoh, 13.
service authorities did nothing to prevent the dangerous material entering

for those whose work commitments prevent them from following the normal
they must be turned regularly to prevent the embryo sticking to the shell
simple erm and are designed to prevent radon getting from the ground up
the only solution. And attempts to prevent them from leaving may create an
out that only one man could now prevent war in the Gulf – and that man is
may consider tabling legislation to prevent unmerited pay rises. The
process. No one who is concerned to prevent the disintegration of an
sick. The state had no authority to prevent the plant from burning chlorinated
States Supreme Court in an effort to prevent Klansmen from striking all the
seek help, and seek it quickly to prevent further damage to them.
schism to extend our power. And to prevent the Cybernetic Universal Church
social forces will by themselves prevent excessive mongrelization from
to attract a mate, failing to prevent cuckoldry, or failing to keep a
was content to use its influence to prevent any Senate amendments adding
objectives in Louisiana: first, to prevent New Orleans from turning into an
that he has legal rights which prevent such demeaning, mix and match
bundle the leaves in the winter to prevent snow and water getting into the
own way. A lone Labor voter prevented a clean sweep in Birdsville,
V.P. Singh if the temple project is prevented or if the pilgrimage by its
at least some batterings could be prevented, but now local advocacy groups

PREVENT . . . INCIDENT

have prevented. Talking about the incident became, in its own way, a part of
predict or prevent that damage. The incident spoiled my self-satisfaction,
oxygen system to **prevent a similar** incident. Verdict: Natural causes.
should help **prevent further** incidents of the kind that Mr Rowe so
The MPs hope to **prevent** incidents such as the attack on Daniel
in an attempt to **prevent** potential incidents of 'bar rage'. Plain- clothes
would help **prevent a repeat of** incidents like the collapse of the State
to act to **prevent such** violent incidents **again.**" Local MLA Vince
and thought to **prevent such** incidents **in future**, Itar-Tass news agency
should take steps 'to **prevent such** incidents as the assassination of Rabin'.
to have been unable to **prevent such** incidents. The fundamentalists who patrol
two countries to **prevent similar** incidents **in the future**. DOMINICAN
concerned to **prevent further such** incidents. The Secretary General of the
decisive measures to **prevent** these incidents. Simon Long reports from Peking:
could do far more to **prevent such** incidents. However the fact that this
responsibility to **prevent such** incidents. Yesterday, the Lebanese
to be failsafe and **prevent such** incidents from happening. It is a
spy Rudolf Abel. To **prevent** incidents **like this**, air forces in the US
guidelines which can help **prevent** incidents **like this one**. In the Persian
Post Office can do to **prevent such** incidents. FRED VAN DE PUTTE, Postal
was in its own interest to **prevent** incidents from occurring on the premises,
To **prevent** terrorist incidents and to convict those responsible
will be enough to **prevent any more** incidents. I don't think Eric ever

What the teacher 'wants' the learner to see in these lines are the
presence of the patterns *prevent something, prevent something
happening* and *prevent something from happening* and the absence
of the pattern *prevent something to happen*. The teacher may also
wish the learner to note ways of expressing recurrence, as in *prevent*

incidents like this, prevent such incidents or *prevent a similar incident.* In other words, there are two foci of attention: the patterns of the verb and the ways of expressing the whole idea.

Once the concordance lines have been obtained, the learner may be asked simply to notice the patterns. With very advanced students, or students who have worked with concordance lines before, this may be a successful strategy. With other students, more detailed instructions may have to be given. For example, the student may be given these pattern phrases – *prevent an incident, prevent an incident happening, prevent an incident from happening* and *prevent an incident to happen* – and be asked to match each pattern phrase with concordance lines. This would draw the student's attention to what is relevant to pattern in the sample lines. If lines with *incident* have been selected, the student can also be instructed to underline, for example, all words and phrases indicating 'happen again'. Finally, the student can be asked to re-word the problem sentence in one or more ways.

Example 2: not any *and* no

This task replicates Dodd's idea of asking learners to check grammar book information in a corpus. The grammar book used is the *Longman English Grammar* (1988: 93–94) which notes that negatives can be formed using *not . . . any* or with *no,* as in *There aren't any buses after midnight* and *There are no buses after midnight.* A useful learner project might be to check a corpus for any differences between these alternative phraseologies. The corpus used here is the spoken corpus from the Bank of English. The first thing to be noticed is the difference in frequency. In this corpus, *there's no* is much more frequent than *there isn't any* (over 2,000 lines compared with fewer than 100). (This finding concurs with Biber et al 1999: 172.) Secondly, *there isn't any* frequently occurs at the end of a clause, with *any* being used cohesively, referring back to something earlier in the discourse, as in these (slightly edited) examples:

A: I mean what would you want them to do to help themselves?
B: Well perhaps look round for accommodation instead of just sitting on the street.
A: But **there isn't any.**

I dunno whether it's maybe just that the subtext of the Archers is much more clumsy or that **there isn't any.**

Take my point about there is no trust for the police. **There isn't any.**

There's nowhere within a few minutes walk of here that's selling sweets. And I've just been on the prowl to find somewhere and **there isn't any.**

A: What's the point of that?
B: **There isn't any.**

He said Can't we have some sprouts. I said No **there isn't any.**

A: What about the state of the streets litter er garbage collection that kind of thing?
B: **There isn't any.**

Apart from that, the phrase is used with a variety of nouns, as in these lines:

we go into school <M01> There isn't any **bus** that comes that way is
category but there there isn't any clear **perception** that say in
here is it? No. <M01> Cos there isn't any **decrease** in the number of kids
the seventeenth of February. Now there isn't any **fiddle** going on because the
it was probably because there isn't any free **parking** is there there
War of course illustrates that there isn't any **government** at that level it's
kind of because there isn't any **hot water** nothing got
often things like noise and dust there isn't any **limit** or isn't any compliance
different ways. <M0X> Mm I bet there isn't any **newspaper** in another language
use that argument both ways. There isn't any one **reason** why it's become
there isn't anything. There isn't any **other word** so if you had to
<F01> Yeah. <M0X> Erm. <F01> There isn't any **possibility** I mean this is
on Villa to sell although there isn't any **pressure** if erm if Doug takes
<F01> And it's so unfair and there isn't any **redress** <F06> No that's
you're doing a spoken one I mean there isn't any **sensible way** of sampling
So I think you I think <F06> But there isn't any **such thing** yet is there John?
is pressing her <M01> Mhm. <F01> there isn't any **time** you see this is the
train of thought really because there isn't any **train of thought** very much.
re actually bound booklets so there isn't any **V A T.** I don't think so
re saying FX? Yes because there isn't any **water** under the rim.

The phrase *there's no*, on the other hand, is frequently followed by abstract, discourse nouns such as *need, point, problem, reason* and *way*, rather than nouns referring to physical objects. The following lines illustrate this:

know between as far as I know there's no **comparison** between the nature
to make the point that there's no **evidence** whatsoever that humans can
also be some colour although there's no **example** of it in this er particular
actually. <M01> Mm. Well there's no **hurry** is there. <M02> No.
s no <M01> Mm. <M02> er there's no **measure** of cloud liquid water in the
it down in writing so that there's no er **misunderstanding** <M01> Mm
half a dozen times. You know there's no **need** for it because by the time it
at the end of the day there's no **need** for any er people say you know
I'm not going at seven. There's no **point** in having a wide receiver
so was there there's no **point** in actually looking and sort
arrest <M01> Mm. <F01> erm there's no **problem** with it but er I mean provi
so you're already identified there's no **problem** at all really. <M01> No of
s got a key and he gets in and there's no **problem.** So I think it might be my
that's how it works and there's no **reason** why it shouldn't work like
Mm. <F0X> starter. <F0X> There's no **sign** of them. <F0X> That's mine in
from the courts they said so there's no **use** even putting in for it 'cos you

I miss a lot of things and there's no **way** the patient can ring me as well
I hadn't got access to a car there's no **way** I could cart up bottles and <M01>
s <M01> Yeah. <M02> there's no **way** of knowing precisely which detail
ll have to <F0X> Yeah because there's no **way** in which – You've got to teach

This small investigation illustrates the general rule that details of usage can account for observations of frequency and can make those observations more directly useful. This in turn illustrates the need to move between quantitative and qualitative information.

As was noted in chapter 1, Owen (1996) warns that encouraging advanced students to look in a corpus can lead to problems. He notes that a native speaker would probably find a sentence such as *Further experiments require to be done* unacceptable and might direct the student to a corpus in order to discover that *REQUIRE* is not used with a passive infinitive, whereas *NEED* is. The problem is that the student looking at the relevant concordance lines in the Bank of English would actually find a number of lines that appear to break the rule, such as these:

that at some stage you would require to be admitted to hospital for
must raise other questions which require to be answered. Among them, he
and women in these hospitals did not require to be cared for in such secure
of the modifications that we require to be carried out on the yeast
of the minority of patients who require to be detained in hospital or
at the commercial potential that may require to be developed at a number of
<p> Where media and cultural studies require to be distinguished is in their
me as Official Receiver, would require to be funded. I have approached
drugs are available. However, they require to be given for rather a prolonged
been derived are too well known to require to be indicated. Countless letters
require maintenance but it does require to be kept well moist and
you can take unstable vaccines that require to be kept in the refrigerator and
model. These may be prisoners who require to be kept apart for their own
small air inclusions which will require to be made good in this way during
legal position of the monarchy would require to be made by legislation enacted
certain needs and goals that they require to be met <M01> Right
that a large number of laws would require to be passed by a two-thirds
<p> A Yes, your cordon pears do require to be pruned in summer. This
as the physical health of the people require to be remedied.
the fact that these prisoners require to be segregated for their own

In other words, the corpus information does not seem to accord with native-speaker intuition. Looking at the corpus may therefore confuse the student and undermine the authority of the teacher. Closer examination of lines such as those above suggests a resolution of the problem, in that in each line the past participle is of a verb indicating a specific action (e.g. *vaccines require to be kept, pears require to be pruned, prisoners require to be segregated*) rather than of a general verb such as *do*. In each case the subject of the clause indicates an entity which is the goal of a process. The problem sentence *Further experiments require to be done* is different, not only because the verb is a general one but also because the subject expresses the range of the verb (in Halliday's terms) rather than the goal. The phrase *do an experiment* expresses a single action rather than an action done to something. Although this may solve Owen's dilemma, it is true that his question 'How many instances in a corpus are enough to show that something is correct English?' becomes a pressing, and awkward, one when learners investigate a corpus for themselves. An extreme example of this is clauses introduced by *like*, such as *They head for me like I'm a magnet or something*. This is usually considered to be 'incorrect' in English, the correct version being *They head for me as if I was a magnet or something*. The Bank of English has numerous examples of the incorrect usage, which is very common, especially in spoken English. Distinguishing between what is said and what is accepted as standard may need the assistance of a teacher or a grammar book.

Designing materials based on corpus data

The alternative to encouraging learners to explore a raw corpus is to select the evidence, that is, to give learners materials based on concordance lines which the teacher has selected, and to add questions which will guide the learners towards noticing relevant information in the lines. Johns (1997a: 101) gives some examples of question types (e.g. 'How many different verbs are shown with this structure?' and 'Which word is present in the right context of citations 1–8 that is not present in the right context of citations 9–16?') and notes that '[s]uch tasks are, of course, "closed" in the sense that the result is known to the teacher in advance'. The advantage of selecting concordance lines is that lines with exceptionally difficult vocabulary can be left out, as can lines that exemplify usages that the teacher would prefer the student to ignore at this stage. This selection allows concordance lines to be used with students who are not advanced enough to benefit from 'raw' concordance data.

The teacher may choose to begin with a word that is already familiar to learners. The following lines illustrate one use of the adjective *angry*:

> At first I thought her parents were angry with her
> But you get so angry with me!
> how can you be angry with the man you love
> Ian gets angry with the television sometimes

These lines have been selected because they do not contain difficult language and because there is a whole sentence or clause in one line. The lines have been cut so that there is no extraneous information in them. Learners, having identified the sequence *angry with* as the key point here, can be asked to look at other lines with a similar pattern, such as:

> I'm more annoyed with myself you know
> I was annoyed with him.
> I knew my father would be annoyed with me.
> But Americans also are annoyed with George Bush
> He says he's never been bored with the job
> I got a bit bored with popular music
> I get bored with cooking
> She's highly intelligent and gets bored with television
> I was clearly becoming rather impatient with rejections.
> Charlie could be impatient with others.
> There are countless times when I get impatient with my husband, Ken
> increasingly impatient with the slow pace of change

A simple exercise is to ask learners to list the adjectives used in this way. If they are able, they might be asked to predict other adjectives that they might expect to have the same pattern, and these can be checked against a corpus, or against a dictionary. Further exercises could include underlining the verbs that come before the adjectives (*BE, GET, BECOME*). If the concordance lines are extended, learners can note a longer phraseology, such as prepositional phrases beginning with *for* that express the reason for anger, as in these extended lines:

> Was he not even angry with his mother for not explaining things t
> I do not feel angry with him for what he has done.
> I feel angry with her for not standing up to him.
> looked at him as if she were annoyed with him for letting it happen.

Learners are building up an extended phrase here that might be expressed as 'be angry with someone for something' or 'be angry with someone for (not) doing something'.

Exercises such as this one can be enjoyable, but they are also time-consuming for the teacher to write, so it is worthwhile bearing in mind this caveat from Dave Willis (personal communication):

One of the major problems with DDL, or with consciousness-raising in general, is what to focus on. Exercises of this kind are very time consuming in the classroom. A sequence like that starting with *angry* and leading on to *angry with someone for something* might not repay the time taken. . . . I would not argue that exercises like this are not worth doing. I am saying that time in classrooms is very limited and that there is a danger of spending too long on generalisations which may be of limited value . . .

To avoid a wasteful expenditure of effort, writers of DDL materials frequently focus on items which are known to be difficult for students with a particular language background, or items which are particularly frequent or otherwise important in a given subject area.

DDL exercises can be integrated into the rest of the lesson if the starting point for the activity is a word or phrase met in a reading or listening text, or in another classroom activity. For example, a reading passage with a group of students studying science through the medium of English may contain the sentence *Salt water has a lower freezing point than normal water.* The teacher may consider the phraseology of the phrase *freezing point*, and its close relatives *boiling point, melting point* and so on, to be important enough to warrant the development of DDL materials. It is a simple matter to select some concordance lines:

```
          soil to raise the temperature above freezing point, the planetary permafrost
               hunt. Temperatures remained at freezing point, prompting Kobe doctor
      As the temperature dropped below freezing point at night, local reside
                    drops in your area below freezing point for seven consecutive
              water, still liquid below its freezing point, and in a false state
         freezer since alcohol has a lower freezing-point than water and therefore
         imparting taste. They lower the freezing point of a food to keep it l
   on runways and aircraft, push the freezing point of ice down to 13 degrees
         increased pressure lowers the freezing point of water. This is the
      cold – don't you know what the freezing point of alcohol is? As we s
       the period never rose above the freezing point of water (32F). Certainly
       to car antifreeze, to lower their freezing point, to prevent large ice
         and play in temperatures near to freezing point. That's not a whinge
       that, sometimes nearly down to freezing point on a cold night. And s
      reduce the temperature inside to freezing point in seconds. 'Imagine
```

Questions for students could include the following:

• Underline the lines where *freezing point* does not have *a* or *the* or *its* or *their* in front of it. In the lines, which words come before freezing point?
• Complete these sentences:
  The temperature dropped .... *freezing point.*
  The temperature rose .... *freezing point.*
  The temperature remained .... *freezing point.*
  The heater raised the temperature .... *near freezing point.*
• Look at the lines containing the phrase *the freezing point.* What words come after this phrase?
• Complete these sentences:
  The freezing point of alcohol is .... *than the freezing point of water.*
  .... *will lower the freezing point of water.*

Table 7.1 Data from a French–English parallel corpus of *Le Petit Prince*/*The Little Prince*: on

French	English
1. On en avale une par semaine et l'on n'éprouve plus le besoin de boire.	You need only swallow one pill a week, and you would feel no need of anything to drink.
2. Il faut s'astreindre régulièrement à arracher les baobabs dès qu'on les distingue d'avec les rosiers auxquels il ressemblent beaucoup quand ils sont très jeunes.	You must see to it that you pull up regularly all the baobabs, at the very first moment when they can be distinguished from the rose-bushes which they resemble so closely in their earliest youth.
3. On épargne cinquante-trois minutes par semaine.	With these pills, you save fifty-three minutes in every week.
4. Quand on veut faire de l'esprit, il arrive que l'on mente un peu.	When one wishes to play the wit, he sometimes wanders a little from the truth.
5. Quand le mystère est trop impressionnant, on n'ose pas désobéir.	When a mystery is too overpowering, one dare not disobey.
6. Ils répètent ce qu'on leur dit . . .	They repeat whatever one says to them . . .
7. Donc, quand la moralité de l'explorateur paraît bonne, on fait une enquête sur sa découverte.	Then, when the moral character of the explorer is shown to be good, an inquiry is ordered into his discovery.
8. On note d'abord au crayon les récits des explorateurs.	The recitals of explorers are put down first in pencil.
9. On attend, pour noter à l'encre, que l'explorateur ait fourni des preuves.	One waits until the explorer has furnished proofs, before putting them down in ink.
10. On s'assoit sur une dune de sable. On ne voit rien.	One sits down on a desert sand dune, sees nothing, hears nothing.
11. On risque de pleurer un peu si l'on s'est laissé apprivoiser. . .	One runs the risk of weeping a little, if one lets himself be tamed . . .
12. C'est dur de se remettre au dessin, à mon âge, quand on n'a jamais fait d'autre tentatives que celle d'un boa fermé et celle d'un boa ouvert, à l'âge de six ans!	It is hard to take up drawing again at my age, when I have never made any pictures except those of the boa constrictor from the outside and the boa constrictor from the inside, since I was six.
13. On disait dans le livre : "Les serpents boas avalent leur proie tout entière, sans la mâcher."	In the book it said: "Boa constrictors swallow their prey whole, without chewing it."

Table 7.1 (continued)

French	English
14. C'est très utile, si l'on est égaré pendant la nuit.	If one gets lost in the night, such knowledge is valuable.
15. S'il s'agit d'une brindille de radis ou de rosier, on peut la laisser pousser comme elle veut.	If it is only a sprout of radish or the sprig of a rose-bush, one would let it grow wherever it might wish.
16. Voici mon secret. Il est très simple: on ne voit bien qu'avec le coeur.	"And now here is my secret, a very simple secret: It is only with the heart that one can see rightly;
17. Tu sais . . . quand on est tellement triste on aime les couchers de soleil . . .	"You know – one loves the sunset, when one is so sad . . ."
18. Tantôt je me dis: "On est distrait une fois ou l'autre, et ça suffit!"	But at another time I say to myself: "At some moment or other one is absent-minded, and that is enough."
19. Quand on a terminé sa toilette du matin, il faut faire soigneusement la toilette de la planète.	When you've finished your own toilet in the morning, then it is time to attend to the toilet of your planet, just so, with the greatest care.
20. Or un baobab, si l'on s'y-prend trop tard, on ne peut jamais plus s'en débarrasser.	A baobab is something you will never, never be able to get rid of if you attend to it too late.

(adapted from Rézeau – http://www.uhb.fr/joseph.rezeau/concord.html)

The integration of activities of this kind into a lesson and a syllabus will be discussed below.

Reciprocal learning and parallel concordances

Perhaps one of the most exciting innovations in language teaching of recent years is the development of reciprocal learning. Reciprocal learning occurs when two language learners are paired, each helping the other learn their language. For example, a French speaker learning English may be paired with an English speaker learning French. Parallel corpora may be used to aid reciprocal learning, and they are also useful for teaching translation or for more conventional language-learning in situations where all learners share a common first language.

As an example, Table 7.1 shows some sentences extracted from parallel corpora in French and English, which have been identified by searching on the French pronoun *on*. This pronoun has several translation equivalents in English, and the examples in Table 7.1 are used to alert both English and French learners to this fact. (Note that these sentences have not been translated for the purposes of the exercise – they are the genuine translations made by the original translator.) This example comes from exercises written by Joseph Rézeau (http://www.uhb.fr/joseph.rezeau/concord.html; see Rézeau 2001 for more examples).

From the examples in Table 7.1 it can be seen that the French word *on* has been translated into English by *one* (4, 5, 6, 9, 10, 11, 14, 15, 16, 17, 18); *you* (1, 3, 19, 20); *I* (12); impersonal *it* (13); and by the passive (2, 7, 8). For the learner of French, this indicates that *on* has a wider range of uses than might be supposed. For the learner of English, it indicates that English has a range of expressions where French prefers the single word *on*.

A common objection to the use of parallel corpora is that the translations found are just that, translations, and that they may be less than felicitous. A present-day speaker of English may object to the frequent use of *one* in these examples, preferring perhaps *you* in example 11 or a paraphrase such as *Someone who is so sad loves sunsets* for example 17. Such examples can be discussed by the reciprocal learners. It is important that the translations are not assumed to be the only correct version, but that they indicate a range of possibilities.

Another example, this time from Tim Johns' web-site (http://www.bham.ac.uk/johnstf), is the French word *dont*, which I select because I personally find it extremely informative. A selection only is given in Table 7.2.

From these examples, learners are first asked simply to identify the various ways in which *dont* is expressed in English. Further tasks follow, focusing on the translations using *whose* and those using *of which*. The final task is to put missing words into French or English sentences. Here are a few examples:

(i) Dans la salle des États, oeuvres de la Renaissance dont la Joconde de Léonardo de Vinci.
In the Salle des États are Renaissance works, _____ the Mona Lisa by Leonardo da Vinci.

(ii) Hérodote advoua son ignorance de la façon dont le nom d'Europe fut donnée au continent occidental.
Herodotus admitted his ignorance of the way _____ which the name 'Europe' was given to the western continent.

Table 7.2: Data from a French–English parallel corpus: *dont*

French	English
'La Guerre des mondes' (1898) dont la libre adaptation sur les ondes par Orson Welles sema la panique aux Etats-Unis en 1938.	The War of the Worlds (1898), whose 1938 radio adaptation by Orson Welles created a wave of panic in the United States.
Inspiré par la pensée humaniste, le programme des décors, dont beaucoup ont été détruits, multipliait les allégories érudites, les références à la mythologie et à l'histoire antique ou contemporaine, ainsi que les louanges à la gloire du Roi.	Inspired by humanist thought, the allegorical decorations, many of which have been destroyed, represent mythology and ancient and modern history, as well as the glories of the king.
Traverser la cour de la Fontaine, dont l'eau pure était jadis réservée aux rois.	Cross the Fountain Courtyard, where the remarkably fresh water issuing from this fountain was reserved for the king.
De ce plan d'eau partent trois "rivières" dont le Rio Grande qui sépare l'Hotel Santa Fe et l'Hotel Cheyenne.	Three "rivers" run out of this lake, including the Rio Grande which separates the Hotel Santa Fe from the Hotel Cheyenne.
Dans la tradition française, les accouchements royaux étaient publics: dans cette chambre sont ainsi nés dix-neuf enfants de France, dont Louis XV et Philippe V d'Espagne.	In France, royal births were public events: in this room nineteen children of France were born, among them Louis XV and Philip V of Spain.

(adapted from Johns – http://web.bham.ac.uk/johnstf/dont.htm)

(iii) *"Nous sommes trop loin, effectivement," admit Ortiz, dont la voix _____.*
"In fact we are too far off," Ortiz admitted, his voice trembling.

(iv) *Drogo regardait se profiler sur la poussière de la route l'ombre nette des deux chevaux dont les têtes, à chaque pas, faisaient "oui oui".*
Drogo watched the clear-cut shadows of the two horses on the dust of the road, their heads _____ at every step.

(v) *L'héritage dont il s'_____ est un héritage contesté . . .*
The heritage in question is a disputed heritage . . .

As I mentioned above, I regard reciprocal learning and the use of parallel corpora as two of the most exciting innovations in language teaching and learning in recent years. Learners teaching each other are truly empowered, and are likely to be genuinely motivated to make discoveries about each other's language. The role of the teacher becomes that of materials-provider. My excitement about parallel concordances is a personal response to seeing English–French concordances, and finding from them enormous amounts of information about French. The use of *dont* before a noun phrase, translated as *including* or *among them*, and the use of *dont* + clause in translating 'their heads nodding' and so on were new to me. Moreover, this is not simply a matter of learning how to translate.[2] As a learner of French, having my attention drawn to these examples through their translations gives me a better 'feel' for how the word *dont* is used. The obvious restriction on reciprocal learning, however, is that it can be undertaken only in a context where there are students learning each other's language. This is not the situation in most contexts where English is being taught.

Corpora and language teaching methodology

Many teachers have two main reservations when considering the use of DDL in the classroom. The first is the means by which DDL can be integrated into the plan for an ordinary lesson. The second concerns the language points that seem to be the topic of DDL materials. These tend to deal with the minute details of the phraseology of particular words, and may be difficult to reconcile with the 'big themes' of language teaching, such as 'tenses' or 'articles'. In this section some answers to these questions are offered. The section draws largely on the work of Dave and Jane Willis in considering the place of corpus-based materials in language teaching.

DDL as consciousness-raising

DDL does not 'teach' a language feature, but presents learners with evidence and asks them to make hypotheses and draw conclusions. As an activity, it therefore fits best with a lesson that has such learner-centred activities built into it. An example of such an approach is the framework for task-based learning proposed by J. Willis (1996). Willis defines a task as 'a goal-oriented activity in which learners use language to achieve a real outcome' (1996: 53). She proposes a framework consisting of three stages (1996: 53):

---

2 It is interesting that Johns' proposals re-visit traditional grammar-translation methods.

Pre-task: Introduction to the topic and task
Task cycle: Task → Planning → Report
Language Focus: Analysis and practice

For the Language Focus stage, Willis and Willis (1996) propose that 'consciousness-raising activities' should be used, designed to draw learners' attention to some of the language features in the texts (written and spoken) that they have been engaged with when doing the task. Because a particular feature may occur only once or twice in the text, additional corpus material may be useful to help the learner to see a pattern rather than relying on a single occurrence.

As an example, here is one of the texts used as an illustration by Willis and Willis (1996: 71). It is a fairly simple (if frightening) story:

Auto-pilot

The flight ran several times a week taking holiday-makers to various resorts in the Mediterranean. On each flight, to reassure the passengers all was well, the captain would put the jet on to auto-pilot and he and all the crew would come aft into the cabin to greet the passengers.

Unfortunately on this particular flight the security door between the cabin and the flight deck jammed and left the captain and the crew stuck in the cabin. From that moment, in spite of efforts to open the door, the fate of the passengers and crew was sealed.

Willis and Willis suggest a variety of activities designed to encourage students to think about the lexis and grammar of the story. Below is an additional short sequence of activities, each one making use of corpus material in addition to the story itself.

The sequence begins by underlining the phrase: *left the captain and the crew stuck in the cabin*. This phrase from the story has been chosen because the verb *left* here occurs in a useful pattern, in which the verb is followed by a noun group and then by a past participle (*stuck*). Looking at the concordance lines for *LEAVE* in this pattern, it is striking that the past participles are usually words with a negative evaluation, such as *exhausted, crippled, paralyzed, shocked*. Here are some carefully selected examples:

The masked men left her bound and gagged.
A serious operation left her confined to a wheelchair.
A childhood illness has left her crippled . . .
The war left 300,000 homes destroyed.

The bitter winds left many anglers frozen to their seats.
An earthquake . . . killed around 170 people and left thousands homeless.

The subject may be a human being doing something intentionally (*the masked men*) but is more often an inanimate object without intentions (*a serious operation . . . a childhood illness*). The last example above uses a different but very similar pattern, in which the noun group is followed by an adjective instead of a past participle.

The teacher could draw attention to the pattern by asking learners to complete a table which isolates elements of the pattern, thus:

The security door	*left the captain and the crew*	*stuck in the cabin.*
A serious operation	*left her*	*confined to a wheelchair.*
The bitter winds	*left many anglers*	*frozen to their seats.*
An earthquake	*left thousands*	*homeless.*

This could be taken a step further by looking at other verbs with the same pattern. Here are some examples of *KEEP* and *FIND*:

Russian troops have kept the town sealed off since Saturday.
. . . a social life which kept us and others entertained . . .
I kept myself fit all summer.
She kept that world completely hidden from her friends.
He found himself immediately surrounded by opposing players.
Ray found himself charged with murder.
American soldiers found themselves hopelessly outnumbered.
At some point, he found himself drawn into conversation with Nina and her new friend.

Willis and Willis (1996: 66) refer to the 'grammar of class' as being an important component of pedagogic grammar. Here we are looking at a verb that belongs to a particular 'class': the class of verbs that are followed by a noun and a past participle or adjective.

Another important target of consciousness-raising mentioned by Willis and Willis is collocation. An example of a fixed collocation in the 'Auto-pilot' text is *fate . . . sealed*. This collocation is in danger of being missed by a reader of the text because the individual words are separated by a fairly long noun group: *of the passengers and crew*. (Lewis 1996: 14 makes the point that phenomena like this blur the 'word partnership'.) To make the word partnership, or collocation, clearer, the teacher might show these concordance lines:

These groups, who sealed the fate of President Marcos, have also lo
night appears to have sealed their fate. Buoyed up by the survival of t
Mr Wilson had sealed his fate shortly before the murder when he
nd that politics have sealed his fate – all these features being peculi

ncer that should have sealed the fate of the tan once and for all, we
of the border that sealed Collins' fate. And the other directors
If ever Sir Richard's fate was sealed it was at that moment
to happen. But now my fate was sealed. In the morning the
rian regimes, and its fate was sealed for a time by the defe
1945, and in 1951 its fate was sealed, even though Labour
Alas, they cried, our fate is sealed. For the sake
She was convinced her fate was sealed and so she shut her eyes

Having been asked to identify the common pattern in these lines, the learners can be asked to find a similar example in the reading text.

The pedagogic corpus

In the examples given above, the concordance lines are taken from the Bank of English. D. Willis (1993, cited in Willis and Willis 1996: 67) suggests an alternative source: what he calls the learner's pedagogic corpus. This consists of all the language that a learner has been exposed to in the classroom – mainly the texts and exercises that the teacher has used. If the teacher has used authentic texts with a class, the corpus will consist of authentic language. If specially written texts have been used, the corpus will consist of invented language. The advantage of a pedagogic corpus is that, when an item is met in one text, examples from previous (and future) texts can be used as additional evidence for the learner to draw conclusions. The disadvantage of the general corpus – the unfamiliarity of the language in it – is overcome. Instead the teacher draws together for the learner aspects of the learner's past language experience to enable the learner to see patterns.

As an example, here are some concordance lines extracted from the first 50 pages of a Malaysian coursebook in English for post-elementary students (Khong et al 1987). The first set of lines is for the word *at*. These lines are taken from all parts of the course book, that is, from the rubrics to students as well as from the reading samples in the book.

I think we should leave it at the office.
Turn right at the junction.
ppens around 9:15am on Saturday mornings at the following places?
e lives at 23 Jalan Berenang. Norliza studied at the SRJK Jalan Cawang.
Ramlee's family will move into the house at No.1 Jalan Kiambang.
The school office is at the end of the corridor.
At the end of the corridor, turn left
t time does the afternoon session start? At ten minutes past one.
Doesn't the class begin at 9 am?
ident that happened one Saturday morning at around 9:15am.

> She laughed as she looked at the timetable.
> notice board. Some students are looking at it excitedly.
> Look at these important benefits.
> Read the passage and look at the plan of the neighbourhood.
> How good are you at describing things. Let's find ou
> I've one brother, no sisters at all.

By this point in the course book, the learners have met *at* in the following contexts:

* to indicate place;
* to indicate time;
* after *look*;
* after *good*;
* in the frame *no . . . at all.*

If a teacher wants to draw attention to the use of *at* in a new text, these concordance lines could be used as supplementary information.

The second example comes from the second 50 pages of the same book. Suppose the learners now meet an '-ing' form following *when* (e.g. *When reading this passage,* . . .). The teacher wishes to remind them of this use of *when* and similar words. Here are the examples from the course book:

Put back the newspapers after reading them.
Look left, right and left again before crossing the road.
He has also written down what one should not do while playing the game.
When asking questions, ask only wh-questions.
A student dropped her purse when getting into the school bus.

These examples are somewhat stilted because none of the texts in this course book are authentic. They might be supplemented with a few genuine examples:

When buying a chair, you should first consider its function and the price.
If you suffer from headaches when reading . . .
When buying clothes for your baby, I'd definitely go for convenience . . .
Take care when using traditional remedies.
Wear rubber gloves when washing up.

Corpora and syllabus design

In this chapter so far we have been taking the view-point of the classroom teacher and materials writer, and we have seen the contribution that materials based on concordances may make to the language class. There are, however, wider issues at stake. If, as Sinclair (1991: 100) says, 'language looks different when you look at a lot of it at once', then the experience of using corpora should lead to rather different views of syllabus design. One type of syllabus whose design is based on concepts arising from corpus studies is the 'lexical syllabus'.

The notion of a 'lexical syllabus' was proposed in a paper by Sinclair and Renouf (1988), and finds its fullest exposition in D. Willis (1990). The term is occasionally (mis-)used to indicate a syllabus consisting only of vocabulary items, but as Sinclair, Renouf and Willis use the term, it comprises all aspects of language, differing from a conventional syllabus only in that the central concept of organisation is lexis. At its most simple, the argument is that it makes sense to teach the most frequent words in a language first. Sinclair and Renouf argue that 'the main focus of study should be on (a) the commonest word forms in the language; (b) the central patterns of usage; (c) the combinations which they usually form' (1988: 148). Their point is that the most frequent words have a variety of uses, so that learners acquire a flexibility of language fairly easily. In addition, the main uses of the most frequent words cover the main points of grammar, if in an unfamiliar form. Sinclair and Renouf quote *MAKE* as an example of a word with many uses, some of which are rarely covered in most beginners' courses. The most frequently occurring use of this verb is in combinations such as *make decisions, make discoveries, make arrangements*, rather than in the more concrete *make a cake* etc. In Sinclair's terminology, *MAKE* is used as a delexical verb more frequently than as an ordinary verb. An English course that focuses only on the concrete sense of *MAKE* denies the learner the opportunity to express sophisticated meanings with a simple verb.

Another example of a frequent word with multiple uses is *back*. This is a very frequent word: according to Sinclair 1999, it is 95th in frequency in the Bank of English, ahead of, for example, *get, may, how, think, even* and *us*. The reason for this frequency is that it is used in phrases such as *get the bus back, come/go back, look back, move back, turn back*, as well as as a noun: *behind your back, at the back*. Teaching the typical uses of *back* therefore introduces the learner to a large amount of language though not a massive vocabulary. Sinclair and Renouf make the point:

> Almost paradoxically, the lexical syllabus does not encourage the piecemeal acquisition of a large vocabulary, especially initially. Instead, it concentrates on making full use of the words that the learner already has, at any particular stage. It teaches that there is far more general utility in the recombination of known elements than in the addition of less easily usable items. (1988: 155)

Turning to the issue of grammar in a lexical syllabus, Sinclair and Renouf argue that in a lexical syllabus, a separate listing of grammatical items is unnecessary:

If the analysis of the words and phrases has been done correctly, then all the relevant grammar etc should appear in a proper proportion. Verb tenses, for example, which are often the main organizing feature of a course, are combinations of some of the commonest words in the language. (1988: 155)

D. Willis (1990) takes up the issue of lexis and grammar (see also chapter 6). He points out that 'English is a lexical language', meaning that many of the concepts we traditionally think of as belonging to 'grammar' can be better handled as aspects of 'vocabulary'. For example, the passive can be seen as *BE* plus an adjective or past participle, rather than as a transformation of the active (1990: 17). Conditionals can be handled by looking at the hypothetical meaning of *would*, rather than by proposing a rule about sequence of tenses, that often does not work (1990: 18–19). He also argues that what is traditionally termed 'grammar' can often be called 'pattern' (1990:51). For example, a pattern consisting of 'noun phrase + *am/ are/is + . . .ing*' is what is more usually called the present continuous tense. Other patterns that are less often treated as basic grammar might include other frequent words, such as *way*, e.g. *'the + adjective + way + of + . . .ing*' (*the best way of getting to Birmingham . . .*), *'the only way + that*-clause + *is/was + *to-infinitive clause*' (*the only way you'll do that is to get the train*). In other words, Willis argues that the most productive way to interpret grammar in the classroom is as lexical patterning and, conversely, that all patterns involving frequent lexical items are important in the classroom, not only those that are traditionally covered by 'grammar'. Because patterns attach to all lexical items in the language, learning the lexis means learning the patterns and therefore the grammar.

Perhaps Willis' most radical suggestion is that a syllabus can, in effect, consist of a corpus (1990: 70). In other words, if the course designer collects pieces of authentic language that contain instances of the most frequent patterns of the most frequent words, then that collection (corpus) will exemplify what the learner needs to know. The job of the teacher or materials writer, then, is to devise ways of encouraging the learner to engage with the material in the corpus (e.g. by setting tasks) and of helping the learning to 'notice' (Schmidt 1990; Bernadini 2000) the patterning of language (e.g. by consciousness-raising activities). A description of the syllabus would, in effect, be a description of the corpus. If the syllabus was expressed as a list of items, it would be as a list of the most frequent word-forms in the corpus, along with their most typical phraseologies. As the texts making up the corpus were presented to the learners, the syllabus would inevitably be covered. This alters the respective roles of the syllabus designer and materials writer quite considerably. Instead of the syllabus designer selecting items of language description and the materials writer choosing texts to illustrate them, the materials writer will choose interesting texts and the syllabus designer will keep a check on the balance of the overall collection of texts, ensuring that its most frequent word-forms, and their typical phraseologies, match what the learners require. Here, of course, there is an element of subjectivity. The syllabus designer may aim to mirror the distribution of structures, word frequency and phraseology in a larger, general corpus, or may decide that the learners' age, or specific needs, makes a different target corpus more appropriate. This subjectivity is no more than syllabus designers always employ, however, and has the advantage of making an appeal to principle, rather than to conventional wisdom. A syllabus of this kind would have the advantage of answering Long and Crookes' (1992: 33) objection that a lexical syllabus leads to artificial teaching materials if language is written specially to demonstrate key lexical items. Indeed, Willis' concept of a collection of texts is not dissimilar from the task-based syllabus proposed by Long and Crookes, though it would be a more concrete entity.

One problem in employing a corpus as syllabus is knowing how to describe the relevant frequencies in the corpus. A word-by-word account is very lengthy. One useful piece of supplementary information is a list of frequently occurring sequences. Sequences of this kind are of recent increasing interest to corpus linguists. De Cock et al (1998, also de Cock 1998) compare 'prefabs' in native-speaker and learner corpora, to test the hypothesis that learners tend not to use formulae as frequently as native speakers do. Biber et al (1999: 993–994) examine 'lexical bundles' in conversation and academic prose, using the Longman Grammar Corpus. They find that three-word bundles are much more frequent than four-word, that both kinds of bundles are more frequent in conversation than in academic prose, and that in conversation the bundles comprise more of the total word-count (28%) than they do in academic prose (20%). Some of the very frequent bundles in conversation include: *I don't know, I don't think, do you want, I don't want, don't want to, don't know what, and I said, I was going to, are you going to*; the frequent bundles in academic prose are, unsurprisingly, very different, and include: *in order to, one of the, part of the, the number of, the presence of, in the case of, on the other hand*.

D. Willis (1998) has done a similar study using the somewhat larger Bank of English corpus, but not differentiated by register. Some of the very frequent four-word combinations are:

Phrase	Number of occurrences	Phrase	Number of occurrences
the end of the	2,074	an awful lot of	514
a lot of people	1,834	in the middle of	510
nice to talk to	1,650	in the first place	477
that sort of thing	1,531	that kind of thing	441
a lot of the	1,189	this sort of thing	437
quite a lot of	1,098	per cent of the	392
a bit of a	1,089	got a lot of	389
end of the day	896	a little bit more	382
of the things that	654	a couple of years	366
the rest of the	608	a lot of time	351
a lot of money	595	a lot of things	346
a little bit of	570	most of the time	346
in terms of the	565	used to go to	337
to go to the	549	think a lot of	325
no no no no	536	to make sure that	324

The importance of these bundles or phrases is, firstly, that a syllabus designer working with a pedagogic corpus would wish to ensure that the corpus reflected these sorts of figures, if necessary differentiated by register, and secondly, that a materials designer would wish to draw attention to them as useful formulae for learners to use.

Challenges to the use of corpora in language teaching

Although corpora are widely acknowledged to be a valuable resource in describing language, there is less consensus on the value of corpus findings in the description of language for learners or on the use of corpus-based material in language classrooms. Among others, Widdowson (2000) and Cook (1998) have spoken against what they term an 'extreme' attitude towards using corpora in language teaching.[3] At the risk of over-simplification, their arguments can be summarised thus:

---

[3] For Widdowson, this is part of a more general argument against the uncritical use of theoretical linguistics in applied linguistics. Interestingly, Borsley and Ingham (forthcoming) regard corpora as the preoccupation of Applied Linguistics as opposed to theoretical linguistics.

1. A corpus is 'real language' only in a very limited sense. Language in a corpus is de-contextualised and must be re-contextualised in a pedagogic setting to make it real for learners. In Widdowson's (2000) terms, a corpus comprises traces of texts, not discourse.

2. Teachers (and course book writers etc) should not accept corpus evidence uncritically, but should appraise it in the light of other sources of information about language such as introspection and elicitation. In particular, frequency should not be the only factor in deciding what to teach: how salient a language feature is should also be taken into account, as should how highly valued a language item is. Learners should be encouraged to be creative in their language use, and should not be restricted to clichéd utterances.

3. Corpora tend to comprise the language of native speakers only, whereas many learners will never communicate with a native speaker and/or are not interested in native speaker norms. In particular, the details of phraseology or collocations may be unimportant to a non-native speaker of English. Too strong a dependence on corpora of native-speaker English tends to de-value the language of non-native-speakers and to perpetuate colonialist attitudes towards English.[4]

4. In a similar vein, learners should be allowed to approach language in a way they feel comfortable with. In many cases, this will be via grammatical rules and lists of lexical items. Learners should not be forced to approach English via 'lexical chunks' exclusively.

Some of these points can be taken as common ground. It would be very odd to suggest that language should not be contextualised within the classroom or that teachers should approach corpus evidence uncritically. Previous chapters in this book have stressed the need for caution in extrapolating from a corpus to a language and the importance of careful thought in interpreting corpus evidence. As Barlow (1996: 2) comments, 'using such powerful tools should not cause the researcher to become complacent and imagine that "language" is now in the computer'.

There are, however, three points here that deserve closer attention. These are: the issue of native-speaker corpora; the issue of frequency versus saliency, value and creativity; and the issue of lexis, grammar and 'lexical chunks'. Each of these will be dealt with in turn below.

I would not wish to argue against Cook's (1998) concern that

---

[4] See, for example, Hall and Eggington (eds.) 2000.

corpora tend to treat native-speaker language as overly valuable.[5]
Cook seems to imply, however, that the English of non-native
speakers (sometimes called International English, and exemplified by
interactions between a Japanese manufacturer and a Turkish whole-
saler) does not contain those features that corpus linguists claim for
native-speaker English, such as variation between registers, restric-
tions on co-occurrence, association between pattern and meaning,
and so on. Hunston and Francis (1999: 268–270) suggest that
although patterning in International English might be different from
that found in any native-speaker variety, it would still exist and be
worth teaching as patterning. Their argument is that the process of
'doing corpus research' has a value that is independent of the value of
the product on which that research is currently carried out. If
currently available corpora are inadequate, and in this respect they
very clearly are, then there is a strong argument for compiling more
adequate corpora, in this case of International English, rather than
simply abandoning corpora altogether. I suspect that compiling such
a corpus would be fraught with difficulties, ranging from 'Who
would consider such an enterprise worth funding?' to 'Whose
language should be collected?', but the very existence of such
questions, and the problems they raise, is itself usefully revealing of
attitudes towards International English.

The second interesting question that Cook raises is that of the
importance of frequency. It is very commonly argued by those who
advocate using corpus evidence in teaching that what is most
frequent should be taught first, and that learners' attention should be
drawn most to frequently occurring phenomena. The opposing
argument is that certain aspects of English are important even though
they are not frequent, either because they carry a lot of information
or because they have a resonance for a cultural group or even for an
individual. Wray and Perkins (2000, and citing Hickey 1993 and
Howarth 1998) make a similar argument when they suggest that a
sequence of words may constitute a 'formula' for an individual or a
cultural group, even if the sequence is attested only rarely. Items
which are important though infrequent seem to be those that echo
texts which have a high cultural value. A good example is the co-
occurrence of *death* and *adventure* in the following extract from J. K.
Rowling's *Harry Potter and the Philosopher's Stone*:

---

[5] It is worth adding, perhaps, that this argument applies only to English, because of its
unique hegemony in the modern world. Learners of French, German, Japanese etc might
be less disconcerted by having access to a corpus of language produced by native speakers
only.

Death is but the next great adventure.

For many (though not all) readers, *death* and *adventure* may effectively be collocates, because of an intertextual reference to the classic children's play *Peter Pan*, by J. M. Barrie, which includes the line:

To die will be an awfully big adventure.

There are a handful of similar instances in the Bank of English, some specifically quoting Barrie, but too few to have statistical significance. The resonance of Rowling's phrase, then, apparently comes from its cultural salience, not its frequency.[6]

In many cases, however, cultural salience is not so clearly at odds with frequency. Examples of salient items sometimes given are: proverbs such as 'Too many cooks spoil the broth'; slogans such as the American Express 'That will do nicely', which has a resonance arising from the frequency with which the advertisement was repeated and mimicked; and headlines such as 'Gotcha!' (the *Sun* newspaper's infamous response to the sinking of the Argentinian ship the Belgrano prior to the Malvinas/Falklands conflict in 1982). In each case, salience does seem to be reflected in statistical measures. *Spoil* is a significant collocate of *broth* (occurring two places to the left of *broth* with a high MI-score of 12, indicating a strong collocation, and a t-score of 3.3, indicating a certainty just above the cut-off point of 2), and the proverb is not only quoted but exploited with variation, as these concordance lines illustrate:

> Too many musical heroes can spoil the broth, but not on Bill Laswell's late
> cordon bleu chef might just spoil the broth. I don't think anybody really
> workers: Too many computers spoil the broth. WASHINGTON, DC
> Will one more TV cook spoil the broth? Not if it's TODAY columnist
> penicillin, and too many cooks spoil the book advances. When every other
> part of PR. Too many cooks spoil the menu; There's a recipe for

Similarly, *do* occurring immediately to the left of *nicely* has a t-score significance of 10.7, with most examples clearly echoing the advertising slogan, either directly or through exploitations such as *tatt will do nicely*, *data'll do nicely* or *American Express won't do nicely*. *Gotcha* occurs in the Bank of English 128 times, including in the phrase *gotcha journalism*.

In these examples, the corpus examples do not explain why a phrase is significant, but the frequency information does seem to follow the salience. The fact that salient phrases are often subject to variation is also illustrated, in turn showing that English is about creativity as well as cliché.

---

[6] I am grateful to Hsin Chin Lee for bringing this example to my attention.

Another aspect of saliency is discussed by Barlow (1996) and Shortall (1999), though not using that terminology. Barlow suggests that learners create schemata for grammatical features of a language, contrasting this with the 'parameter setting' hypothesis. These schemata are based partly on the evidence that the learner meets when experiencing authentic examples of the language, but also on the prototypes or expectations that the learner has about what meaning distinctions might be made. Arguing that both induction and expectation have a role in language learning, Barlow comments: 'the learner is not seen as just a passive pattern extractor, but is, in addition, a cognizer with the ability to make numerous cognitive distinctions' (1996: 17–18). Shortall goes further in relating this to teaching syllabuses. He points out that all language users have 'prototypes' about aspects of language use, and that these may conflict with the evidence of what is most frequent. For example, he finds that, when asked to produce a sentence with *there*, most people use a concrete noun and a prepositional phrase, as in *there are three books on the table*, whereas in the Bank of English corpus *there* constructions are more frequently used with abstract nouns and clauses, as in *there is evidence to suggest that* . . . Shortall expresses the teacher's resulting dilemma in the form of two conflicting statements: 'If concrete nouns are prototypical, and if this is the kind of noun people first think of, perhaps these should be taught first in EFL textbooks' and 'If abstract nouns are more frequent in real language (or in the corpus) perhaps these should be given priority.' He argues that prototypes are so strong that learners should be taught them first and only later introduced to the more frequent usages. In this, Shortall demonstrates the discerning attitude towards corpus evidence that Widdowson and Cook advocate.

The third point I wish to debate here is Cook's observation that learners should not be forced to restrict their learning experience to 'lexical chunks'. If a learner wishes to perceive English in terms of grammatical rules supplemented by vocabulary lists, she or he should be allowed to do so, and not be forced into ignoring rules and learning only phrases. If researchers into corpora did advocate a 'phrase-book' approach to language learning, then Cook's criticism would be legitimate, but this is far from the case. The essence of the 'idiom principle' and of 'units of meaning', as discussed in chapter 6, is that the patterning of language is more flexible and also more pervasive than the concept of 'lexical chunks' would suggest. Again, Barlow (1996: 15) expresses this well:

Part of the motivation for [this] approach . . . is a rejection of the distinction between a creative, compositional, productive component of the grammar and a component consisting of a collection of fixed idiomatic forms. The claim is that *most* of language consists of semi-regular, semi-fixed phrases or units . . . [words] have an affinity for each other and are linked together, but not so strongly as to form an identifiable lexical unit.

Barlow's discussion of the use of reflexive pronouns illustrates this phenomenon. Reflexive pronouns are used predominantly with some verbs rather than others (see Francis et al 1996 for detailed lists), but these do not constitute 'fixed phrases'.

Another point to be made here is that where phrases are advocated as a useful input to language learning (see, for example, the discussion of Willis above), the notion of language teaching is somewhat different to that apparently envisaged by Cook. It is not recommended that teachers 'present' phrases as a teaching item, but that phrases are among the variety of lexical and grammatical features which are amenable to consciousness-raising (D. Willis, personal communication). Thus, the learner's predilection for viewing language in a particular way is not thwarted, but may be encouraged to expand.

Widdowson argues that the importance of corpora 'lies not in the answers they provide but in the questions they provoke' (2000: 23). I would agree with the words here, though not in the way Widdowson means them: possibly the most far-reaching influence of corpora is not the individual observations that have been made using them, but the radical questions they have raised about the nature of language itself (see chapter 6). One of the questions provoked for Widdowson is 'If they do not represent real language for the learner, then what *does*?' (2000: 23). Given the ambiguity of this question, it is one that we can all probably agree is worth answering.

Conclusion

In this chapter, general issues concerning the way that corpora can inform classroom teaching have been discussed, as they affect the syllabus designer, the materials writer and the teacher. In the next chapter, more specific issues relating to language teaching will be taken up, focusing on English for Academic Purposes and language testing. The use of learner corpora will also be demonstrated.

8 Corpora and language teaching: Specific applications

This chapter looks at two specific applications of corpora: to English for academic purposes (EAP) and language testing, and at the specific area of learner corpora.

Corpora and EAP

For the teacher of English for academic purposes, the issue of 'what to teach' (as opposed to 'how to teach') is of particular significance. If a student is required to write an essay, a thesis, or an academic paper, what are the salient features of those genres that the student needs to be aware of? One answer to this question is to be found in the work of genre analysts (e.g. Swales 1990; Bhatia 1993). Further information can come from corpus linguistics. Some of the most interesting work in this area focuses on very specific kinds of writing, such as academic papers in individual disciplines.[1]

In looking at some of the work in this area, I shall borrow Halliday's notions of the ideational and the interpersonal. Some corpus studies of the documents in academic disciplines focus on the typical phraseologies of these disciplines, and this leads them to a discussion of the ideational meanings made (e.g. Gledhill 1995; 1996; Luzon Marco 2000). Other studies focus on an interpersonal meaning (e.g. Hyland 1998; Charles in preparation), and compare disciplines to see how this meaning is made. Thus the two approaches, whether intentionally or not, highlight different kinds of variables in the discourse construction of a discipline.

Ideational meanings in EAP

Because corpora of articles from a particular discipline tend to be relatively small, researchers often begin their studies with the most frequent words, that is, the grammatical words. The aim of the study is not to investigate the use of these words themselves so much as the phraseologies of which they are a part. Because the words themselves

---

[1] Spoken academic English is now being investigated at the Universities of Michigan and Warwick.

are so frequent, their phrases are relatively frequent also, even if the individual lexical words occurring in these phrases are relatively infrequent.

Luzon Marco (2000), for example, takes Renouf and Sinclair's (1991) notion of 'frames' and examines the most frequently occurring frames in a corpus of medical research articles. One of these is *the . . . of*, which is used with nouns expressing particular meanings:

* measurement and quantification, such as *the amount of, the degree of, the extent of, the frequency of, the majority of, the rate of*;
* medical procedures, such as *the addition of, the administration of, the diagnosis of*;
* qualities or properties, such as *the ability of, the abnormality of, the effectiveness of*;
* existence or non-existence, such as *the absence of, the lack of, the occurrence of, the presence of*;
* a moment of time in a process, such as *the beginning of, the end of, the onset of*;
* focus on an aspect of the research, such as *the cause of, the effect of, the risk of*.

Other frames examined in the same way include *BE . . . to, a . . . of, we . . . that* and *the . . . that*. In this way the typical phraseology of the discipline is established.

Gledhill (1995; 1996) uses a small, very specialised corpus of research articles in the field of cancer research. The corpus is divided so that titles, abstracts, and the sections Introduction, Method, Results and Discussion can be treated separately, allowing comparisons to be made between them. Gledhill uses the 'Keywords' program in the Wordsmith Tools package of corpus software (Scott 1996; and see chapter 4). Using this program on each sub-corpus compared with the whole corpus, Gledhill identifies words which are most significantly found in each part of the research article. He notes, for example, that in method and results sections, the following kinds of words are significant (1995: 19):

* research process verbs such as *added, performed, incubated, obtained, dried*;
* verbs of observation such as *shown, described, reported, expected*;
* specific methodological terms such as *solution, temperature, buffer*.

In introduction and discussion sections, however, these words are significant:

- auxiliaries, including modals, such as *is, would, might*;
- items which signal cohesion and the logical connection between one part of the discourse and another, such as *because, then, each*.

Gledhill then obtains concordance lines for the grammatical items that are frequent in each of the research article sections. As discussed above, he chooses grammatical items because these demonstrate lexical patterning in a small corpus. For example, *a lot of, several of, a great deal of* would all be found in concordance lines for *of* even if the number of instances of *lot, several, great* or *deal* was each fairly small. A few examples of the many phraseologies found by Gledhill for the preposition *in* (1996) in different sections of the research article are as follows:

- In abstracts, one use of *in* is in expressions of measurement, such as: *significant increase in toxicity; reduction in levels; differences in cytotoxicity; decrease in uptake.*
- Another use in abstracts is in the phrase *in the treatment of*, which in turn frequently follows an expression defining the use of a new drug, as in: *APD a commonly used drug in the treatment of cancer; [drug X] is a new H2 used in the treatment of cancer; [drug X] is a recent antagonist used in the treatment of gastric and duodenal cancer.*
- In results sections, one use of *in* is in comparative expressions indicating an increase, as in *increase in, higher concentrations in*. The phrase *increase in* in turn often follows a verb showing a result: *resulted in an increase in, produced a linear increase in, led to an overall increase in* and so on. The whole sequence typically occurs after a noun group indicating an experimental treatment and before a noun group indicating a measurable experimental outcome, as in: *treatment with butyrate resulted in an increase in relative tumor weights; 2 weeks' exposure produced a linear increase in the total number of tumors; treatment with carcinogens led to an overall increase in alkaline phosphase activity* and so on.
- In discussion sections, one phrase involving *in* is PLAY *a . . . role in*. The noun *role* is modified by an adjective such as *major, important*, and there is often modality in the sentence, indicating that this phrase is used to express a judgement on the part of the writer. Examples are: *Our findings suggest that CsA might play a role in the differentiation of cells; . . . accumulation of p53 alterations may play an important role in regulation of the cells.*
- Another phrase frequent in discussion sections is BE *present in*, which is typically used to talk about substances or changes, and which is not typically used with modality. Examples are: *. . . p53*

mutations were present in the majority of cancer cells; . . . a small amount of contaminating mouse skin was present in the tissue.

There are four main points that need to be made about Gledhill's work. Firstly, he points out that variation exists between the sections of a research article. It is not possible to make a connection between the presence of a word and its significance without knowing which section the word occurs in. Secondly, he shows how phraseology builds up. For example, *in* is used in the phrase *an increase in*, which is part of a larger phrase beginning with a verb such as *produced* or *led to*, which in turn is part of the larger phraseology exemplified by *2 weeks' exposure produced a linear increase in the total number of tumors.* The actual wording of this sentence may well be unique, but phrases similar to each of its component parts are frequently found. When one typical phrase leads on to another, Gledhill terms the phenomenon 'collocational cascade' (1995: 24).

Thirdly, Gledhill's work suggests that in approaching choices between present and past tense, for example, the teacher may be better advised to concentrate on phraseology rather than time reference. In abstracts, for example, *is* is used in two ways: in expressions with *there* such as *there is no evidence, there is no indication, there is no significant difference*; and in expressions with *it* such as *it is apparent that, it is expected that* and so on. The past tense *was* is not used in these ways but forms passives with past participles indicating the process of research (*was observed, was found, was studied* etc) or indicating a biochemical process (*was metabolically expressed, was immunologically reacted* and so on). In other words, *is* and *was* do not occur in similar environments, suggesting that for the writer they do not constitute a paradigm from which a choice needs to be made. (This point was discussed in chapter 6 under the heading 'How far can you go?'.) Finally, Gledhill makes the point that phraseology is not 'neutral' or accidental but is interwoven with the ideology of the discipline under study. This point is taken further by writers concerned with comparisons between disciplines.

According to Swales (1990), a genre is the voice of a discourse community and, conversely, a discourse community may be defined as the people who participate in the production of certain genres. Examining the professional writing in, say, history or biology, should give a profile of the concerns of the discourse community in question. Conrad (1996; Biber et al 1998) notes that history research articles have more of the features associated with narrative than ecology ones do, although they score much lower on the 'narrative –

non-narrative' dimension than fiction does. This is because history articles mix narrative concerns (what happened) with interpretation (what it means). Comparing the two disciplines in terms of impersonality, ecology comes out higher than history. History has relatively more non-impersonal features because the subject matter of history discourse is often 'people' and their activities. The actions and ideas of the researchers, however, are written about as impersonally in history as in ecology.

Williams (1998) uses collocation to compare research papers in two disciplines – molecular biology of parasitic plants and physiology of parasitic plants – and papers in which the members of each discourse community (and others) come together at a conference to form a third community with an interest in a common topic. Williams (1998: 154) comments:

> In so far as the lexis of a discourse is not stable, but changes in function of [sic] the needs of that community, the language tends to change in the same direction or break up as the D[iscourse] C[ommunity] breaks up to reform into new DCs with new frames of reference.

In other words, examining the collocates of key lexical items in two or three corpora can help to indicate the relationship between the discourse communities that produced the corpora. Williams takes items that appear frequently in each corpus, such as *DNA* and *plants*, finds their collocates and the collocates of those collocates, ending up with a network of connected items. These networks can then be compared between the discipline-based discourse communities and the topic-based community. In the molecular biology corpus, *plants* is part of the network for a more important item *genes*. Williams notes that this is to be expected, as molecular biologists are concerned with the cell structure of plants, not with individual plant species. Collocates to the left of *plants* reflect molecular biological concerns: *higher, land, host, parasitic, autotrophic* and *photosynthetic*. In the topic-based corpus, *plants* is the centre of a large network with a wide range of left collocates, including those also found in the molecular biology corpus, but also including items such as *field, flowering, tobacco* and *tomato*. In short, the collocations in the topic-based corpus reflect the varied concerns and methods of the different discipline discourse communities.

Interpersonal meaning in EAP

The studies of Luzon Marco, Gledhill, Conrad and Williams highlight those words and phrases which constitute the Field of the discipline concerned (using Halliday's terminology). They explore in great detail what it is that a discipline is about, and how it differs from related disciplines. Other researchers focus on the way that the writers in different disciplines construct their relationship with their readers: what might be called the interpersonal meanings made in the discourse.

Hyland (1998) studies the broad semantic category of 'hedging' in a corpus of Biology research articles, compared with a more general corpus of scientific English and the academic components of the Brown and LOB corpora. His quantitative studies of items such as modal auxiliaries (*may, might, could* and so on), epistemic lexical verbs (*SUGGEST, INDICATE* and so on), and epistemic adjectives, adverbs and nouns (*possible, possibly, possibility* and so on) suggest that hedging is all-pervasive in research articles. Drawing on work by sociologists of science such as Latour and Woolgar (1979) and of discourse analysts such as Myers (1990), Hyland also suggests that the function of hedging is essential to what science is about. He points out that:

[a]ppropriate hedging . . . constitutes a central dimension in audience design and in negotiating the acceptance of claims between a writer and reader . . . Hedging in scientific discourse is not simply a means of distinguishing the factuality of claims, but is a rational interpersonal strategy, crucial to defining a relation with other researchers and their work. (1998: 63–64)

Hyland proposes a number of functions that hedging might perform in a research article, which might be briefly summarised as follows:

• To indicate the sometimes imprecise relation between what is said and what has occurred during empirical work, that is, the degree of fit between the word and the world (Hyland 1998: 164; see also Hunston 1993a: 61).
• To indicate the degree of confidence that the writer has in their claims (Hyland 1998: 166).
• To limit personal commitment when the writer is taking risks, such as when a novel claim is being made, or other researchers are being criticised. This enables writers to make as strong a claim as is possible, as early in the research process as possible, while being protected from the negative consequences of the claim subsequently being disproved (Hyland 1998: 176).
• To construct a persona for both the writer and the reader as individuals conforming to the norms of the scientific community. Hyland (1998: 178) describes writers as '[soliciting] collusion' and

'[conforming] to research community expectations' when presenting claims in a conventionally hedged form.

In short, for Hyland, hedging allows the writer to negotiate a set of relationships: between the proposition and the world, between the writer and the proposition, between the writer and the reader, and between the writer and their peers.

Charles (in preparation) takes a somewhat different approach from Hyland but in some respects enlarges on his concept of writer and reader persona, in different disciplines. She compares indicators of stance, such as evaluative adjectives and adverbs, personal pronouns, discourse labels, and connectors, in theses written by native speakers of English studying politics and materials science. She finds consistent differences between the two disciplines and interprets them in terms of the nature of the discourse community in each discipline. For example, Charles notes that adverbs such as *even, in fact, indeed, really* and *clearly, obviously, of course* are much more frequent in her politics corpus than in her materials science corpus. These adverbs compare what is said with what is expected, either contrasting the two (as in <u>*Even*</u> *Churchill remained unwilling to oppose Eden in Cabinet meetings*) or showing alignment (as in *The Suez war is <u>obviously</u> the case in point*). Charles describes adverbs such as these as 'consensus-building', in that they indicate what attitude a member of the discourse community is expected to have (that Churchill could be expected to oppose Eden; that the Suez war is a good example of a particular phenomenon). The thesis writer in each case shows great skill in subtly demonstrating a knowledge of the background discourse of the discipline. Why are these adverbs more frequent in politics than in materials science? Charles argues that it is because in politics the discipline advances through argument, whereas in materials science it advances through an accumulation of empirical data. It is therefore more crucial that the writer in politics sets his or her argument in the context of what the discipline expects. In Charles' materials science corpus, on the other hand, adverbs such as *generally, usually* and *typically* are more frequent than they are in the politics corpus. Charles suggests that this reflects the concern with accumulation of knowledge in science disciplines.

The techniques of corpus investigation are ideally suited to examining specific, fairly homogenous discourses. Specialised corpora can be compiled relatively easily and connections can be made between the phraseology of the discourse and the ideology of the discourse community. The results are clearly applicable to the needs of those seeking to be socialised into that community.

Corpora and language testing

It is only recently that corpus studies have assumed significance in the world of language testing, and the work reported here is mostly in its early stages.

One role that corpora can play in language testing is by allowing a measurement of typicality of the materials used, whether or not these have been specially written for the test. Several major projects in the US are currently investigating the kinds of text often used in the TOEFL test in order to establish criteria for the kind of language that should appear in them. One example is the investigation of modals in service encounters, with the aim of having service encounters in tests comply with genuine usage as far as possible (Clark and Friginal forthcoming).

Another preoccupation of large testing organisations is the quality of the marking of tests, particularly when the marking is to some extent holistic, as is the case when essays or spoken interactions are assessed. The assessor relies on judgement, rather than on a single 'right answer', to give a mark. Even when there is a high degree of inter-assessor reliability it may be difficult to tell which factors in the testee's performance are influencing the assessors most. A study currently being undertaken for the UCLES examinations board compares high- and low-scoring essays written for the IELTS test, to establish what features differentiate them. The findings might be used to assess the validity of the test, in that the significant features can be compared with the expectations of educational institutions that use IELTS as an entry qualification.[2]

Finally, testing procedures can be developed which utilise corpus-based findings about language. Rees (1998), for example, has developed cloze tests in which the deleted item is selected on the basis of the presence or absence of collocates in the test text. This allows deletion to be 'rational' rather than arbitrary, yet able to be applied in a principled way, rather than simply in accordance with the intuition of the tester. Rees has established that items selected on the basis of

(a) their frequency in a large general corpus,
(b) the strength of collocation in the test text,
(c) the amount of repetition of the target word in the text, and
(d) the word-class

---

[2] This work is being carried out by Chris Kennedy, Tony Dudley-Evans and Dillys Thorpe at the University of Birmingham.

give good results in terms of discrimination between strong and weak test candidates.

Rees' work demonstrates that the insights about language derived from corpora can be used to test aspects of learners' work that might have gone unnoticed before. Howarth (1998) examines essays written by learners of English for correct and incorrect uses of restricted lexical collocations (such as *blow a fuse*), in which one item has a small range of collocates when used with a particular meaning. He attempts to correlate his results with the learners' test scores, but finds that the one is a poor predictor of the other. He comments that:

> it could be that appropriate collocational performance, in the sense of approximating to NS norms of conventionality, is a highly individual matter of style, which follows a quite separate path of development from measurable levels of general language proficiency. (Howarth 1998: 36)

Further insights from studies of learner language will be considered in the next section.

The evidence of learner corpora

This section deals with corpora composed of the speech or writing of people who are learning a language, in this case English. These corpora can give information about the difference between learners and between learners and native speakers. The most important work in this area has been done by Sylviane Granger of the Université Catholique de Louvain in Belgium, whose edited volume (Granger ed. 1998) contains papers reporting most of the research done on comparisons between native-speaker English and learner English. (See also Flowerdew 2000; Seidlhofer 2000.)

The essence of work on learner corpora is comparison: between corpora produced by different sets of learners, and between corpora produced by learners and those produced by native or expert speakers. Comparability between the corpora is important. Many of the papers in Granger (ed. 1998) use the International Corpus of Learner English (ICLE) database. This comprises 500-word non-technical argumentative essays produced by advanced learners of English as a foreign (not second) language who are studying English language and literature at undergraduate level and who are about 20 years old (Granger 1998b: 9–10). The ICLE database is divided into corpora, each produced by learners from one country or with one first language. Each corpus comprises 200,000 words. For the native-speaker data, the studies use the LOCNESS Corpus, which is a collection of essays of a type similar to those in ICLE, written by undergraduate students in Britain and the US. The LOCNESS Corpus comprises 300,000 words (Granger 1998b: 13).

The studies in Granger's collection are quantitative rather than qualitative in nature, but there are interesting qualitative generalisations to be made. Firstly, as might be expected, the learner corpora show a greater use of a smaller range of vocabulary items. The most frequent lexical words in the corpora of learner English account for a greater proportion of the total text than in the corpus of native-speaker English (Ringbom 1998). For example, the verb *THINK* occurs 6 times per 10,000 words in the native-speaker corpus, but between 21 and 30 times per 10,000 words in the French, Spanish, Finish, Swedish and German corpora. Similar findings occur if two-, three-, four- and five-word combinations ('prefabs') are considered (de Cock et al 1998). Learners and native speakers both use these prefabs, but learners tend to use the same ones more frequently. Altenberg and Tapper (1998) find that Swedish speakers of English use a few, informal, connectors, such as *but*, with great frequency, but others, such as *however*, *though* and *yet*, less frequently than native speakers do.

A second set of findings relates to the style of the discourse. Learners tend to use certain vocabulary items of high generality, such as *people* and *things*, with a very high frequency (Ringbom 1998), giving their discourse a sense of vagueness. On the other hand, they use prefabricated phrases such as *and stuff like that* or *sort of thing* less frequently than native speakers do, reducing the sense of vagueness (de Cock et al 1998). Lorenz (1998) notes that learners tend to modify adjectives more frequently than native speakers do, giving their discourse a sense of 'over-statement' and of too much information. Flowerdew (2000) concurs that a corpus of Hong Kong learners' writing shows an underuse of hedging devices, leading to writing that is 'too direct' (2000: 151).

More specifically, several papers suggest that learners use features which are more typical of spoken English than of academic written English. Petch-Tyson (1998) finds that learners use features associated with high writer/reader involvement, such as pronouns, emphatic particles, and reference to the situation of writing or reading. In other words, their written prose is more interactive than is typical in the native-speaker corpus. Similar findings come from Granger and Rayson's study of the distribution of word-classes in the ICLE and LOCNESS corpora, where the learner use of nouns, verbs and pronouns is more similar to that expected in speech than that typical of academic written English (Granger and Rayson 1998).

Aarts and Granger (1998) study the most frequent sequences of word-class tags in the various corpora. Among their findings are that the learners use sentence-initial sequences such as *But today, But anyhow, And so, And still*, which are informal rather than formal, more than native speakers do under the same circumstances. They use sequences with prepositions, associated with heavily packed noun phrases, less frequently than native speakers do.

All of this is confirmed by Biber and Reppen's (1998) study, although they approach comparability of register more explicitly. They use the Longman Learner Corpus, which is a collection of essays written by intermediate and advanced learners of English, but instead of comparing the output with a comparable corpus of essays written by native speakers, they use the Longman Grammar Corpus, the much larger corpus of native-speaker texts divided into four registers (academic, fiction, journalism and conversation) mentioned in chapter 5. Although they cannot compare like with like directly, they have the advantage of being able to compare the learners' essays with a variety of English registers. Their study focuses on complementation clauses, that is, that-clauses, to-clauses, *ing*-clauses and *wh*-clauses following verbs such as *THINK, SAY, KNOW, SHOW* and *HOPE*. In the Longman Grammar Corpus, that-clauses following *THINK, SAY* and *KNOW* are much more frequent in conversation than in academic prose. *HOPE* is rarely used in either register with a that-clause. All these patterns occur frequently, however, in the corpora of essays written by native speakers of French, Spanish, Chinese and Japanese. In other words, *THINK that, SAY that* and *KNOW that* are used in a way that is more like English conversation than English academic prose, whilst *HOPE that* is used with a frequency that is unlike any register of English. Comparisons such as these make it possible to make hypotheses about interference from other registers of English as well as about over-generalisations or transfer from other languages.

Although these results are interesting, it is not always easy to see how they could be translated into pedagogic issues. In the case of some underused items (for example, nouns that summarise bits of text, such as *argument, controversy*), it is possible to imagine teaching materials that would focus on these items. It would also be possible to compile lists of frequently used adverb-adjective combinations that might point learners away from combinations such as *absolutely easy*. In many cases, however, more investigation is needed before advice to learners can be given. For example, if a group of learners overuses *thing*, there is no point in simply saying 'Use *thing* less often'. The teacher would need to know the precise circumstances when native speakers would typically choose an alternative to *thing*, and what that alternative would be.

More immediately practical, perhaps, (though see the discussion of Granger and Tribble's paper below) is Flowerdew's (1998) discussion of expressions of cause and effect in a corpus of learner English and one composed of comparable native-speaker texts. She finds that learners use *because* and *therefore* more frequently than native speakers, who prefer reduced relative clauses (such as *resulting in* . . .). In addition, words such as *therefore* are used to link two clauses by learners, whereas the native speakers use them to make more global discourse links. The word *reason* is used by learners to give a reason, whereas native speakers prefer the alternative use, in which *reason* indicates the presence (or absence) of a reason, but not the reason itself, as in *there are many reasons* and *there is no reason why* . . . Such differences, linked to a specific language function, provide a useful starting point for materials preparation.

Examples of concordance-based materials using a learner corpus and a comparative native-speaker corpus are given in Granger and Tribble (1998). Likely sources of error are first identified by comparing the two corpora in statistical terms. Then comparable concordance lines are used to encourage the learners to be aware of the differences between native and non-native usage. One example is based on the patterns following the verb *accept*. The concordance lines from the native-speaker corpus show that *accept* is followed by a noun (e.g. *learn to accept their traditions*) or by a that-clause (e.g. *Hugo cannot accept that the party line has changed*). The learner corpus lines include examples of *accept* followed by a to-infinitive (e.g. *He could never accept to be inferior*). Learners are asked to notice the different patterns and, presumably, change their own usage so that it is more like the native-speaker usage.

Another example given by Granger and Tribble is based on the observed overuse of certain adjectives, such as *important*, in the learner corpus. As noted above, it is probably not useful to tell learners not to use *important* as much as they do. Instead, Granger and Tribble advocate finding the alternatives to *important* that native speakers use and which the learners should start using more. They provide concordance lines from a native-speaker corpus based on words such as *serious, major* or *critical*. Then, concordance lines which include *important* are taken from the learner corpus. The node word, *important*, is removed, and learners are asked to replace it with one of the alternatives suggested: *critical, crucial, major, serious, significant* and *vital*.

These examples illustrate the need to identify what resources both

Table 8.1. Comparative frequencies of modals in the EVA corpora

Modal verb	Corpus of learners' spoken English	Corpus of native speakers' spoken English
can	245	111
could	39	30
may	12	1
might	5	13
must	41	6
should	57	28
will	56	13

learners and native speakers have at their disposal and to make comparisons between them. To demonstrate this further, I shall use data from the EVA corpus available on the worldwide web (http://kh.hd.uib.no/eva/). The corpus consists of transcripts of Norwegian 14- and 15-year olds performing various information-transfer and discussion tasks in English. There is also a corpus of British schoolchildren performing the same tasks. A comparison of some modal verbs in the two corpora reveals some surprising differences in frequency, as Table 8.1 shows.

The learners use more of these modals than the native speakers do; in particular *can, must, should* and *will* occur more frequently in the learner corpus than in the native-speaker corpus. Closer examination shows differences that are more interesting than the simple frequency. For example, the modal verb *should* is used by both groups to express obligation, in a context of giving an opinion about parents' authority over children. The following example is from the learner corpus, but is typical of both:

I think parents should decide er what time the teenagers would come in and er it should be a agreement between the the parents and the teenager.

There are also, however, clear divergences of usage. The native speakers use *should* to indicate that something is probably the case or, more specifically, that something will happen if all goes well, or if the speaker has gauged the situation correctly. Examples are as follows:

[about taking a dog for a walk] half an hour should do
that should be about right
he should be back soon
if you go to the second drawer it should be there

This is the second most frequent use of this modal for the native speakers, but it is rarely used by the learners.

Conversely, the learners frequently use *should* when giving instructions for how a procedure, such as loading a washing machine, takes place. Examples are:

you are laying it with the things you should wash
you should decide which program
then you should pull the button

The native speakers do not use *should* in this way. The equivalent set of instructions in the native-speaker corpus is expressed like this:

it's got buttons on it and it erm puts it on different cycles and that, and you put your clothes in and you shut the door.

Here instruction is expressed through a description of the machine and the process.

The difference between the two groups is perhaps best exemplified by two pairs of examples, in which the speakers use *should* in similar contexts, but with a different meaning:

1a (learner): the train you <u>should</u> take comes to Birmingham it leaves at 15:37 and arrives at Birmingham at 19:10
1b (native speaker): then to get from Coventry to Slode, use a taxi. that <u>should</u> take you there to my house
2a (learner): first of all you <u>should</u> know where the necklace (= dog lead?) is, it's behind the door and the dog food is in . . .
2b (native speaker): if I go in door, I go to the kitchen, I <u>should</u> find the dog food. is that right

In both cases, the learner uses *should* to indicate obligation or need, whereas the native speaker uses it to indicate what can reasonably be expected to happen. Although the learners in this corpus have used *should* so much, they are still restricted in the range of meanings they can make with this modal. They also appear to be restricted in the means at their disposal for expressing certain meanings, such as how to carry out a process.

The drawback to Granger's approach, and the *should* example above, is that is assumes that learners have native-speaker norms as a target. The writers in Granger's book use the verbs 'overuse' and 'underuse' when comparing learners' discourse with that of native speakers. Leech (1998: xix–xx) comments:

[These terms] should not be used in a judgmental spirit. They should be interpreted, to my mind, not prescriptively but descriptively, as a convenient shorthand for 'significantly more/less frequent use by NNSs [non-native speakers] than by NSs [native speakers].

These comments notwithstanding, it is difficult sometimes to remember that information about differences between learner and native-speaker usage is not necessarily to be taken as a criticism of the learners involved.

On the other hand, the use of corpora in this context has two major advantages over other methods of examining learner language use. Firstly, it makes the basis of the assessment entirely explicit: learner language is compared with, and if necessary measured against, a standard that is clearly identified by the corpus chosen. If that standard is considered to be inappropriate (if, for example, the appropriate target for Norwegian schoolchildren is considered to be expert Norwegian speakers of English rather than British speakers of English), then the relevant corpus can be replaced. Secondly, the basis of assessment is realistic, in that what the learners do is compared with what native/expert speakers actually do rather than what reference books say they do. Many of the parameters of difference noted, such as vocabulary range, or word-class preference, do not appear in most grammar books.

Conclusion

This chapter has provided further evidence for the importance of corpora for language teaching. It has shown how relatively small but highly specialised corpora can be used in certain situations, for example in describing the language of specific discourse communities or in comparing native-speaker and non-native-speaker usage. The chapter has highlighted once again the need to move between quantitative information, which can alert the user to potential points of interest, and qualitative information, which is needed to provide explanation of those points.

9 An applied linguist looks at corpora

In this final chapter I shall try to answer briefly the question: What difference have corpora made to the working lives of applied linguists?

1. Corpora have made language investigations possible that were not possible before

Examples of new possibilities include all kinds of quantitative linguistic work, such as obtaining accurate frequency counts for words, lemmas and grammatical features, or comparing one speaker/ writer's usage against a norm. This can be used to identify register differences, or to characterise the style of an individual writer, with applications in literary stylistics, forensic linguistics and literary translation.

2. Corpora have changed the way we look at language and, for teachers at least, the way we see our own roles

In terms of language, new concepts such as the 'unit of meaning' or 'semantic prosody' are dependent on the availability of large quantities of language which can be manipulated electronically. These concepts in turn bring into question traditional language units such as the phrase and the clause.

For the language teacher, data-driven learning and reciprocal learning necessitate a re-evaluation of the teacher's role. More generally, whatever role a corpus plays in the learning process, the very activity of designing and compiling corpora forces attention upon the assumptions in place. Without an explicit corpus, for example, the question of what varieties of English a learner should have as a model may remain implicit, or may be different in theory and in practice. If, however, a pedagogic corpus is designed, the question of what goes into that corpus cannot be fudged.

Corpora can be authoritarian or empowering. If they are thought to contain all that is possible in a language, their use may hamper creativity. Learners (or teachers) may even think they should not say anything which is not attested in a corpus. More positively, corpora put into the hands of learners the raw data which lie behind pedagogic assertions. Even where corpus data is mediated, there are increasing possibilities for revealing the evidence that lies behind statements of language description. For example, electronic dictionaries may give, not only definitions and a few examples, but samples of concordance lines. Learners may choose to compile their own corpora, thereby selecting for themselves the kind of English they wish to have access to. Of course, the downside to these developments is that they are dependent on resources which are relatively costly – computers, Internet access, a consistent electricity supply and so on. The empowerment of corpora may be restricted to the rich, or at least to the relatively well off.

3. Corpora have made life simpler

With a corpus, a translator can see quickly to what extent words that seem to be translations of each other are in fact equivalent. A critical linguist who wishes to investigate, say, a writer's use of modal verbs can easily get all those modals together in one place for inspection. The act of evidence gathering is made simple, freeing the researcher's effort for the act of interpretation. A teacher wishing to demonstrate to a learner why a particular usage is incorrect can show evidence instead of resorting to tortuous, and possibly inexact, explanations. In these and other ways, the life of the applied linguist is made simpler by the use of corpora. On the other hand . . .

4. Corpora have made life more complex

With corpora we can see that language is patterned in a much more detailed way than might have been suspected. A simple, general rule of thumb often turns out to apply only in certain contexts. Here is an example: the final one in this book, and from personal experience. A student of mine writes that a particular author *is under the influence of Halliday*. This strikes me as odd, indeed comically so, and using intuition I correct the phrase to 'is influenced by Halliday', adding a helpful note that *under the influence of* is used only of bad things such as alcohol and drugs. Later, I consult the Bank of English corpus. To my dismay, I find that although examples such as *under the influence of alcohol* and *under the influence of drugs* are the most typical, there are also numerous examples that appear to be very like the student's, in that the influence is exerted by a person, and is positive rather than negative:

. . . Baker is improving steadily under the influence of Bill Ferguson, who used to coach Colin Montgomerie. (*Times*)

. . . As a gospel singer and evangelist, he came under the influence of C. I. Scofield. (US books)

. . . The Royal Herbert Hospital . . . built <u>under the influence of</u> Florence Nightingale in 1865 . . . (*Guardian*)

. . . he was awarded a scholarship to the department of landscape at the University of Pennsylvania, where he came <u>under the influence of</u> Ian McHarg, as did many other young landscape architects of his generation. (*Times*)

Closer examination of these examples suggests that the presence or absence of the verb *BE* may be a contributory factor. I therefore compare two phrases: *BE under the influence of* and *COME under the influence of*. In the case of *BE under the influence of*, the most frequent nouns following *of* are *alcohol, drink* and *drugs*. There are a few lines in which the noun following *of* indicates a person. In nearly every case there is evidence that the influence is not benign. Here are some examples:

. . . the only way that can be achieved is <u>under the influence of</u> a parent not so much supportive as desperate . . .

. . . girl was said to have been <u>under the influence of</u> an older woman, and killed Mr Sacco as 'a proof of her love' . . .

. . . only slightly less harmful was the disinformation spread by Louis Fischer who is said to have been <u>under the influence of</u> his wife . . .

Sports reporting provides the only exception:

. . . he knows the game and that's not surprising having been <u>under the influence of</u> Jim McLean when he was at the peak of his powers . . .

Turning to *COME under the influence of*, I find about half the number of instances as with *BE*, most of which have a noun indicating a person, group, or ideological position occurring after *of*. About half the lines indicate a bad influence, such as these:

. . . Hal Hartley's latest film is about a garbage collector, Simon, who comes <u>under the influence of</u> egomaniac Henry Fool . . .

. . . about a young man coming <u>under the influence</u> of a malign older man . . .

but the others indicate a good or neutral influence, e.g.:

. . . his early teaching career at Manchester University, where he came <u>under the influence of</u> the great historian of eighteenth-century political life, Sir Lewis Namier . . .

. . . like many of his contemporaries he also came <u>under the influence of</u> Raphael . . .

At the end of this search, then, my original intuition proves to be mainly but not entirely correct. Although the phrase *BE under the influence of* has a negative connotation, the phrase *COME under the influence of* can describe either a negative or a positive process. The corpus search led me along some interesting byways (not reported on here), such as the use of *influence* and *influenced* in science writing, which distracted from the point of the investigation and took some hours (and the search is not, of course, by any means complete). My intuitive response to the student took a few seconds.

For the applied linguist, then, a corpus provides a rich resource for investigating language. As a result, new ideas about language emerge and the old ones may need re-evaluation. Our own roles may change. In some ways, our lives become simpler: questions such as 'Under what circumstances is this expression preferred to that one?' become much easier to answer. On the other hand, our lives become more complex, simply because it is much harder to ignore the endless intricacy of language itself.

List of relevant web-sites

Note: Entering 'corpora and language teaching' into a search engine finds links to articles available on the world wide web and to details of conferences. Entering 'corpora and translation' finds a number of articles on parallel corpora and on translation.

http://www.ruf.rice.edu/~barlow/corpus.html
A collection of information about available corpora and software, with a lot of links to other sites.

http://www.sslmit.unibo.it/zanettin/cl.htm
A guide to software, available corpora, associations and conferences, with links to other sites.

http://www.rc.kyushu-u.ac.jp/~higuchi/text7/corpus.html
A collection of links to available corpora.

http://clwww.essex.ac.uk/w3c/general.html
Part of a project to make corpora available on the worldwide web. Includes information on corpora, available courses, and a bibliography.

http://web.bham.ac.uk/johnstf
Tim Johns' home page, with details of data-driven learning, parallel concordancing and reciprocal learning, as well as links to other sites.

http://www.uhb.fr/campus/joseph.rezeau/
Joseph Rézeau's home page, with information about concordancing and language teaching, and links to other sites.

http://www.liv.ac.uk/~ms2928/wordsmith/screenshots/
Mike Scott's home page, with information about Wordsmith Tools.

http://juppiter.fltr.ucl.ac.be/FLTR/GERM/ETAN/CECL/cecl.html
Information on learner corpora, including an extensive bibliography.

http://www.lancs.ac.uk/postgrad/tono/
A list of resources relating to learner corpora.

http://www.benjamins.com/jbp/journals/Ijcl_info.html
The web-site for the *International Journal for Corpus Linguistics*.

http://www.cobuild.collins.co.uk
Information about the Bank of English corpus and Cobuild publications.

http://info.ox.ac.uk/bnc/index.html
Information about the British National Corpus.

http://www.paddocks64.freeserve.co.uk/CompSIG2/callsig.htm
The web-site for the Computers Special Interest Group of IATEFL, an organisation of English language teachers interested in corpora and other applications of computer technology to language teaching.

http://www.hd.uib.no/icame.html
Information about the International Computer Archive of Modern and Medieval English – an organisation of linguists working with corpora.

References

Aarts J. and Granger S. 1998. 'Tag sequences in learner corpora: a key to interlanguage grammar and discourse' in Granger (ed.) 132–142.

Aarts J., van Halteren H. and Oostdijk N. 1998. 'The linguistic annotation of corpora: the TOSCA analysis system' *International Journal of Corpus Linguistics* 3: 189–210.

Adams D. 1979. *The Hitch Hiker's Guide to the Galaxy*. London: Pan.

Ahmed K. and Davies A. 1997. 'The role of corpora in studying and promoting Welsh' in Wichmann et al (eds.) 157–172.

Aijmer K. 1996. *Conversational Routines in English: Convention and creativity*. London: Longman.

Aijmer K. and Altenberg B. 1991. *English Corpus Linguistics*. London: Longman.

Altenberg B. and Tapper M. 1998. 'The use of adverbial connectors in advanced Swedish learners' written English' in Granger (ed.) 80–93.

Aston G. 1995. 'Say "thank you": some pragmatic constraints in conversational closings' *Applied Linguistics* 16: 57–86.

Baker M. 1993. 'Corpus linguistics and translation studies: implications and applications' in Baker et al (eds.) 233–252.

Baker M. 1995. 'Corpora in translation studies: an overview and some suggestions for future research' *Target* 7: 223–243.

Baker M. 1999. 'The role of corpora in investigating the linguistic behaviour of professional translators' *International Journal of Corpus Linguistics* 4: 281–298.

Baker M., Francis G. and Tognini-Bonelli E. (eds.) 1993. *Text and Technology: in honour of John Sinclair*. Amsterdam: Benjamins.

Barlow M. 1996. 'Corpora for theory and practice' *International Journal of Corpus Linguistics* 1: 1–37.

Barnbrook G. 1996. *Language and Computers: A practical introduction to the computer analysis of language*. Edinburgh: Edinburgh University Press.

Barnbrook G. and Sinclair J.M. 1995. 'Parsing Cobuild entries' in J.M. Sinclair, M. Hoelter and C. Peters (eds.) *Studies in Machine Translation and Natural Language Processing*. Luxembourg: European Commission. 13–58.

Barth D. 1999. 'Investigating the concessive relation in a corpus of spoken English discourse'. Paper read at the BAAL/CUP seminar 'Investigating discourse practices through corpus research: methods, findings and applications', University of Reading, May 1999.

Baugh S., Harley A. and Jellis S. 1996. 'The role of corpora in compiling the

Cambridge International Dictionary of English' *International Journal of Corpus Linguistics* 1: 39–59.

Bazerman C. 1988. *Shaping Written Knowledge: the genre and activity of the experimental article in science*. Madison, WI: University of Wisconsin Press.

Bernadini S. 2000. *Competence, Capacity, Corpora*. Bologna: CLUEB.

Bhatia V. 1993. *Analysing Genre: language use in professional settings*. London: Longman.

Biber D. 1988. *Variation in Speech and Writing*. Cambridge: CUP.

Biber D. 1992. 'Using computer-based text corpora to analyze the referential strategies of spoken and written texts' in Svartvik (ed.) 213–252.

Biber D. 1996. 'Investigating language use through corpus-based analyses of association patterns' *International Journal of Corpus Linguistics* 1: 171–197.

Biber D. and Finegan E. 1988. 'Adverbial stance types in English' *Discourse Processes* 11: 1–34.

Biber D. and Finegan E. 1989. 'Styles of stance in English: lexical and grammatical marking of evidentiality and affect' *Text* 9: 93–124.

Biber D., Conrad S. and Reppen R. 1998. *Corpus Linguistics: investigating language structure and use*. Cambridge: CUP.

Biber D., Johansson S., Leech G., Conrad S. and Finegan E. 1999. *Longman Grammar of Spoken and Written English*. London: Longman.

Biber D. and Reppen R. 1998. 'Comparing native and learner perspectives on English grammar: a study of complement clauses' in Granger (ed.) 145–158.

Borsley R.D. and Ingham R. forthcoming. 'Grow your own linguistics? On some applied linguists' views of the subject' *Lingua*.

Brien D. et al 1992. *Dictionary of British Sign Language/English*. London: Faber and Faber.

Brown P. and Levinson S. 1987 [1978]. *Politeness: Some universals in language usage*. Cambridge: CUP.

Burgess G.J.A. 2000. 'Corpus analysis in the service of literary criticism: Goethe's *Die Wahlverwandtsschafen* as a model case' in Dodd (ed.) 40–68.

Burnard L. (ed.) 1995. *Users' Guide to the British National Corpus* Oxford: Oxford University Computing Services.

Burnard L. and McEnery T. (eds.) 2000. *Rethinking Language Pedagogy from a Corpus Perspective*. Frankfurt: Peter Lang.

Burrows J.F. 1992. 'Computers and the study of literature' in C. Butler (ed.) *Computers and Written Texts*. 167–204.

Butler C. 1998. 'Collocational frameworks in Spanish' *International Journal of Corpus Linguistics* 3: 1–32.

Caldas-Coulthard C.R. 1996. ' "Women who pay for sex. And enjoy it": transgression versus morality in women's magazines' in C. Caldas-Coulthard and M. Coulthard (eds.) 250–270. Reprinted in A. Jaworski and N. Coupland (eds.) *The Discourse Reader*. London: Routledge. 523–540.

Caldas-Coulthard C.R. and Coulthard M. 1996. (eds.) *Texts and Practices: Readings in critical discourse analysis.* London: Routledge.

Caldas-Coulthard C. and Moon R. 1999. 'Curvy, hunky, kinky: using corpora as tools in critical analysis'. Paper read at the Critical Discourse Analysis Meeting, University of Birmingham, April 1999.

Cameron L. and Deignan A. 1998. 'Metaphor-signalling devices in talk', paper read at the 31st BAAL Annual Meeting, Manchester, September 1998.

Campanelli P. and Channell J. 1994. *Training: an exploration of the word and the concept with an analysis of the implications for survey design.* London: Department of Employment.

Carter R. 2000. 'The CANCODE Project', paper read at the University of Birmingham, March 2000.

Carter R. and McCarthy M. (eds.) 1988. *Vocabulary and Language Teaching.* London: Longman.

Carter R. and McCarthy M. 1995. 'Grammar and the spoken language' *Applied Linguistics* 16: 141–158.

Channell J. 2000. 'Corpus-based analysis of evaluative lexis' in Hunston and Thompson (eds.) 38–55.

Charles M. in preparation. 'The author's voice in academic writing with reference to theses in politics and materials science'. Unpublished PhD thesis, University of Birmingham.

Cicourel A. 1982. 'Language and belief in a medical setting'. In H. Byrnes (ed.) *Contemporary Perceptions of Language: Interdisciplinary dimensions.* Georgetown: Georgetown University Round Table on Language and Linguistics. 48–78.

Clark V. and Friginal E. forthcoming. 'Service encounter talk: a closer look' in Reppen et al (eds.).

Clear J. 1993. 'From Firth principles: computational tools for the study of collocation' in Baker et al (eds.) 271–292.

Clear J. 1994. 'I can't see the sense in a large corpus' in F. Kiefer, G. Kiss and J. Pajzs (eds.) *Papers in Computational Lexicography: COMPLEX '94.* Budapest: Research Institute for Linguistics, Hungarian Academy of Sciences.

Clear J., Fox G., Francis G., Krishnamurthy R. and Moon R. 1996. 'Cobuild: the state of the art' *International Journal of Corpus Linguistics* 1: 303–314.

Cobb T. 1997. 'Is there any measurable learning from hands-on concordances?' *System* 25: 301–315.

Cobb T. and Horst M. 2001. 'Reading academic English: carrying learners across the lexical threshold' in J. Flowerdew and M. Peacock (eds.) *Research Perspectives on English for Academic Purposes.* Cambridge: Cambridge University Press. 315–329.

Coniam D. 1998. 'Partial parsing: boundary marking' *International Journal of Corpus Linguistics* 3: 229–249.

Conrad S. 1996. 'Academic discourse in two disciplines: professional writing and student development in Biology and History'. Unpublished PhD dissertation, Northern Arizona University.

Conrad S. 2000. 'Will corpus linguistics revolutionize grammar teaching in the 21st century?' Paper read at the 2nd North American Symposium on Corpora and Language Teaching, Northern Arizona University, March 2000.

Conrad S. and Biber D. 2000. 'Adverbial marking of stance in speech and writing' in Hunston and Thompson (eds.) 57–73.

Cook G. 1998. 'The uses of reality: a reply to Ronald Carter' *ELTJ* 52: 57–64.

Cook, G. 2001. ' "The philosopher pulled the lower jaw of the hen." Ludicrous invented sentences in language teaching' *Applied Linguistics* 22: 366–387.

Coulthard M. 1994. 'On the use of corpora in the analysis of forensic texts' *Forensic Linguistics* 1: 27–44.

Coulthard M. 1997. 'A failed appeal' *Forensic Linguistics* 4: 287–302.

Cowie, A.P. 1988. 'Stable and creative aspects of vocabulary use' in Carter and McCarthy (eds.) 126–139.

Crowdy S. 1993. 'Spoken corpus design' *Literary and Linguistic Computing* 8: 259–265.

De Beaugrande R. 1999. 'Reconnecting real language with real texts: text linguistics and corpus linguistics' *International Journal of Corpus Linguistics* 4: 243–259.

De Cock S. 1998. 'A recent word combination approach to the study of formulae in the speech of native and non-native speakers of English' *International Journal of Corpus Linguistics* 3: 59–80.

De Cock S., Granger S., Leech G. and McEnery T. 1998. 'An automated approach to the phrasicon of EFL learners' in Granger (ed.) 67–79.

Dodd B. 1997. 'Exploiting a corpus of written German for advanced language learning' in Wichmann et al (eds.) 131–145.

Dodd B. 2000. 'When *Ost* meets *West*: a corpus-based study of binomial and other expressions before and during German unification' in Dodd (ed.) 69–95.

Dodd B. (ed.) 2000. *Working with German Corpora.* Birmingham: University of Birmingham Press.

Fairclough N. 1995. *Critical Discourse Analysis.* London: Longman.

Fairclough N. 2000. *New Labour, New Language?* London: Routledge.

Farr F. and O'Keeffe A. forthcoming. 'Corpora and linguistic variety: hedging the issues' in Reppen et al (eds.).

Fillmore C.J. 1992. ' "Corpus linguistics" or "Computer-aided armchair linguistics" ' in Svartvik (ed.) 35–60.

Finlay S. 2000. 'CopyCatch in use'. Manuscript, CFL Software Development.

Fitzmaurice S. forthcoming. 'The textual resolution of structural ambiguity in 18th century English: a corpus-linguistic study of patterns of negation' in Reppen et al (eds.)

Flowerdew J. 1997. 'The discourse of colonial withdrawal: a case study in the creation of mythic discourse' *Discourse and Society* 8: 453–477.

Flowerdew J. 1998. *The Final Years of British Hong Kong: The discourse of colonial withdrawal.* Basingstoke: Macmillan.

Flowerdew L. 1998. 'Integrating expert and interlanguage computer corpora findings on causality: discoveries for teachers and students' *English for Specific Purposes* 17: 329–345.

Flowerdew L. 2000. 'Investigating referential and pragmatic errors in a learner corpus' in Burnard and McEnery (eds.) 145–154.

Foucou P.Y. and Kübler N. 2000. 'A web-based environment for teaching technical English' in Burnard and McEnery (eds.) 65–74.

Fowler R. 1987. 'Notes on critical linguistics' in R. Steele and T. Threadgold (eds.) *Language Topics: Essays in honour of Michael Halliday* Vol II. Amsterdam: Benjamins. 481–492. Reprinted with modifications as 'On critical linguistics' in Caldas-Coulthard and Coulthard (eds.) 3–14.

Fox G. 1987. 'The case for examples' in Sinclair (ed.) 137–149.

Francis G. 1993. 'A corpus-driven approach to grammar – principles, methods and examples' in Baker et al (eds.) 137–156.

Francis G. 1994. 'Labelling discourse: an aspect of nominal-group lexical cohesion' in M. Coulthard (ed.) *Advances in Written Text Analysis.* London: Routledge. 83–101.

Francis G., Hunston S. and Manning E. 1996. *Collins* COBUILD *Grammar Patterns 1: Verbs.* London: HarperCollins.

Francis G., Manning E. and Hunston S. 1997. *Verbs: Patterns and Practice.* London: HarperCollins.

Francis G., Hunston S. and Manning E. 1998. *Collins* COBUILD *Grammar Patterns 2: Nouns and adjectives.* London: HarperCollins.

Garside R., Fligelstone S. and Botley S. 1997. 'Discourse annotation: anaphoric relations in corpora' in Garside et al (eds.) 66–84.

Garside R., Leech G. and McEnery A. (eds.) 1997. *Corpus Annotation: linguistic information from computer text corpora.* London: Longman.

Garside R. and Smith N. 1997. 'A hybrid grammatical tagger: CLAWS4' in Garside et al (eds.) 102–121.

Geisler C. forthcoming. 'Investigating register variation in nineteenth-century English: a multi-dimensional comparison' in Reppen et al (eds.).

Gerbig A. 1993. 'The representation of agency and control in texts on the environment'. Paper read at the AILA Congress, Amsterdam, August 1993.

Ghadessy M. (ed.) 1988. *Registers of Written English: situational factors and linguistic features.* London: Pinter.

Ghadessy M. (ed.) 1993. *Register Analysis: theory and practice.* London: Pinter.

Gledhill C. 1995. 'Collocation and genre analysis: the phraseology of grammatical items in cancer research abstracts and articles' *Zeitschrift für Anglistik und Amerikanistik* 43: 11–29.

Gledhill C. 1996. 'Science as collocation: phraseology in cancer research articles' in S. Botley, J. Glass, T. McEnery and A. Wilson (eds.) *Proceedings of the Teaching and Language Corpora 1996.* UCREL Technical Papers 9: 108–126.

Gomez-Gonzalez M.A. 1998. 'A corpus-based analysis of extended multiple themes in PresE' *International Journal of Corpus Linguistics* 3: 81–113.

Graddol D. 1999. 'The decline of the native speaker' in D. Graddol and U.H. Meinhof (eds.) *English in a Changing World*. AILA Review 13. Association Internationale de Linguistique Appliquée.

Granger S. 1998a. 'Prefabricated patterns in advanced ELT writing: collocations and formulae' in A.P. Cowie (ed.) *Phraseology: Theory, analysis, and applications* Oxford: Clarendon Press. 145–160.

Granger S. 1998b. 'The computer learner corpus: a versatile new source of data for SLA research' in Granger (ed.) 3–18.

Granger S. (ed.) 1998. *Learner English on Computer*. London: Longman.

Granger S. and Rayson P. 1998. 'Automatic profiling of learner texts' in Granger (ed.) 119–131.

Granger S. and Tribble C. 1998. 'Learner corpus data in the foreign language classroom: form-focused instruction and data-driven learning' in Granger (ed.) 199–209.

Greenbaum S., Nelson G. and Weitzman M. 1996. 'Complement clauses in English' in Thomas and Short (eds.) 76–91.

Gross M. 1993. 'Local grammars and their representation by finite automata' in Hoey (ed.) 26–38.

Hall J.K. and Eggington W.G. (eds.) 2000. *The Sociopolitics of English Language Teaching*. Clevedon: Multilingual Matters.

Haller J. 2000. 'Research and development in the field of controlled languages: language technology at IAI'. Paper read at 3rd Rencontres Internationales de Linguistique Appliquée, University Paris 7, July 2000.

Halliday M.A.K. 1976 [1966]. *System and Function in Language* (edited by G. Kress). Oxford: OUP.

Halliday M.A.K. 1985. *Spoken and Written Language*. Geelong, Vic.: Deakin University Press. Republished 1989. Oxford: Oxford University Press.

Halliday M.A.K. 1987. 'Language and the order of nature' in N. Fabb, D. Attridge, A. Durant and C. MacCabe (eds.) *The Linguistics of Writing: arguments between language and literature*. Manchester: Manchester University Press. 135–154.

Halliday M.A.K. 1992. 'Language as system and language as instance: the corpus as a theoretical construct' in Svartvik (ed.) 61–78.

Halliday M.A.K. 1993. 'Quantitative studies and probabilities in grammar' in Hoey (ed.) 1–25.

Halliday M.A.K. 1994. *In Introduction to Functional Grammar*. 2nd edition. London: Arnold.

Halliday M.A.K. and Hasan R. 1976. *Cohesion in English*. London: Longman.

Halliday M.A.K. and James Z.L. 1993. 'A quantitative study of polarity and primary tense in the English finite clause' in J.M. Sinclair, M. Hoey and G. Fox (eds.) *Techniques of Description: Spoken and written discourse*. London: Routledge. 32–66.

Halliday M.A.K., McIntosh A. and Strevens P. 1964. *The Linguistic Sciences and Language Teaching*. London: Longman.

Halliday M.A.K. and Martin J.R. 1993. *Writing Science: Literacy and discursive power*. London: The Falmer Press.

Hanks P. 1987. 'Definitions and explanations' in Sinclair (ed.) 116–136.

He A.P. and Kennedy G. 1999. 'Successful turn-bidding in English conversation' *International Journal of Corpus Linguistics* 4: 1–27.

Hermanns F. 1994. *Schlüssel-, Schlag- und Fahnenwörter: Zur Begrifflichkeit und Theorie der lexikalischen Semantik*. Arbeiten aus dem Sonderforschungsbereich 245: Sprache und Situation. Heidelberg/Mannheim: Bericht Nr. 81.

Hickey T. 1993. 'Identifying formulas in first language acquisition' *Journal of Child Language* 20: 27–41.

Hoey M. 1993. 'How the word *reason* is used in texts' in J.M. Sinclair, M. Hoey and G. Fox (eds.) *Techniques of Description: spoken and written discourse*. London: Routledge. 67–82.

Hoey M. (ed.) 1993. *Data, Description, Discourse*. London: HarperCollins.

Holmes D.I. 1998. 'The evolution of stylometry in humanities scholarship' *Literary and Linguistic Computing* 13: 111–117.

Howarth P. 1998. 'Phraseology and second language proficiency' *Applied Linguistics* 19: 24–44.

Hsia C.H.L., Chitravelu N., Lee A. and Ibrahim A. 1989. *English Form 3*. Kurikulum Bersepadu Sekolah Menegah. Kuala Lumpur: Pena Modal Sdn. Bhd.

Hudson R. 1984. *Word Grammar*. Oxford: Blackwell.

Hundt M. and Mair C. 1999. '"Agile" and "uptight" genres: the corpus-based approach to language change in progress' *International Journal of Corpus Linguistics* 4: 221–242.

Hunston S. 1993a. 'Evaluation and ideology in scientific writing' in M. Ghadessy (ed.) *Register Analysis: theory and practice*. London: Pinter. 57–74.

Hunston S. 1993b. 'I must say I'm a little sceptical: an investigation of a discourse use of some modal auxiliaries'. Paper read at the BAAL Annual Meeting, Salford, September 1993.

Hunston S. 1993c. 'Professional conflict: disagreement in academic discourse' in Baker et al (eds.) 115–136.

Hunston S. 1993d. 'Projecting a sub-culture: the construction of shared worlds by projecting clauses in two registers' in D. Graddol et al (eds.) *Language and Culture*. Clevedon: Multilingual Matters/BAAL. 98–112.

Hunston S. 1995a. 'A corpus study of some English verbs of attribution' *Functions of Language* 2: 133–158.

Hunston S. 1995b. 'Grammar in teacher education: the role of a corpus' *Language Awareness* 4: 15–32.

Hunston S. 1997. 'What makes English difficult? (and how to make it easier)'. Paper read at the conference *Learners and Language Learning*, RELC, Singapore, April 1997.

Hunston S. 1999a. 'Corpus evidence for disadvantage: issues in critical interpretation'. Paper read at the BAAL/CUP seminar 'Investigating discourse practices through corpus research: methods, findings and applications', University of Reading, May 1999.

Hunston S. 1999b. 'Local Grammars: the future of corpus-driven grammar?'. Paper read at the 32nd BAAL Annual Meeting, University of Edinburgh, September 1999.

Hunston S. 2000. 'Phraseology and the modal verb: a study of pattern and meaning' in C. Heffer and H. Sauntson (eds.) *Words in Context: a tribute to John Sinclair on his retirement*. University of Birmingham CD-ROM.

Hunston S. 2001. 'Colligation, lexis, pattern and text' in G. Thompson and M. Scott (eds.) *Patterns of Text: in honour of Michael Hoey*. Amsterdam: Benjamins. 13–33.

Hunston S., Francis G. and Manning E. 1997. 'Grammar and vocabulary: showing the connections' *ELTJ* 51: 208–216.

Hunston S. and Francis G. 1998. 'Verbs Observed: A corpus-driven pedagogic grammar' *Applied Linguistics* 19: 45–72.

Hunston S. and Francis G. 1999. *Pattern Grammar: A corpus-driven approach to the lexical grammar of English*. Amsterdam: Benjamins.

Hunston S. and Sinclair J.M. 2000. 'A local grammar of evaluation' in Hunston and Thompson (eds.) 75–101.

Hunston S. and Thompson G. (eds.) 2000. *Evaluation in Text: Authorial stance and the construction of discourse*. Oxford: OUP.

Hyland K. 1998. *Hedging in Scientific Research Articles*. Amsterdam: Benjamins.

Ivanic R. 1998. *Writing and Identity. The discoursal construction of identity in academic writing*. Amsterdam: Benjamins.

Jackson J. 1997. 'Corpus and concordance: finding out about style' in Wichmann et al (eds.) 224–239.

Johansson S. 1981. 'Word frequencies in different types of English texts' *ICAME News* 5: 1–13.

Johansson S. 1993. '"Sweetly oblivious": Some aspects of adverb-adjective combinations in present-day English' in Hoey (ed.) 39–49.

Johansson S., Ebeling G. and Hofland K. 1996. 'Coding and aligning the English-Norwegian parallel corpus' in K. Aijmer, B. Altenberg and M. Johansson (eds.) *Languages in Contrast: papers form a symposium on text-based cross-linguistic studies, Lund, March 1994*. Lund: Lund University Press. 87–112.

Johns T. 1991. '"Should you be persuaded": two samples of data-driven learning materials' in T. Johns and P. King (eds.) 1–16.

Johns T. 1997a. 'Contexts: the background, development and trialling of a concordance-based CALL program' in Wichmann et al (eds.) 100–115.

Johns T. 1997b. 'Multiconcord: the Lingua Multilingual Parallel Concordancer for Windows' http: //www.bham.ac.uk/johnstf/ltext.htm

Johns T. 1997c. '*Reason for* and *reason to*' http://web.bham.ac.uk/johnstf/revis021.htm

Johns T. and King P. (eds.) *Classroom Concordancing* ELR Journal 4. University of Birmingham.

Johnson A. 1997. 'Textual kidnapping: a case of plagiarism among three student texts?' *Forensic Linguistics* 4: 210–225.

Kennedy G. 1991. '*Between* and *through*: the company they keep and the functions they serve' in Aijmer and Altenberg (eds.) 95–110.

Kennedy G. (ed.) 1997. *Dictionary of New Zealand Sign Language*. Auckland: University of Auckland Press.

Kennedy G. 1998. *An Introduction to Corpus Linguistics*. London: Longman.

Kenny D. 2000. 'Translators at play: exploitations of collocational norms in German-English translation' in Dodd (ed.) 143–160.

Khong C. P., Lee J.K.S. and Chan P. 1987. *Launch Into KBSM English: Form 1*. Petaling Jaya: Eastview Publications Sdn. Bhd.

King P. 1997. 'Parallel corpora for translator training' *PALC '97*: 393–402.

King P. and Woolls D. 1996. 'Creating and using a multilingual parallel concordancer' in B. Lewandowska-Tomaszczyk and M. Thelen (eds.) *Translation and Meaning, part 4: Proceedings of the Lodz session of the 2nd International Maastricht-Lodz Duo Colloquium on Translation and Meaning, Lodz, September 1995* Amsterdam: Benjamins. 459–466.

Knowles G. 1997. 'Using corpora for the diachronic study of English' in Wichmann et al (eds.) 195–210.

Knowles G., Wichmann A. and Alderson P. (eds.) 1996. *Working with Speech: Perspectives on research into the Lancaster/IBM Spoken English Corpus*. London: Longman.

Kress G. 1994. 'Text and grammar as explanation' in U. Meinhof and K. Richardson (eds.) *Text, Discourse and Context: Representations of poverty in Britain*. London: Longman. 24–46.

Kress G. and van Leeuwen T. 1994. *Reading Images: The design of visual communication*. London: Routledge.

Krishnamurthy R. 1996. 'Ethnic, racial and tribal: The language of racism?' in Caldas-Coulthard and Coulthard (eds.) 129–149.

Kruyt T. 2000. 'Towards the integrated language database of 8th–21st century Dutch'. Paper read at the 3èmes Rencontres Internationales de Linguistique Appliquée, Paris, July 2000.

Latour B. and Woolgar S. 1979. *Laboratory Life: the social construction of scientific facts*. Beverly Hills: Sage.

Laviosa S. 1997. 'How comparable can "comparable corpora" be?' *Target* 9: 289–319.

Lawson A. 2000. '"Die schöne Geschichte": a corpus-based analysis of Thomas Mann's *Joseph und seine Brüder*' in Dodd (ed.) 161–180.

Lee W.L. 1999. 'A corpus-based study of synonymous words'. Unpublished MA thesis, University of Birmingham.

Leech G. 1992. 'Corpora and theories of linguistic performance' in Svartvik (ed.) 105–122.

Leech G. 1997a. 'Grammatical tagging' in Garside et al (eds.) 19–33.

Leech G. 1997b. 'Introducing corpus annotation' in Garside et al (eds.) 1–18.

Leech G. 1997c. 'Teaching and language corpora: a convergence' in Wichmann et al (eds.) 1–23.

Leech G. 1998. 'Preface' in Granger (ed.) xiv-xx.

Leech G. and Eyes E. 1997. 'Syntactic annotation: treebanks' in Garside et al (eds.) 34–52.

Leech G., McEnery T. and Wynne M. 1997 'Further levels of annotation' in Garside et al (eds.) 85–101.

Leech G., Rayson P. and Wilson A. 2001. *Word Frequency in Written and Spoken English: Based on the British National Corpus*. London: Longman.

Leech G. and Short M. 1981. *Style in Fiction*. London: Longman.

Levi J.N. 1994. 'Language as evidence: the linguist as expert witness in North American courts' *Forensic Linguistics* 1: 1–26.

Levin B., Song G. and Atkins B.T.S. 1997. 'Making sense of corpus data: a case study of verbs of sound' *International Journal of Corpus Linguistics* 2: 23–64.

Lewis M. 1996. 'Implications of a lexical view of language' in Willis and Willis (eds.) 10–16.

Long M.H. and Crookes G. 1992. 'Three approaches to task-based syllabus design' *TESOL Quarterly* 26: 27–56.

Lorenz G. 1998. 'Overstatement in advanced learners' writing: stylistic aspects of adjective intensification' in Granger (ed.) 53–66.

Louw B. 1993. 'Irony in the text or insincerity in the writer? – the diagnostic potential of semantic prosodies' in Baker et al (eds.). 157–176.

Louw B. 1997. 'The role of corpora in critical literary appreciation' in Wichmann et al (eds.) 140–251.

Lowe J.B., Baker C.F. and Fillmore C.J. 1997. 'A frame-semantic approach to semantic annotation'. http://www.icsi.berkley.edu/~framenet/docs/siglex.html

Luzon Marco M.J. 2000. 'Collocational frameworks in medical research papers: a genre-based study' *English for Specific Purposes* 19: 63–86.

Martin J.R. 1982. 'Process and text: two aspects of human semiosis' in J.D. Benson and W.S. Greaves (eds.) *Systemic Perspectives in Discourse vol. 1: selected theoretical papers*. Norwood, NJ: Ablex. 248–274.

Martin J.R. 2000. 'Beyond exchange: APPRAISAL systems in English' in Hunston and Thompson (eds.) 143–175.

Mason O. 1999. 'Parameters of collocation: the word in the centre of gravity' in J.M. Kirk (ed.) *Corpora Galore: analyses and techniques in describing English*. Amsterdam: Rodopi. 267–280.

Mautner G. 2000. 'Market-driven education: the discourse of mission statements and deans' messages on Business Schools' internet web pages'. Paper read at the 33rd BAAL Annual Meeting, Cambridge, September 2000.

McEnery T. and Wilson A. 1996. *Corpus Linguistics*. Edinburgh: Edinburgh University Press.

McEnery T., Baker J.P. and Hutchinson J. 1997. 'A corpus-based grammar tutor' in Garside et al (eds.) 209–219.

Mindt D. 2000. *An Empirical Grammar of the English Verb System*. Berlin: Cornelsen.

Mitkov R. 1999. 'Towards automatic annotation of anaphoric links in corpora' *International Journal of Corpus Linguistics* 4: 261–280.

Moon R. 1998. *Fixed Expressions and Idioms in English: A corpus-based approach*. Oxford: Clarendon Press.

Morrison A. and Love A. 1996. 'A discourse of disillusionment: Letters to the Editor in two Zimbabwean magazines 10 years after independence' *Discourse and Society* 7: 39–76.

Myers G. 1990. *Writing Biology: texts in the social construction of scientific knowledge*. Madison: University of Wisconsin Press.

Nattinger J. and DeCarrico J. 1989. 'Lexical phrases, speech acts and teaching conversation' in P. Nation and R. Carter (eds.) *AILA Review 6: Vocabulary Acquisition*. Amsterdam: AILA. 118–139.

Nattinger J. and DeCarrico J. 1992. *Lexical Phrases and Language Teaching*. Oxford: OUP.

Noguchi J. 2001. The Science Review Article: an opportune genre in the construction of science. Unpublished PhD thesis, University of Birmingham.

Nordlinger R. and Traugott E.C. 1997. 'Scope and development of epistemic modality: evidence from *ought to*' *English Language and Linguistics* 1: 295–317.

Oakes M.P. 1998. *Statistics for Corpus Linguistics*. Edinburgh: Edinburgh University Press.

Orpin D. 1997. 'The lexis of corruption in the news: a corpus-based study in ideology'. Unpublished MA dissertation, University of Birmingham.

Owen C. 1996. 'Does a corpus require to be consulted?' *ELTJ* 50: 219–224.

Partington A. 1998. *Patterns and Meanings*. Amsterdam: Benjamins.

Pawley A. and Syder F.H. 1983. 'Two puzzles for linguistic theory: nativelike selection and nativelike fluency' in J.C. Richards and R.W. Schmidt (eds.) *Language and Communication*. London: Longman. 191–227.

Pearson J. 1998. *Terms in Context*. Amsterdam: Benjamins.

Pearson J. 2000. 'Surfing the Internet: teaching students to choose their texts' in Burnard and McEnery (eds.) 235–239.

Petch-Tyson S. 1998. 'Writer/reader visibility in EFL written discourse' in Granger (ed.) 107–118.

Peters A.M. 1983. *The Units of Language Acquisition*. Cambridge: CUP.

Pidd M., Robinson P., Stubbs E. and Thompson C.E. 1997. 'Digital imaging and the manuscripts of *The Canterbury Tales*' *Literary and Linguistic Computing* 12: 197–201.

Piper A. 2000a. 'Lifelong learning, human capital, and the soundbite' *Text* 20: 109–146.

Piper A. 2000b. 'Some have credit cards and others have giro cheques: 'Individuals' and 'people' as lifelong learners in late modernity' *Discourse and Society* 11: 515–542.

Poos D. and Simpson R. forthcoming. 'Cross-disciplinary comparisons of hedging: some findings from the Michigan Corpus of Academic Spoken English' in Reppen et al (eds.).

Prescott A. 1997. '*The Electronic Beowulf* and digital restoration' *Literary and Linguistic Computing* 12: 185–195.

Quirk R., Greenbaum S., Leech G. and Svartvik J. 1972. *A Grammar of Contemporary English*. London: Longman.

Rayson P., Leech G. and Hodges M. 1997. 'Social differentiation in the use of English vocabulary: some analyses of the conversational component of the British National Corpus' *International Journal of Corpus Linguistics* 2: 133–150.

Rees J. 1998. 'A new approach to rational deletion in cloze tests'. Paper read at the University of Birmingham, 1998.

Renouf A. 1987. 'Corpus development' in Sinclair (ed.) 1–40.

Renouf A. and Sinclair J.M. 1991. 'Collocational frameworks in English' in Aijmer and Altenberg (eds.) 128–144.

Reppen R. 1994. 'Variation in elementary student language: a multi-dimensional perspective'. Unpublished PhD dissertation, Northern Arizona University.

Reppen R., Biber D. and Fitzmaurice S. (eds.) forthcoming. *Using corpora to Explore Linguistic Variation*. Amsterdam: Benjamins.

Rézeau J. 2001. 'Concordances in the classroom: the evidence of the data' in A. Chambers and G. Davies (eds.) *ICT and Language Learning: A European perspective*. Lisse: Swets & Zeitlinger. 147–166.

Ringbom H. 1998. 'Vocabulary frequencies in advanced learner English: a cross-linguistic approach' in Granger (ed.) 41–52.

Rissanen M. 1991. 'On the history of *that*/zero as object clause links in English' in Aijmer and Altenberg (eds.) 272–289.

Rizomilioti V. in preparation. 'Epistemic Modality in Academic Writing: a corpus-based approach'. Unpublished PhD thesis, University of Birmingham.

Rudanko J. 1996. *Prepositions and Complement Clauses: A syntactic and semantic study of verbs governing prepositions and complement clauses in present-day English*. New York: State University of New York Press.

Rudanko J. 2000. *Corpora and Complementation: Tracing sentential complementation patterns of nouns, adjectives and verbs over the last three centuries*. Lanham, Maryland: University Press of America.

Schmidt R. 1990. 'The role of consciousness in second language learning' *Applied Linguistics* 11: 129–158.

Scott M. 1996. *Wordsmith Tools*. Oxford: OUP.

Scott M. 2000. 'Focusing on the text and its key words' in Burnard and McEnery (eds.) 103–121.

Sealey A. 2000. *Childly Language: Children, language and the social world*. London: Longman.

Seidlhofer B. 2000. 'Operationalizing intertextuality: using learner corpora for learning' in Burnard and McEnery (eds.) 207–224.

Short M., Semino E. and Culpeper J. 1996. 'Using a corpus for stylistics research: speech and thought presentation' in Thomas and Short (eds.) 110–134.

Shortall T. 1999. 'Protogrammar, frequency, and the acquisition of structure'. Workshop given at the 25th JALT conference, Maebashi, Japan.

Simpson P. 1993. *Language, Ideology and Point of View*. London: Routledge.

Simpson P. and Montgomery M. 1995. 'Language, literature and film: the stylistics of Bernard MacLaverty's *Cal*' in P. Verdonk and J. J. Weber

Twentieth-Century Fiction: From text to context. London: Routledge. 138–164.

Sinclair J.M. 1987a. 'Grammar in the dictionary' in Sinclair (ed.) 104–115.

Sinclair J.M. 1987b. 'The nature of the evidence' in Sinclair (ed.) 150–159.

Sinclair J.M. (ed.) 1987. *Looking Up: An account of the COBUILD project.* London: HarperCollins.

Sinclair J.M. 1991. *Corpus Concordance Collocation.* Oxford: OUP.

Sinclair J.M. 1992. 'The automatic analysis of corpora' in Svartvik (ed.) 379–397.

Sinclair J.M. 1993. 'Written discourse structure' in J.M. Sinclair, M. Hoey and G. Fox (eds.) *Techniques of Description.* London: Routledge. 6–31.

Sinclair J.M. 1994. 'A search for meaningful units of language'. Paper read at the International Symposium on Phraseology, University of Leeds, April, 1994.

Sinclair J.M. 1999. 'A way with common words' in H. Hasselgård and S. Oksefjell (eds.) *Out of Corpora: Studies in honour of Stig Johansson.* Amsterdam: Rodopi. 157–179.

Sinclair J.M. 2000. 'The computer, the corpus and the theory of language' in G. Azzaro and M. Ulrych (eds.) *Transiti Linguistici e Culturali* Volume II. *Proceedings of the 18th AIA Congress. Anglistica e metodi e persorsi comparatistici nelle lingue, culture e letterature di origine europpa.* Trieste: EUT. 1–15.

Sinclair J.M. and Coulthard M. 1975. *Towards the Analysis of Discourse.* Oxford: Oxford University Press.

Sinclair J.M. and Renouf A. 1988. 'A lexical syllabus for language learning' in R. Carter and M. McCarthy (eds.) *Vocabulary and Language Teaching.* London: Longman.

Sinclair J.M. et al 1990. *Collins COBUILD English Grammar.* London: HarperCollins.

Somers H. 1998. 'Further experiments in bilingual text alignment'. *International Journal of Corpus Linguistics* 3: 115–150.

Sripicharn P. 1998. 'Concordance-based materials and learner self-correction in EFL writing'. Unpublished MA dissertation, University of Birmingham.

Stevens V. 1991. 'Concordance-based vocabulary exercises: a viable alternative to gap-fillers' in Johns and King (eds.) 47–62.

Storey-White K. 1997. 'KISSing the jury: advantages and limitations of the 'keep it simple' principle in the presentation of expert evidence to courts and juries' *Forensic Linguistics* 4: 280–286.

Stubbs M. 1995. 'Collocations and semantic profiles: on the cause of the trouble with quantitative studies' *Functions of Language* 2: 1–33.

Stubbs M. 1996. *Text and Corpus Analysis.* Oxford: Blackwell.

Stubbs M. 1997. 'Whorf's children: critical comments on critical discourse analysis' in A. Ryan and A. Wray (eds.) *Evolving Models of Language.* Clevedon: Multilingual Matters/BAAL. 100–116.

Stubbs M. 1999. 'Society, education and language: the last 2,000 (and the next 20?) years of language teaching'. Plenary lecture given at the 32nd Annual Meeting of the British Association for Applied Linguistics, University of Edinburgh, September 1999.

Stubbs M. and Gerbig A. 1993. 'Human and inhuman geography: on the computer-assisted analysis of long texts' in Hoey (ed.) 64–85.

Summers D. 1996. 'Computer lexicography: the importance of representativeness in relation to frequency' in Thomas and Short (eds.) 260–265.

Sutarsyah C., Nation I.S.P. and Kennedy G. 1994. 'How useful is EAP vocabulary for ESP? – a corpus-based case study' *RELC Journal* 25: 34–50.

Svartvik J. (ed.) 1992. *Directions in Corpus Linguistics. Proceedings of Nobel Symposium 82, Stockholm, 4–8 August 1991*. Berlin: Mouton de Gruyter.

Swales J. 1990. *Genre Analysis*. Cambridge: CUP.

Swan M. 1994. 'Design criteria for pedagogic language rules' in M. Bygate, A. Tonkyu and E. Williams (eds.) *Grammar and the Language Teacher*. Hemel Hempstead. Prentice Hall: 45–55.

Taylor L. 1996. 'The compilation of the Spoken English Corpus' in Knowles et al (eds.) 20–37.

Teubert W. 2000. 'A province of a federal superstate, ruled by an unelected bureaucracy: Keywords of the Eurosceptic discourse in Britain' in A. Musolff, C. Good, P. Points and R. Wittlinger (eds.) *Attitudes Towards Europe: Language in the Unification Process*. Aldershot: Ashgate. 45–86.

Thomas J. and Short M. (eds.) 1996. *Using Corpora for Language Research*. London: Longman.

Thomas J. and Wilson A. 1996. 'Methodologies for studying a corpus of doctor-patient interaction' in Thomas and Short (eds.) 92–109.

Thomas P. 1992. 'Computerized term banks and translation' in J. Newton (ed.) *Computers in Translation: a practical appraisal*. London: Routledge.

Thompson G. 1994. *Reporting*. COBUILD *Guides 5. London: HarperCollins*.

Tognini-Bonelli E. 2001. *Corpus Linguistics At Work*. Amsterdam: Benjamins.

Toolan M. 1988. *Narrative: a critical linguistic introduction*. London: Routledge.

Tottie G. 1991. *Negation in English Speech and Writing: a study in variation*. San Diego: Academic Press.

Tribble C. 2000. 'Genres, keywords, teaching: towards a pedagogic account of the language of project proposals' in Burnard and McEnery (eds.) 75–90.

Ure J.N. 1971. 'Lexical density and register differentiation' in G.E. Perren and J.L. Trim (eds.) *Applications of Linguistics: Selected papers of the Second International Congress of Applied Linguistics*. Cambridge: Cambridge University Press. 443–452.

Van Dijk T. 1991. *Racism and the Press*. London: Routledge.

Van Leeuwen T. 1996. 'The representation of social actors' in Caldas-Coulthard and Coulthard (eds.) 32–70.

Weinert R. 1995. 'The role of formulaic language in second language acquisition' *Applied Linguistics* 16: 180–205.

Wichmann A., Fligelstone S., McEnery T. and Knowles G. (eds.) 1997. *Teaching and Language Corpora*. London: Longman.

Wickens P. 1998. 'Comparative analysis of the use of projecting clauses in pedagogic legal genres'. Paper read at the 25th International Systemic-Functional Congress, University of Wales, Cardiff, July 1998.

Widdowson H.G. 1979. *Explorations in Applied Linguistics*. Oxford: Oxford University Press.

Widdowson H.G. 2000. 'On the limitations of linguistics applied' *Applied Linguistics* 21: 3–25.

Williams B. 1996. 'The formulation of an intonation transcription system for British English' in Knowles et al (eds) 38–57.

Williams G.C. 1998. 'Collocational networks: interlocking patterns of lexis in a corpus of plant biology research articles' *International Journal of Corpus Linguistics* 3: 151–170.

Williams R. 1976. *Keywords*. London: Fontana.

Willis D. 1990. *The Lexical Syllabus: a new approach to language teaching*. London: HarperCollins.

Willis D. 1993. 'Syllabus, corpus and data-driven learning' *IATEFL Conference Report: Plenaries*.

Willis D. 1994. 'A lexical approach' in M. Bygate, A. Tonkyn and E. Williams (eds.) *Grammar and the Language Teacher*. London: Prentice Hall. 56–66.

Willis D. 1998. 'The idiom principle: a pedagogic approach'. Paper read at the University of Birmingham, November 1998.

Willis D. and Willis J. 1996. 'Consciousness-raising activities in the classroom' in Willis and Willis (eds.) 63–76.

Willis J. 1996. 'A flexible framework for task-based learning' in Willis and Willis (eds.) 52–62.

Willis J. and Willis D. (eds.) 1996. *Challenge and Change in Language Teaching*. London: Heinemann.

Wilson A. and Thomas J. 1997. 'Semantic annotation' in Garside et al (eds.) 53–65.

Woolls D. and Coulthard M. 1998. 'Tools for the trade' *Forensic Linguistics* 5: 33–57.

Wray A. and Perkins M.R. 2000. 'The functions of formulaic language: an integrated model' *Language and Communication* 20: 1–28.

Index

DATE DUE

HIGHSMITH #45115